To Danny:
Happy 60th B-day!
Hope you grow some great Agaves!

Greg Star

8/30/19

Gift from my sister Debbie Lesko
on my 60th Birthday!!
thanks :)

Agaves

**Living sculptures
for
landscapes
and containers**

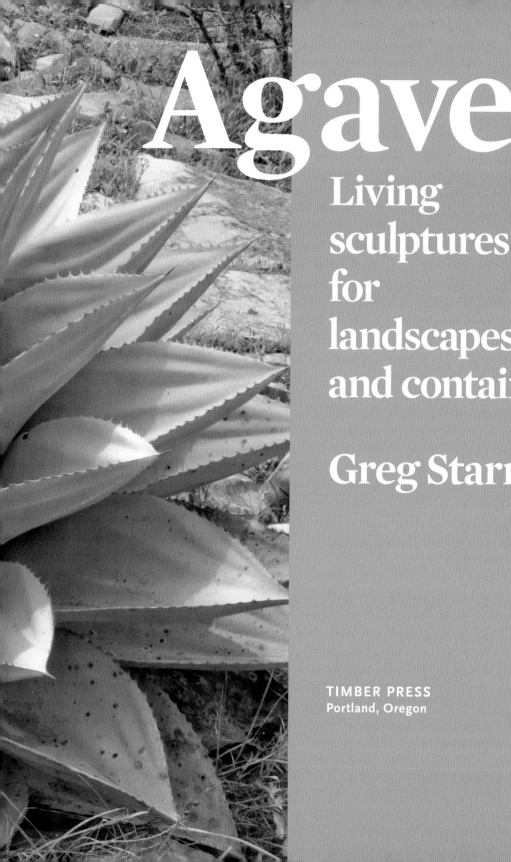

Agaves

Living sculptures for landscapes and containers

Greg Starr

TIMBER PRESS
Portland, Oregon

To Carol: You are my best friend, and your love, patience, and support have given me the strength, drive, and wisdom to tackle another time-consuming project and to understand what love really is. I love you with all of my heart.

To Brian: Your enthusiasm for life has enriched mine; your insight and interest in this book have driven me to see it to fruition.

Frontispiece: *Agave ovatifolia*

All photographs by the author
Climate zone map by Julie Hecimovich

Published in 2012 by Timber Press, Inc.

The Haseltine Building
133 S.W. Second Avenue, Suite 450
Portland, Oregon 97204-3527
timberpress.com

Printed in China
Second printing 2017

Library of Congress Cataloging-in-Publication Data

Starr, Greg, 1957–
    Agaves: living sculptures for landscapes and containers/Greg Starr.
        p. cm.
    Includes bibliographical references and index.
    ISBN-13: 978-1-60469-198-6
    1. Agaves. 2. Agaves—Varieties. I. Title.
    SB317.A2S73 2010
    633.5′77—dc23   2011034310

A catalog record for this book is also available from the British Library.

Contents

Preface

"Why do you like agaves?"

Scott Calhoun, my friend and a fellow plant freak, posed that question to me a while back. If asked a dozen times, I will have a dozen different answers.

Each species has a distinctive feature that draws me in repeatedly like a moth to a flickering flame, letting go briefly as my interest flashes to a different species before pulling me back in time and time again. In several species, what draws me in is the perfect symmetry of the rosette, regardless of the leaf size. Narrow or wide, the mathematical precision as the leaves spiral around the central point, revealing an affinity for Fibonacci patterns, is quite mesmerizing. Many broad-leaved species sink their gnarly, wicked teeth deep into my flesh as I work with them, causing me to pause, mumble a few choice words, and then inspect the intricacies of the teeth and the decorative impressions they left on the surrounding leaves. These impressions, called bud prints, form while the leaves are soft and malleable as they sit tightly wrapped in the developing leaf cone, and remain for the life of the leaf.

Some make incredible landscape specimens, creating year-round visual interest that can be complemented by flowering perennials and shrubs. When these are used together effectively, the garden periodically bursts into a field of color. And after this color fades away, the agaves remain standing boldly, awaiting the next wave.

When I am traveling around the southwestern United States and Mexico, the variation of form, color, and texture in these plants is a visual treat. Leaf colors include deep, dark, avocado green, apple green, red grape red, purplish red, silvery blue, and frosty ice blue. With its

Agave victoriae-reginae

deep green leaves with intricate white stripes lovingly hand-painted by Mother Nature, *Agave victoriae-reginae*, named for Queen Victoria and showing regal features not unlike the queen herself, is a perennial favorite.

Agaves have long been of interest to me. It all began in 1980 when my wife, Carol, and I attended a talk sponsored by the Arizona Native Plant Society. The speaker was Howard Scott Gentry, and he spoke to us about agaves. He was captivating, telling stories of his travels in search of agaves throughout the southwestern United States, Mexico, and Central America while he worked for the United States Department of Agriculture.

Shortly after that talk, I entered graduate school to study horticulture and got a job working for University of Arizona Landscape Architecture professor Warren Jones. He was heading a project to collect, test, and evaluate desert plants for landscaping in the southwestern United States. Warren took me along on a couple of collecting trips, and I was hooked.

My first real expedition south of the United States–Mexico border was in October of 1981, when I was invited on a research trip to Baja California with a group of scientists, botanists, and plant enthusiasts. The trip was organized by Tony Burgess, who under the tutelage of Ray Turner was examining the agaves of Baja California in preparation for his doctoral dissertation. At that time, collecting a handful of seeds from some plants was no big deal, and on *Agave cerulata* I did manage to find a few seeds, which I then grew. Nearly thirty years later, I still have a small cluster growing at my house.

In 1982, Howard Scott Gentry's *Agaves of Continental North America* was published by the University of Arizona Press. That book was a catalyst for my interest in agaves, and one day not long after it came out, I was working at the University of Arizona herbarium when in walked Dr. Gentry himself. He was in good humor and quite engaging that day, and even though we had never met, he spent some time entertaining me with stories of his travels, describing how he would spend many days riding on burros in search of new crops and studying agaves along the way. He had a way with words that enlivened the conversation, evoking visions of exciting exploration which intrigued me.

After finishing graduate school, I opened a nursery specializing in unusual landscape plants. For years, desert landscapes in my hometown of Tucson and in the rest of southern Arizona had consisted of either cactus and succulents or drought-tolerant trees and shrubs, and "never the twain shall meet." My own plant interest ebbed and flowed from succulents to trees, shrubs, and perennials and back again—and during my early trips throughout the southwestern United States and Mexico, my focus was more on the leafy plants, with only a side interest in agaves, nolinas, yuccas, and cactus: anything that would make a nice addition to the somewhat bland southwestern landscapes was fair game. Over time, as my interest in agaves and related plants grew, I began to gravitate more toward the succulent end of the plant spectrum until using succulents in garden landscapes became no less important to me than using their leafy counterparts.

One day in 2000, I received an email with a picture of what I was sure was an undescribed species of agave. This exceptionally attractive specimen looked to be about 3 feet (1 m) tall and nearly 5 feet (1.5 meters) across, with extra wide, deeply cupped, silvery blue leaves. I contacted Carl Shoenfeld at Yucca Do Nursery, who had some insight into the origin of the plant. He said that Lynn Lowery, a plantsman in Texas, had brought it back from one of his expeditions into Mexico. More research revealed that he frequently traveled to a private ranch in the mountains of northeastern Mexico, and so—determined to find this agave—I arranged to go with my frequent traveling partner, Ron Gass, to Lampazos in Nuevo León. There we met with Mexican botanist José Angel Villarreal and ventured to the ranch where we found the population of plants, some beginning to flower. José Angel and I formally described this plant as *Agave ovatifolia*. Since then, I have been returning to Mexico to study agaves in habitat, and with every trip I learn something new.

After the publication in 2000 of *Agaves, Yuccas, and Related Plants* by Mary Irish and Gary Irish, interest in the cultivation of agaves was pushed to the forefront of horticulture in the southwestern United States. In turn, a new breed of landscape designers have been designing more complete landscapes that incorporate agaves, yuccas, and cactus with trees, shrubs, and perennials.

From the great foundation laid by Irish and Irish, this book is a natural progression—covering exciting new species, including more photos, and incorporating updated horticultural and taxonomic information. With the growing interest in these plants, the influx of some really cool and exciting artificial hybrids, and updated horticultural information that has come as a result of more experience with growing these beauties, it is time to take a new look at agaves.

An Introduction to Agaves

The genus *Agave* was first named by the Swedish botanist Carolus Linnaeus in his 1753 *Species Plantarum*, in which he recognized four species. One legend says it was named after Agave (Agaue from the ancient Greek) who, according to Greek mythology, was the daughter of Cadmus, the founder and king of the Greek city of Thebes, and his wife, Harmonia.

At various times the genus has been placed in the families Amaryllidaceae, Liliaceae, and Asparagaceae, but is now more universally accepted as belonging to the family Agavaceae along with the related genera *Bravoa, Furcraea, Hesperaloe, Hesperoyucca, Manfreda, Polianthes, Prochnyanthes, Pseudobravoa*, and *Yucca*. These genera are united by their arrangement of five long and twenty-five short chromosomes, and are all native to the New World. Some botanists include the genera *Calibanus, Dasylirion, Dracaena*, and *Nolina*, while other botanists put those in their own family, the Dracaenaceae. A detailed taxonomic discussion of placement is beyond the scope of the book, and this is no place to settle a family quarrel. Therefore, we will focus on the genus *Agave* itself.

Agave ocahui, a non-offsetting type

A Closer Look

Agaves are extra small to extra large plants consisting of thick or thin, succulent or fibrous leaves arranged in a spiral, forming a rosette. This rosette, which can be as small as 3 inches (7.5 cm) tall by 4 inches (10 cm) across or as large as 10 feet (3 meters) tall and 12 feet (3.5 meters) across, usually sits atop a short, indistinct trunk. A handful of species, including *Agave decipiens, A. fourcroydes, A. karwinskii,* and *A. tequilana,* have tall trunks, while a couple others such as *A. cerulata* and *A. shawii* have long ones that can be found snaking along the ground.

The range of sizes from extra small to extra large, the variation in color, and the amazing array of leaf shapes, sizes, and armature can yield some fascinating and very sculptural looks. The leaves alone are a study in diversity, ranging from the extremely narrow, needle-like leaves of *Agave striata* to the super-broad ones of *A. ovatifolia.* Leaf color is quite variable as well, from the light green of *A. bracteosa* through the Granny Smith apple green of *A. mitis* to the dark green of *A. montana* or the

Agave shawii, an offsetting type, with its pups

nearly black-green of *A. nickelsiae* (synonyms: *A. victoriae-reginae* forma *nickelsiae* and *A. ferdinandi-regis*), and from the frosty blue of *A. colorata* to the light, powder blue of *A. parryi*, the alabaster white of *A. titanota*, and the purplish red found on some forms of *A. striata*. Even in death, flowering agaves can be quite colorful as shades of red, orange and yellow burst forth while the green chlorophyll breaks down—signaling a final farewell as life slowly drains from the once-proud plant.

Sometimes the teeth along the leaf edges are nonexistent, replaced by marginal threads, while in other cases they are very wickedly curved like something seen on Halloween night. The terminal spine can also be lacking as in *Agave bracteosa*, long and wiggly as in *A. utahensis* var. *eborispina*, or stout and lethal as seen on *A. gentryi*.

To add to the variation, there are two basic vegetative types: the solitary or non-offsetting ones, and those that produce offsets in the leaf axils or baby plants connected to the mother plant by underground stems.

Nearly all agaves, along with most bromeliads such as the pineapple, are somewhat peculiar in their flowering habit. They grow vegetatively for many years (though not the hundred years that gave rise to the common name of century plant) without producing a single flower, and then when they get the urge to reproduce, they send forth an enormous stalk with hundreds and hundreds of them. These plants that flower and set seed only once in their lives are called monocarpic; Gentry coined the term *multiannual* specifically for agaves.

As always, there are some exceptions to the rule. Agaves from two groups, the Polycephalae and the Striatae, produce axillary branching in the rosette, much as a shrub produces side branches when the main stem is terminated by a flower or flower stalk, resulting in large, many-headed clusters. Two prime examples are *Agave mitis* of the Polycephalae and *A. striata* of the Striatae.

The flower stalk is distinctly phallic, beginning with the first signs of its emergence from the center of the plant and continuing until the stalk is fully erect. Some stalks are quite skinny and short while others are much thicker and taller. Intermediate types of inflorescence exist, too. The two extremes are described as spicate (those that have the flowers on short pedicels on the main shaft) and paniculate (those that have the flowers on side branches attached to the main shaft).

The continental North American agaves are separated into two general groups based on their type of inflorescence. Plants in the subgenus

Littaea have a spicate type while those in the subgenus *Agave* have a paniculate type, and hybrids between a species in *Littaea* and a species in *Agave* often have intermediate inflorescences. These plants' fabulous inflorescences usually signal their death, as all of the carbohydrates that have been made over the years are directed towards the flurry of sexual activity. Depending on the species, this free-for-all, no-holds-barred approach can last a month or more. You have to appreciate this burst of activity as the plants have been celibate all their lives, sometimes for as long as twenty-five or thirty years.

The type of inflorescence does not affect whether a species is solitary or offsetting. There are species in *Littaea*, the spicate inflorescence group, that are solitary and species that produce offsets, and there are species in *Agave*, the paniculate inflorescence group, that are solitary and species that produce offsets.

For most home gardeners, it is important to consider whether the plant is solitary or produces offsets as this characteristic will affect the placement of the plant in the landscape. An offsetting type will benefit from having ample room to allow for full development of the large clusters. This requires careful planning to prevent offsets from popping up in spots into which they will not fit. Meanwhile a solitary species, even if it is extra large, will generally need no more room than its expected maximum size.

Reproduction

These beauties can multiply with or without sex. Some species don't believe in sex or birth control and readily produce copious numbers of babies attached to the mother plant or bulbils on the flowering stalk. These all have identical genetic material, resulting in an endless supply of identical agaves trying to overwhelm the landscape. However, these offsets can be removed and relocated throughout the garden. Make sure to retain some of the umbilical cord (rhizome) with roots when separating the babies so that they will have the best chance of survival in their new spot. Once established, these new plants will proceed to multiply profusely.

Some species haven't quite made up their minds about how they want to reproduce, and will develop small plants on their flower stalk along with seed capsules after the flowers fade. Others are risk-takers, producing thousands of seeds to be scattered about and relying solely on the good graces of Mother Nature to perpetuate their genetic line. This

The spicate inflorescence of *Agave ocahui*

method is chancy because it requires a season of consistent rainfall for the seed to sprout, followed by several years where there is enough moisture for the plant to become established, combined with the good luck to avoid being ravaged by hungry animals. Still other species may rely on two or even all three methods of reproduction.

We can artificially multiply plants either by cutting them up and forcing the production of offsets, or by tissue culture. These two methods are especially useful for generating many plants of an exceptionally nice or unusual form. Because of this ability to reproduce the plants vegetatively, we face an explosion in the naming of some far-out forms and hybrids.

Distribution

The genus *Agave* is wholly New World, with species found in the United States and south into Mexico and Central America, northern South America (Colombia and Venezuela), and the Caribbean. In 2002, Abisaí García-Mendoza estimated that there were about two hundred naturally occurring species with an additional forty-seven subspecies and varieties.

There appear to be four major centers of diversity. The first is in the Tehuacán-Cuicatlán region, an area that straddles the states of Puebla and Oaxaca of south-central Mexico. This region is considered to be semi-arid with a mixture of vegetation communities, all rich in spiny, succulent plants. The cold-hardiness of plants from this region needs to be further explored. Some species seem to be unfazed by frost while others need the protection of frost cloth, burlap, or even a heavily insulated winter jacket when the temperature hits freezing.

With twenty-four species, the state of Sonora in northwestern Mexico is another area of agave richness. This is due in part to the topographic diversity of the state. The elevation ranges from sea level along the Gulf of California in the western part of the state to over 6250 feet (1900 meters) in the Sierra Madre Occidental in the eastern part. Annual rainfall varies from about 3.5 inches (9 cm) in the northwestern part of the state to about 40 inches (100 cm) in the mountains near the Chihuahua border.

A third major center of species richness is the southeastern part of the Chihuahuan Desert Region in east-central Mexico. This area is botanically rich to begin with, again due largely to varied topography and summer rainfall, so it is no surprise that agaves are well represented there.

The paniculate inflorescence of *Agave parryi* var. *couesii*

17

Southwestern Mexico is the fourth area that is rich in *Agave* species, and it seems to be a hotbed for recent discoveries. This area lies is at the intersection of two distinct yet equally rich floristic communities: the lowland tropics and the pine-oak woodlands. For the most part the climate is warm and moist, resulting in species with large leaves and not much frost tolerance.

AGAVE CONSERVATION

The field notes in this book are meant to paint a picture of the habitats in which agaves occur, and a sense of the thrill that one feels when looking for a species in some remote part of the United States or Mexico. If you do make a trip to see plants in habitat, leave the shovel at home and help to conserve the plants in habitat by capturing them with a photograph instead. This is especially important when returning to the United States from south of the border, as it is illegal and punishable by large fines to bring collected plants back into the country.

When you return home, seek out and purchase plants from a reputable nursery. With the rising interest in tissue culture, selected forms of *Agave* are now being mass-produced and are becoming widely available to the general public, making it unnecessary to collect plants.

Horticultural History

Agaves have long been horticulturally popular, especially in the Old World, having first been introduced into European gardens in the late 1700s. Their peak in popularity took place during the 1800s when many plants were sent to Europe from Mexico. (For the most part, the Caribbean and South American species have been neglected in outdoor horticulture. This could be due to the frost sensitivity of these plants, or because obtaining seed is somewhat difficult, or maybe the old adage "out of sight, out of mind" comes into play. Few intrepid explorers have traveled to the Caribbean islands or remote regions of northern South America in search of agaves, preferring to concentrate on the relatively more accessible species from Mexico and the southwestern United States.)

During the period of 1959 to 1964, August J. Breitung produced a thirty-three-part series on agaves in cultivation for the *Cactus and Succulent Journal*. The horticultural encyclopedia *Hortus III* lists seventy-six species, giving brief descriptions and natural distribution ranges. In 1982, Gentry devoted two pages to the culture of agaves, briefly touching on general water use, cold hardiness, and maintenance.

In 2000, Mary Irish and Gary Irish laid the groundwork for future agave research with detailed descriptions and valuable horticultural information. *Agaves, Yuccas, and Related Plants* includes one photograph each for forty-five of the species, and covers synonyms, common names (if known), descriptions of the plants including size, leaves, and flowering, and information on their distribution and cultural requirements. (In *Agaven*, published in 2003, Thomas Heller covered seventy-eight *Agave* species and their cultivation—but unless you read fluent German, live in a cold climate, and grow your plants in pots in a greenhouse, it is of limited value.)

The resurgence in agave interest has resulted in many previously unavailable species making their way into horticultural circles. Because these species have not been around long, the horticultural information is just now becoming more widely known. It is now time to add fuel to the fire by updating horticultural and taxonomic information on many of the species covered by Irish and Irish, by incorporating some of the recently described species and by including new photos of the plants in habitat. In the following pages I cover eighty species, varieties, cultivars, and hybrids that are available to the agave enthusiast, including some species that are most suitable for container culture in areas where frost occurs. As this is a fraction of the nearly three hundred taxa (species and varieties) and numerous cultivars beginning to flood the market, some of your favorites may not be covered—but the line must be drawn somewhere.

Agave Taxonomy

"Of all cultivated plants, none are more difficult to name accurately than species of *Agave*," commented Sir Joseph Dalton Hooker, director of the Royal Botanic Gardens at Kew from 1865 to 1885. With the resurgence of interest in agave cultivation, this statement still rings true.

Historically, naming agaves has been difficult for several reasons. When agave collection and cultivation exploded in Europe in the early to mid-1800s, many of the plants were sent from Mexico with very little locality information. Plants were often sent to two or more renowned botanists or growers at the same time; each would write a brief botanical description and assign a botanical name, so that the same plant would sometimes have multiple names. Sometimes two or more distinct forms of the same plant were mistaken for different species, again resulting in multiple names. What's more, Gentry wrote that these early European botanists would use potted specimens growing in various European gardens, where the growing conditions could be quite different from those in Mexico, so that their descriptions were not always entirely representative of the species. And agaves are relatively difficult to press for herbarium sheets, resulting in relatively scant availability of preserved material compared to shrubs and herbaceous plants.

In 1833, European botanist Joseph Zuccarini studied plants collected in southern Mexico by Wilhelm Friedrich von Karwinsky between 1827 and 1832, and described five new species. By 1834 Prince Joseph Hubert Salm-Dyck had listed thirty-four species, and by 1859 he had increased the total to forty-seven species. The Prussian General Georg von Jacobi was prolific in naming *Agave* species, and by 1867 he had bumped the total to one hundred fifty-seven. While Zuccarini described agave flowers in detail, he apparently did not use floral morphology to determine species, instead relying on vegetative characteristics. In 1877, John Baker was one of the first to actually recognize the two distinct inflorescence types, but still failed to utilize the characteristics in a taxonomic manner and, like others before him, used only vegetative characteristics when writing about the plants.

In 1915 Alwin Berger, curator of the Hanbury Garden at La Mórtola in Italy, produced the monumental *Die Agaven*, listing two hundred seventy-four species in three subgenera: *Littaea, Euagave,* and *Manfreda.* William Trelease, curator at the Missouri Botanical Gardens in St. Louis, traveled and collected in Mexico, the Caribbean, and Guatemala and produced several papers on agaves, culminating in his treatment of one hundred seventy species in Paul Standley's *Trees and Shrubs of Mexico,* published in 1920.

A major milestone in the study of the genus was reached in 1982 when, after nearly fifty years of extensive field work in rough territories of Mexico and Central America, Gentry published his monumental *Agaves of Continental North America.* Gentry collected many herbarium specimens while traveling and exploring in the wild country, often by burro. He did not include the manfredas as a subgenus within *Agave* as Berger had done, preferring to leave them as a separate, sister genus. This left two subgenera: plants with a branching inflorescence fell into the subgenus *Agave* (renamed from *Euagave* as proposed by Baker), while those with inflorescences lacking elongated side branches kept the name *Littaea.* Gentry's work took him to many herbaria throughout the world, where he studied the previous nomenclature and any pressed specimens associated with those early names. Recognizing the many synonyms described over the years, he reduced the species count for continental North America to one hundred thirty-six. Since the publication of Gentry's book, new roads into more remote areas of Mexico have allowed for more exploration, resulting in the discovery and description of twenty-two new species of *Agave* as interpreted in the classic sense.

Currently, some taxonomists consider the genera *Manfreda*, *Polianthes*, and *Prochnyanthes* to be part of *Agave* and place them in the subgenus *Manfreda*. These plants are perennials with harmless, soft, flexible leaves that die off in winter. The flowers are similar and there has been some hybridization, indicating that they are closely related to the agaves with their stout, lethal leaves that can skewer body parts with ease. Other related plants include those from *Beschorneria*, *Furcraea*, *Hesperaloe*, *Hesperoyucca*, and *Yucca*.

Common Names

As confusing as botanical names have been over the years, common names can be just as frustrating. For instance, the word maguey means agave, and a number of Mexican species are called maguey, maguey verde, or maguey de pulque, while others are simply called mescal. Frequently plants are referred to by their local names, and we get some equally hard-to-spell names such as chahuiqui for *Agave multifilifera* and the beautiful Nahuatl name papalometl (butterfly agave) for the equally beautiful *A. potatorum*.

With the rising interest in agaves, growers are looking for unique forms and often give them clever cultivar names so they will be easily remembered. Some examples are *Agave bracteosa* 'Calamar' (a play on the common name of squid agave), *A. geminiflora* 'Spaghetti Strap' (in reference to the very narrow leaves), *A. gentryi* 'Jaws' (a form with extra large teeth), and *A. salmiana* 'Green Goblet' (named for the green leaves and urn-like shape of the plant).

Growing Agaves

While agaves have long been planted in gardens throughout the warmer climes of the desert southwestern United States, they have not long been considered integral parts of landscape design. Instead, they were traditionally relegated to "cactus and succulent gardens" where they were planted singly as part of a one-of-this and one-of-that approach; rarely were they mixed with trees, shrubs, or colorful perennials.

But when you think about it, how often do you find agaves growing in nature with no other plants around? In nearly every instance where I have seen agaves in habitat, they have been part of a landscape including trees, shrubs, and flowering perennials. Accordingly, more and more landscape designers are beginning to view agaves, cactus, and other succulents as key components in a more complete landscape; in the Tucson area, for instance, author/photographer/landscape designer Scott Calhoun has mixed a nice grouping of *Agave schidigera* with a field of the coral-red-flowered *Penstemon superbus*. And at the Desert Botanical Garden in Phoenix in early spring, one can find a strikingly attractive combination of the powdery blue *A. colorata* tucked in a mass of pink-flowered *Penstemon parryi*.

Agave bovicornuta

Many agaves make excellent garden subjects, and owing to their variety of looks these long-lived plants can be used in an array of different ways. Try grouping several plants of one species in among a variety of native flowering shrubs and perennials that will provide colorful interest throughout much of the year. The yellow flowers of *Chrysactinia mexicana* look nice against the silvery blue-gray leaves of *Agave parrasana*, while the rose-purple flowers of *Dalea versicolor* blend well with the slate blue-gray leaves of *A. parryi* var. *truncata*. Try planting the green-leaved species, such as *A. bovicornuta* or *A. mitis*, in shadier spots and mix them with other plants that will provide a tropical or subtropical feel. These are just a few ways in which the bold form of the agave and its colorful flowers can be used to make a visual feast, pleasing the eye of even the most casual observer.

Think of your yard as a blank canvas and use combinations of form, color, and texture much like a painter would to create a beautiful picture. One advantage of painting a picture with plants is that they are living entities, with some dynamic and ever-changing, while others are more static, changing little from season to season. Use the constants as the superstructure, while the more ephemeral plants can be used to keep the landscape in perpetual motion, evolving as seasons change and years progress.

Most agaves can be used in decorative containers, especially in areas that receive substantial amounts of rainfall or experience true winters with the temperature dropping into single digits F (–13 C) or lower. Some species will tolerate winter lows down to 0–10 degrees F (–12 to –18 C), but the selection is limited. Plants in pots can be covered or moved indoors or to protected areas—the most effective solution when you find a species that is just too cool to pass up, even if it is not completely frost hardy in your area.

Where to Grow Agaves

Whether in pots or in the ground, agaves can be grown throughout the world. However, their cultural requirements will vary across regions with the same United States Department of Agriculture (USDA) hardiness zone designation for several reasons. First, the amount of annual rainfall an area receives will affect how a species should be treated. For example, *Agave utahensis* can withstand winter lows well below 0 degrees F (–18 C), but cannot survive the 40 inches (100 cm) of annual rainfall in Raleigh, North Carolina, therefore requiring different care for plants growing there than for plants growing in Las Vegas with its 5 inches

(13 cm) of annual precipitation. In order to keep excess moisture away from the base of the plants, try placing them on a slope or even covering them with a piece of rigid plexiglass.

Second, summer temperatures can be critical to successfully growing agaves. Agaves grow well when the daytime temperature in summer is not too cool, but will shut down when the temperature is too hot. According to U.K. agave grower Paul Spraklin, many agaves can be grown in the southeastern coastal region of England with 20 inches (50 cm) of annual rainfall and daytime highs of 85–90 degrees F (30–32 C) or higher in the summer. Conversely, agaves do not grow as well in the extreme southwestern part of England where annual rainfall totals about 60 inches (150 cm) and summertime highs reach 71–77 degrees F (22–25 C). Agaves seem to shut down when summer temperatures climb above 100 degrees F (38 C), so in much of the desert southwestern United States, the best growing times are in spring and autumn.

While the hardiest species of *Agave* have been grown successfully in many parts of the world that are not frost free, even these plants can suffer over the long term when taken out of their comfort zone and pushed to their limits. For example, Panayoti Kelaidis at the Denver Botanic

Agave utahensis var. *eborispina*

Gardens in zone 5 indicated that an *A. ovatifolia* specimen survived a couple of winters there but then had to expend significant amounts of energy to recover—and eventually was unable to store enough energy during the growing season, leading to its death.

But in general, no matter where you garden, I urge you to look at the recommended hardiness zones for each plant and consider trying those that are rated as one half zone or even one zone warmer than where you live. After all, pushing the envelope and testing the limits of these fantastic plants is a good way to learn more about them.

UNITED STATES

Quite a few species are hardy enough to be grown in the ground in the United States, from the Pacific Northwest, south throughout California, east through Arizona and Texas, into the southeast, and up through the eastern coastal states to parts of North Carolina. However, annual rainfall can sometimes be as great a factor as minimum temperature is in determining where agaves can be grown. When growing agaves in an area with annual rainfall of 20 inches (50 cm) or more, make the extra effort to ensure that excess moisture drains quickly and that water does not sit on the leaves or at the base of the plant.

UNITED KINGDOM AND IRELAND

Most of the United Kingdom and Ireland is in the equivalent of USDA hardiness zones 8–9 (see temperature chart on page 33), but in this region excessive rainfall can be more of a limiting factor than frost. Average annual rainfall can vary from as little as 24 inches (60 cm) to as much as 175 inches (420 cm). Few agaves will tolerate the high end of the spectrum unless the soil is drastically modified—and even then, the much higher humidity will wreak havoc on the more xeric species. The southeastern coast of England is one of the better regions in which to grow agaves.

FRANCE, SPAIN, PORTUGAL, ITALY, AND GREECE

A large portion of these five countries falls within the equivalent of USDA zones 8–9, indicating that a number of species can be grown here without danger of frost damage—so once again annual rainfall totals will be critical. The Mediterranean parts of southern Europe should be ideal for growing agaves; in fact Alwin Berger prepared many pressed specimens from, as Gentry put it, "Mórtola cultivates"—prepared from plants at the Hanbury botanical gardens in La Mórtola, Italy. A number of growers in Spain have been cultivating a wide variety of agaves with great success.

With much of Spain and Portugal falling in zones 9–10, and average annual rainfall ranging from under 20 inches (50 cm) to nearly 40 inches (100 cm), an agave enthusiast should be able to grow a variety of species.

GERMANY AND CZECH REPUBLIC

Few species of *Agave* can be grown unprotected outdoors, and many growers keep their plants potted and in glass houses.

AUSTRALIA AND NEW ZEALAND

Both countries use their own modified versions of the USDA hardiness map. Although the dearth of weather stations in Australia results in a map lacking detail, Australians can use the zone system as a general guideline, much like the system is used in the United States.

The New Zealand system has four zones based on temperature ranges varying from 4 to 6 degrees C, or 39–43 F. The majority of the South Island falls within New Zealand's zone 8 (–10 to –5 C, or 14 to 23 F), with nearly the entire coast considered zone 9 (–5 to –1 C or 23 to 30 F), and the bulk of the North Island zones 9 and 10 (–1 to 4 C or 30 to 39 F). It appears that New Zealand would be a great place to grow agaves.

Planting

The agaves that are hardy to the cold can be planted at any time of year as long as the subsequent watering schedule is appropriate for the season. Those that are considered half-hardy (sustaining some leaf damage at temperatures in the mid- to upper 20s F (–2 to –4 C) should be planted in late spring when the soil is warm enough for good root growth.

Proper planting is as critical for the long-term health of agaves as it is for any other plant. The key is to make sure they are not planted too deep. Dig a hole no deeper than the depth of the root ball, and loosen the soil around the hole. Place the plant so the bottom leaves are slightly above existing grade and fill around the root ball with the soil that was removed from the hole. Do not add any compost or organic matter to the backfill soil, as that will break down, causing the soil and plant to settle too low, which often causes water to collect in the crown and leads to potential crown rot. The soil should have good drainage, allowing excess water to drain away from the center of the plant.

A few species are found naturally growing in cracks or fissures in solid limestone or in limestone-derived soil. These species might not require the limestone, but instead are able to tolerate the conditions better than other species. If your soil is high in organic matter, try mixing in some sharp sand and some commercially bagged lime to increase the drainage and the pH.

Watering

Watering requirements of agaves will vary depending on the species being grown, the soil type, the temperature, the amount of light the plant is receiving, and the elevation zone. Although there are species on either extreme of the water requirements, the majority will grow best when given some supplemental water during their growing season. In general that growing season is when the daytime temperatures are warm but not too hot. In southern Arizona, the plants start to grow in the spring as the daytime temperatures climb high enough to warm the soil sufficiently for the roots to grow and absorb water. They seem to shut down once the temperatures are consistently above about 105 degrees F (40 C).

It is generally best if the plants don't have wet feet. This is especially important for the more xeric species rather than those from more moist climates. Agaves have a shallow, extensive root system so it is best to thoroughly soak an area three or four times the width of the plant to a depth of 1–2 feet (30–60 cm), and then allow the soil to dry before soaking again, rather than watering frequently in small amounts.

Keep standing water away from the center of the leaf rosette all year round, and especially when the weather is cool or cold, to minimize the possibility of rotting the crown. Also, for plants that are in full sun, keep water off the leaf surfaces during the middle of the day. Water drops can act like a magnifying glass, causing burns on the leaves, particularly on broad-leaved species.

Even the most xeric species benefit from supplemental water during the hottest part of the year. One specimen of *Agave palmeri*, which I planted outside my bedroom window in 1985, was given supplemental water the first two summers and then left to survive on scant rainfall ever since. Although it is still alive and looks great, the plant has not quite doubled in size, from 7 inches (18 cm) to 12 inches (30 cm) across—whereas with supplemental water on a consistent basis, a normal *A. palmeri* plant would have reached 3 or 4 feet (0.9 or 1.2 m) across

The Ten Most Xeric Species

Agave applanata
Agave asperrima
Agave colorata
Agave pelona
Agave striata
Agave toumeyana
Agave utahensis
Agave victoriae-reginae
Agave xylonacantha
Agave zebra

The Ten Most Mesic Species

Agave bovicornuta
Agave geminiflora
Agave gentryi
Agave horrida
Agave isthmensis
Agave mitis
Agave montana
Agave petrophila
Agave schidigera
Agave wocomahi

in the same amount of time. In the hot, interior, low elevation zone of the desert southwestern United States, give your agaves a thorough soaking once every seven to ten days from spring through autumn. In the mid-elevation zone, plants will also benefit from some supplemental water once every ten to fourteen days until the summer monsoons hit, and then again once the rainy season is over.

Insects, Diseases, and Other Pests

Because agaves are succulent plants native to the southwestern United States and Mexico, you might expect them to be relatively trouble free. Indeed, if they were only growing in their natural habitat, there would be a natural balance between pests and predators—but with the exponential rise in popularity and subsequent cultivation, there has been a corresponding rise in insect pests, animal pests, and diseases.

The most widely known insect pest is *Scyphophorus acupunctatus*, commonly called the agave snout beetle or agave weevil. This little bugger has a happy relationship with plants out in the wild. Here is a great little bedtime story (which will put most infants and many adults to sleep): when an agave in its natural habitat grows old and flowers, the female beetle of *Scyphophorus acupunctatus* lays her eggs in the stem of the dying plant. The weevils hatch and start eating the stem, digesting the material and turning it into compost. This helps to speed the plant's decay, which would otherwise take a very long time in desert habitats, and in doing so they prevent the dying carcasses from cluttering up an otherwise pristine area. With the increase in agave cultivation, there appears to be an increase in the *Scyphophorus acupunctatus* population, and the use of a systemic insecticide has been the most reliable method of control. Several different products to control the insect are currently available, and with the ever-changing market, the agavologist should look for a grub killer that is also systemic. An infested plant is usually easily spotted, with its characteristic upright central cone with outer leaves flopped to the ground.

Caulotops barberi is known as the agave running bug, and it lives up to its name! If you see it on one side of the leaf and try to get a closer look, it runs around to the other side of the leaf. Although the insect is tough to spot, the damage it causes is really easy to recognize. Look for light-colored spots randomly dotting the leaves as this insect pierces the tissue and sucks out the juice.

Mealy bugs can be found on the leaf cone and nearby leaves, where they tend to hang out socializing and drinking the juice of the young, tender leaves.

It appears that at least three different types of scale insects have been found on various *Agave* species. Soft scale (*Coccid* spp.), felt scale (*Ovaticoccus agavium*) and cochineal scale (*Dactylopius coccus*) are all insect pests that suck the juices from agaves' leaves.

Another pest that has become more prevalent is a species of eriophyid mite (*Aceria* sp.) that resides deep in the leaf cone and scrapes tender tissue, causing unsightly scars that become visible when the leaves grow out. Left untreated, this mite can ruin a prized specimen. This mite is actually related to spiders and not insects, so is best treated with a miticide.

Other spots and disfigurations have been the result of fungal problems. There are at least three species of the fungus *Colletotrichum* that will cause ring spotting on leaves and should be treated with a fungicide specifically for that genus. Another method of control is to simply pull off the infected leaves if the problem is caught early enough that only the outer, lower leaves are affected.

ABOVE An adult agave snout beetle

BELOW A healthy agave (left) and one succumbing to the agave snout beetle (right)

Some species are more palatable to wildlife than others. For instance, packrats will readily demolish young plants of *Agave bracteosa* while those of *A. zebra* are left virtually untouched. The size of the plant does not seem to affect a packrat's choice, either. They will chew out large portions of leaves on adult plants of *A.* 'Sharkskin' as well as totally demolishing young plants. There appears to be little rhyme or reason to the attack of these voracious eaters.

In the desert southwestern United States, rabbits will occasionally eat the leaves of select species. They ate one of my healthy, well-established, fully grown plants of *Agave geminiflora*, giving it a buzz cut similar to the haircut seen on military recruits, from which it finally did recover after a couple of growing seasons. I am happy to report that the plant has not been eaten since and has grown into a beautiful specimen. Reports of javelina and deer eating agaves have been circulating within the xeric plants growers' community, but this seems to be a minor problem for established plants. There is hope: as plants mature and are grown with minimal supplemental water and no fertilizer, they seem to develop a natural deterrent to pesky critters.

ABOVE An adult agave running bug and the damage done to *Agave stricta*

LEFT Mealy bug infestation on the leaf cone of *Agave pygmae*

Size Categories

Agave species that are considered to be extra small have individual rosettes that generally top out at less than 12 inches (30 cm) across. Small species range from about 12 to 30 inches (30–75 cm) across, medium-sized species range from 30 to 48 inches (75–120 cm) across, and those considered large will grow 48–60 inches (120–150 cm) across. In keeping with our penchant for super-sizing just about anything, I reserve a new category of extra large for the giants, or those that get larger than 60 inches (150 cm) across.

As with all living plants (as opposed to dead or plastic ones), agaves refuse to follow religiously the parameters laid down by gardeners and horticulturists. Be aware that there will be exceptions to the not-so-hard-and-fast rules, and some renegade plants will not conform to our neatly defined categories for one reason or another. With that in mind, use these notes as a general guideline and do not come after me with the leaf of *Agave applanata* if, or should I say when, your plant gets larger or stays smaller than the sizes hereby declared as law. A list of agaves according to size category appears at the back of the book.

Cold Hardiness

Because agaves are immensely popular throughout the world, I give general hardiness information using the USDA hardiness zone system, with cold hardiness reduced to a temperature range as shown on the accompanying table. However, these temperatures are general guidelines and do not tell the whole story on cold hardiness. It is always best to see for yourself when it comes to the hardiness of a particular species in your area and under your growing conditions.

In general, the plants from more northern latitudes or from higher elevations tend to be the hardiest, while those from more southern latitudes or more tropical climates tend to be the least hardy. In the following pages, in addition to general advice on growing agaves, I will give additional advice for areas of low, mid-, and high elevation in the southwestern United States, where agaves are widely popular as landscape plants.

Whenever we try to put anything as variable as plants into rigidly defined categories, there are bound to be exceptions. If you have your heart set on a particular plant, experiment with it in more than one place in your landscape. You might find that it survives the cold of winter or the heat of summer, or that it simply grows better in a particular spot than in another. Much of the joy of gardening lies in discovering the intimate details of your landscape, the warm spots and the extra cold spots, and finding the perfect plant for a particular place.

Many horticulturists use three categories when discussing hardiness: hardy, half-hardy, and tender. Although they like to associate temperatures with these categories, hardiness is affected by more than just absolute low temperature. Some of the factors that affect the impact of winter lows on agaves include the duration of the overnight low, the number of consecutive nights at a low temperature, whether or not the plant is actively growing, the elevation from which seed was collected, and the range of hardiness within the species due to its natural distribution.

First, let's look at the duration of the overnight low. *Agave bovicornuta* is considered to be hardy to about the mid-20s F (−3 to −4 C). On some nights, an overnight low of 26 degrees F (−3 C) might occur for a brief time, while on other nights that same temperature might persist for longer. Our *A. bovicornuta* might suffer some damage in the second scenario.

Second, the number of consecutive nights during which the overnight low reaches 26 degrees F (−3 C) can affect the reaction of the plant. Our *Agave bovicornuta* plant might be able to withstand one night at 26 degrees F (−3 C), but would suffer some leaf damage if exposed to that temperature for two or more consecutive nights.

Third, if the plant has been hardened off, or weaned of supplemental water as the temperatures cool in the autumn, thereby reducing the amount of tender, succulent growth, and kept relatively dry through the winter, it might be less affected by the overnight low of 26 degrees F, even if this low temperature is prolonged.

In addition, the elevation from which the seed has been collected can affect the response of a plant to winter cold. For instance, *Agave*

ZONE	TEMP (deg F)	TEMP (deg C)
1	below −50	−45.6 and below
2a	−45 to −50	−42.8 to −45.5
2b	−40 to −45	−40.0 to −42.7
3a	−35 to −40	−37.3 to −40.0
3b	−30 to −35	−34.5 to −37.2
4a	−25 to −30	−31.7 to −34.4
4b	−20 to −25	−28.9 to −31.6
5a	−15 to −20	−26.2 to −28.8
5b	−10 to −15	−23.4 to −26.1
6a	−5 to −10	−20.6 to −23.3
6b	0 to −5	−17.8 to −20.5
7a	5 to 0	−15.0 to −17.7
7b	10 to 5	−12.3 to −15.0
8a	15 to 10	−9.5 to −12.2
8b	20 to 15	−6.7 to −9.4
9a	25 to 20	−3.9 to −6.6
9b	30 to 25	−1.2 to −3.8
10a	35 to 30	1.6 to −1.1
10b	40 to 35	4.4 to 1.7
11	40 and above	4.5 and above

PLANT HARDINESS ZONES
AVERAGE ANNUAL MINIMUM TEMPERATURE

To see the U.S. Department of Agriculture Hardiness Zone Map, go to the U.S. National Arboretum site at http://www.usna.usda.gov/Hardzone/ushzmap.html.

Elevation Zones for the Southwestern United States and Mexico

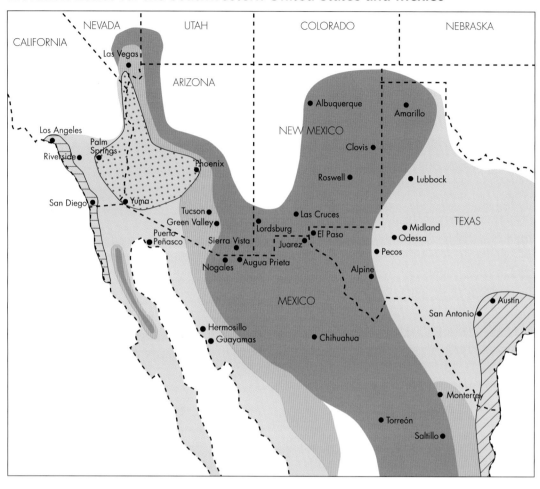

high elevation zone: above 3500 feet (1100 meters)

mid-elevation zone: 2000–3500 feet (600–1100 meters)

low elevation zone: below 2000 feet (600 meters)

The low elevation zone is subdivided
based on temperature and rainfall.

cool, coastal

hot, dry, interior

wet, interior

gentryi that originated at the highest elevation might be hardier to winter temperatures in zone 7b, while those from the lower end of its range might not survive an average winter in the same zone. Another consideration in cold hardiness is the natural range of the species. Some, like *A. asperrima* and *A. parryi*, have long north to south distribution ranges, with the forms from the northern end of the range being generally hardier than those from the southern end.

In her 2002 study of agaves in cold climates, Mary Irish documented several species, with minimum temperature exposed to, locality of the plant, and damage sustained. Some anomalies are difficult to explain. For instance, *Agave lechuguilla*, a Chihuahuan Desert species that should have been able to tolerate a good deal of cold, was listed as dead when exposed to 17 degrees F (–8 C) in the Sierra Foothills in California, yet survived –20 degrees F (–29 C) in Littleton, Colorado, with no damage! In contrast, *A. vilmoriniana*, a Sonoran Desert species that can show slight damage in Tucson, Arizona, when the temperature drops to 17 degrees F (–8 C), survived that same temperature with no damage in the Sierra Foothills in California. Sometimes, a plant that is growing in a zone at the limit of its frost tolerance will survive for several years, but is weakened by the repeated exposure to winter temperatures that are a little too low, eventually resulting in the death of the plant.

All in all, I like the quote from Tony Avent, owner of Plant Delights Nursery in Raleigh, North Carolina: "I consider every plant hardy until I've killed it myself . . . at least three times." I firmly believe that if you like a plant, you should try it in several situations before you give up on it. With that in mind, the accompanying list shows ten species that are considered the hardiest and ten that are the most frost sensitive. (Although sixteen species in my book fall into zone 7, I had to stop at ten.) Check the individual entry in the encyclopedia section for a hardiness guideline—or be like Tony and try them all at least three times!

The Ten Hardiest Species and Cultivars

Agave bracteosa	zone 7b
Agave chrysantha	zone 7b
Agave gentryi	zone 7b
Agave havardiana	zone 7a
Agave montana	zone 7b
Agave polianthiflora	zone 7a
Agave striata	zone 7a
Agave toumeyana	zone 5a
Agave utahensis	zone 5a
Agave victoriae-reginae	zone 7b

The Ten Most Frost-Sensitive Species and Cultivars

Agave bovicornuta	zone 9b
Agave horrida	zone 10a
Agave isthmensis	zone 9b
Agave 'Kichijokan'	zone 10a
Agave macroacantha	zone 9b
Agave marmorata	zone 9b
Agave petrophila	zone 10b
Agave potatorum	zone 9b
Agave stricta	zone 10a
Agave titanota	zone 9b

Encyclopedia of Agaves

I like to think of my book as one would a sumptuous five-course meal. The preface is the pre-meal glass of wine, the introduction is the appetizer, the growing information is the salad, and the encyclopedia is the main course with the pictures being dessert. The main course that follows covers eighty species, cultivars, and hybrids, with field notes, plant descriptions, and information on culture, landscape value, and taxonomic notes when pertinent.

Agave shawii ssp. *goldmaniana*

Because I want to give you a feel for the plants as found in their natural habitat, the field notes are based on personal experience, and include casual observations on soil, exposure, and surrounding vegetation. The descriptions are derived from existing literature and then rounded out with information gleaned from other agavephiles, as well as from my own personal experience.

The sections on culture provide general information for growers worldwide, along with some more specific advice for growers in various parts of the United States. For those gardening with agaves in the American Southwest, information specific to elevation zones is also provided. Although I list temperatures and USDA zones for hardiness, these should be used as guidelines as there are many factors that affect hardiness. Gardeners throughout the world can use these zones, based on the lowest temperatures experienced in a given area. To find your zone, please refer to the chart on page 33.

Advice on landscape value is primarily aimed at gardeners in the arid southwestern United States, especially when it comes to suggested companion plants. For those growing agaves elsewhere, I encourage you to experiment, mixing agaves with native perennials and small shrubs that grow well in your area. You just might hit on a perfect combination that you can then share with your friends.

In each entry, the scientific name, comprising the genus and species, is followed by the name or names of the botanist or botanists who originally described the species. For example, the name *Agave shrevei* Gentry reflects the fact that Howard Scott Gentry described this agave, which he named in honor of Forrest Shreve, a botanist and researcher who worked at the Desert Laboratory in Tucson, Arizona, in the early 1900s. On the other hand, sometimes botanists will derive the species name from a particular characteristic of that species. An example is *A. asperrima*, with *asperrima* referring to the rough, sandpapery feel of the leaves.

For several species, I include taxonomic notes. Some species names have been accepted because they are based on recent, concrete taxonomic work. In other cases, name changes have been rejected even though the author presented an argument for changing the rank from species to subspecies. Taxonomy, after all, is generally a matter of opinion. Many of the agave names are firmly entrenched in horticulture, and to revise them now would increase the frustration that gardeners feel toward botanists constantly changing established names.

Rather than covering only those species that are common and very well known in horticulture, I also include entries for those that are either newly described or gaining in popularity due to the boom in tissue culture making them more commonly available. Some of these include *Agave applanata, A. gentryi, A. montana, A. ovatifolia, A. petrophila, A. utahensis, A. wocomahi,* and *A. zebra.*

I do sprinkle some humor in the following pages. Try not to take it too seriously; for instance, when I suggest using sunscreen on your plants, please do not try that at home, as only trained professionals can apply the correct amount. With that said, let us get on to the good stuff.

Agave albopilosa I. Cabral, Villarreal, & A. E. Estrada

WHITE HAIR AGAVE

Agave albopilosa with its tufts of white fiber at the leaf tips

The appropriately descriptive name *albopilosa* is derived from the Latin *alb*, meaning white, and *pilos*, meaning hairy. This combination refers to the tufts of white fibers at the base of the spine on each leaf.

FIELD NOTES

Because *Agave albopilosa* is rare, highly prized by collectors, and restricted to one small area in northeastern Mexico, the precise locality of these observations will remain undisclosed to prevent further removal of plants within reach. The plant was first found in the mid-1990s, but not described and given a scientific name until 2007. Once the name, description, and photographs were published, the hunt was on and collectors started drooling over this unique plant with the tuft of white hairlike fibers below the terminal spine. Although the plant was not widely cultivated as of 2011, seed is now available from a dealer in Europe, and plants should be hitting the marketplace by 2012.

These small balls of numerous, narrow leaves grow glued to small fissures in a narrow ribbon of sharp limestone rock that juts straight up out of the earth, requiring a rock climber with ropes and special equipment in order to get near all but a few of the plants growing down low. Plants have been found growing in the light shade of sparse trees and in the hot, blazing sun on only two knife-like protrusions between 3300 and 5000 feet (1000–1500 meters) elevation.

DESCRIPTION

My description is based solely on plants in habitat, and eventual size might differ slightly in cultivation. These are small plants forming dense balls to about 6–15 inches high and 10–16 inches across (15–36 by 25–40 cm), and are packed with a hundred or more medium green to yellow-green, linear leaves, each with a small explosion of white fibers at the base of the short terminal spine. As with other closely related species, there are no formidable teeth along the leaf edges; instead they have tiny, sawtooth-like margins that are able to slice a deep "paper cut" in soft skin. The 6–9 inch long by 1/3–1/2 inch wide (14–23 by 0.75–1.25 cm) leaves are terminated by a small, dark gray to black terminal spine that pokes out beyond the tuft of fibers.

Come late spring, dark purple buds eventually open to reveal 1 inch (2.5 cm) long, greenish purple flowers in the upper half of the 18–30 inch (45–80 cm) long, unbranched flower stalk.

CULTURE

Like the plants that surround it in habitat, *Agave albopilosa* should be hardy to at least the high teens F (−7 to −8 C), and probably lower if its association with *A. bracteosa* and *A. victoriae-reginae* is any indication. They can be grown either in the ground or as potted plants in zones 8b–11, and in any frost-free regions throughout the world. Because the plant is so new to horticulture, information on hardiness is scarce, but plants should be able to be grown outdoors throughout the Pacific coast and Gulf coast states that experience mild to moderate frosts. The plants should be perfectly hardy in the low and mid-elevation southwestern U.S. zones without being damaged by frost. As with other species in the group Striatae, the growth rate is moderate to slow. Grow them in partial shade to filtered sun in southwestern U.S. zones, and in full sun in the cool, coastal low elevation zone; in fact, plants will appreciate a bit of light shade no matter where in the world they are grown.

The plants require a moderate amount of supplemental water, though the natural habitat does experience some cool, foggy days which would make this a perfect plant for coastal regions that receive some fog. The soil should have very good drainage, and even some lime added, based on the observation that plants are found perched in cracks of pure limestone.

LANDSCAPE VALUE

Because of its petite size and interesting tufts of fiber on the leaves, *Agave albopilosa* makes an excellent container plant that can be grown in all regions.

OPPOSITE TOP *Agave albopilosa* growing on a limestone wall in northeastern Mexico

BOTTOM LEFT The dark purple flower buds of *Agave albopilosa*

BOTTOM RIGHT The white fibers on *Agave albopilosa* leaves are unique in the genus.

Agave applanata Koch ex Jacobi

MAGUEY DE IXTLE

The stately form of *Agave applanata* makes an excellent focal point.

The name *applanata* is from the New Latin *applanat*, which means flattened, most likely in reference to the flattened leaves on the mature plants.

FIELD NOTES

When traveling the highways of Hidalgo and Puebla in southern Mexico, look for the large, bold form of *Agave applanata* growing on the slopes off the roadway between 6000 and 8200 feet (1800–2500 meters) elevation. In October 2001, Carl Shoenfeld and Wade Roitsch of Yucca Do Nursery took me to see these wild and unusual beauties outside of Tulancingo, Hidalgo, at 7500 feet (2300 meters) elevation. These are unusual in that the plants morph from a cute little juvenile form to a massive adult form that looks radically different from the babies. In cultivation, the juvenile form of *A. applanata* has long been misrepresented as *A. patonii*, *A. parryi* var. *patonii* and *A. parryi* var. *minima*, when in fact the name *A. patonii* is a synonym for *A. parryi*, while the latter two names actually have nothing to do with *A. applanata*.

Scott Calhoun and I revisited the plants near Tulancingo in July 2009 and found no mature plants, but several intermediate-sized ones. We also encountered more populations scattered about the countryside as we headed south towards Oaxaca. Most of the plants were small, but we did spot a few larger plants in flower with the characteristically tall yet narrow panicle. As we traveled further east and then south along Mexico Highway 119 we encountered more plants of *Agave applanata* growing perched on the tops of relatively new roadcuts and others scattered about the open, rolling, grass-covered hills, some with their impressive, candelabra-like flower stalks reaching for the sky.

Howard Scott Gentry indicated that *Agave applanata* had been moved from southern Mexico to the northwestern part of the country by people taking small offsets and planting them, possibly for the use of leaves as a source of strong fiber. This does seem quite likely as plants are frequently found near houses and small settlements in southern and central Mexico.

Plants near the former silver mining town of Mineral de Pozos and on the nearby Cerro El Zamorano are a bit of an anomaly, as they are small to medium-sized with old inflorescences; no giant specimens can be found. In July 2007, I spotted one medium-sized, flowering plant on the drive to Xichú (pronounced See-choo). This plant was about 1½ feet tall by 2 feet across (45 by 60 cm), with an inflorescence shape identical to that of a normal-sized, flowering plant. It looked very much like a juvenile plant making its transition into an adult version of *Agave applanata*

when it decided to send up its flower stalk. Until these plants are studied in more detail to determine whether they are distinct enough to warrant subspecies or varietal status, they should be treated as *A. applanata*.

DESCRIPTION

Don't be fooled by the adorable juvenile form, which will eventually morph into a large or extra large adult plant, reaching about 2.5–4 feet tall and up to 3.5–6 feet across (0.5–1.2 by 1–2 meters), forming a beautifully symmetrical rosette of light whitish blue-gray, sword-shaped leaves that are widest at about the middle of the blade, gradually tapering to the long, sharp tip. Leaves are 16–24 inches long by 3–4 inches wide (40–60 by 7–10 cm), held very stiff and upright in the upper two thirds of the plant, and slightly spreading-upright in the lower one third. Grayish to black, flesh-ripping, marginal teeth are largest above mid-blade, getting smaller both above and below, and can make impressive bud prints on the surrounding leaves. The sharp, stout, grayish to black, 2 inch (5 cm) long terminal spine will pierce muscle and tendons of the careless agavephile. Copious quantities of offsets are frequently produced by the mother plant, creating an incredible garden of tiny, symmetrical rosettes.

The narrow, 13–26 foot (4–8 meter) tall, branched flower stalk resembles a skinny Christmas tree poking up out of the surrounding desert. The 2¼–3 inch (5.5–8 cm) long, bright yellow flowers are densely clustered at the ends of each side branch.

CULTURE

Considered a zone 8a–11 plant, *Agave applanata* has taken winter lows to at least 10 degrees F (–12 C). It can be grown as a landscape plant in mild-winter, dry parts of the Pacific and Gulf coast states as long as the soil is not too wet in winter. All forms can be grown outdoors in the low and mid-elevation range in the southwestern United States, though plants might need some winter protection in the cold, low elevation zone of north Texas.

Agave applanata has a slow growth rate when small, speeding up some as plants morph to adult stage and then slowing a bit once they near mature size. The plants have proven to be quite drought tolerant yet able to utilize extra water if planted with trees, shrubs, or perennials. They are tolerant of full sun in all areas where *A. applanata* can be grown as a landscape plant.

OPPOSITE TOP The juvenile form of *Agave applanata*

BOTTOM LEFT Scott Calhoun next to the adult form of *Agave applanata* in southern Hidalgo

BOTTOM RIGHT The characteristic narrow panicle of *Agave applanata*

My plants, grown in a rocky clay soil in Tucson, receive a thorough soaking once every fourteen days in the summer and once a month or less often in the winter. When grown in the hot, interior, low elevation zone, the plants appreciate water a little more frequently in the summer, maybe once every seven to ten days, while in the cool, coastal, low elevation zone, once every two to three weeks ought to be sufficient. Plants grow fine in most soil types as long as watering is adjusted accordingly and the soil is not kept soggy.

LANDSCAPE VALUE

Use *Agave applanata* in full sun in the most xeric part of a desert landscape. The stiff leaves and symmetrical form will provide visual beauty, drawing the eye to its stately form in the landscape. It can be used as a focal point in a wildflower garden, while the soft gray-green to blue-gray color is perfect for mixing with rich green-leaved perennials and small shrubs with colorful flowers. Some excellent choices include *Berlandiera lyrata*, *Chrysactinia mexicana*, *Glandularia gooddingii*, *Penstemon* species, *Salvia greggii*, *Scutellaria suffrutescens*, and *Tetraneuris acaulis*. Mix in with hardcore desert plants such as the shrubs *Buddleja marrubiifolia*, *Larrea divaricata*, *Leucophyllum frutescens*, and *Simmondsia chinensis*, and trees like *Bauhinia lunarioides*, *Eysenhardtia orthocarpa*, and *Parkinsonia microphylla*.

Plants form majestic specimens composed of stout, lethal, sword-shaped leaves that will skewer even the most experienced desert rat if he or she gets careless.

TAXONOMIC NOTES

Howard Scott Gentry himself was not immune to nomenclatural confusion. In *Agaves of Continental North* America, he included *Agave patonii* as a synonym of *A. parryi* var. *parryi*, but if you continue reading, you will find under *A. parryi* var. *truncata* the following passage: "Other collectors have found this variety, and it may be offered in the succulent trade as *Agave patonii*, as it has been called at Huntington Botanical Gardens, following my suggestion." This is interesting considering that, on the one hand, he rightly subsumed *A. patonii* into the typical *A. parryi*, while on the other suggesting that this name be used for the distinct and more diminutive *A. parryi* var. *truncata*. How the name *A. patonii* came to be so widely used for the juvenile form of *A. applanata* is, and probably shall remain, a mystery.

Agave applanata 'Cream Spike'

Long misrepresented in horticulture as *Agave parryi* 'Cream Spike', this variegated plant is highly ornamental and quite popular as a container plant. Eventual size of the rosette is unknown; however as a potted plant in its juvenile form, it makes a low-growing, almost flat specimen, rounding out just a bit as it ages. To date the largest ones have reached about 12–15 inches tall by 20–24 inches across (30–38 by 50–60 cm). Although the plant has been around for a number of years, it is virtually unheard of as a landscape plant, so not much is known about its full size. The distinguishing feature of this choice cultivar lies in the leaves. Leaves on young plants of 'Cream Spike' are ovate, measuring 2–4 inches long by 1 inch wide (5–10 by 2.5 cm). They are medium blue-green in the center, with broad, butter yellow variegation on either side.

Young plants produce copious quantities of pups which are easily pulled and re-planted elsewhere.

Randy Baldwin at San Marcos Growers in Santa Barbara, California, has indicated that Rick Nowakowski at Nature's Curiosity Shop received this plant from Japan in the 1980s, but the original source of the form is still a mystery.

Plants have proven hardy to at least the high teens F (−7 to −8 C) and should probably be able to withstand slightly lower temperatures. For now, this cultivar should be considered a zone 8b–11 plant, and hardy in the mid- and low elevation southwestern U.S. zones. They seem to grow fine in full sun in the cooler, coastal, low elevation zone and in the mid-elevation zone, but prefer light shade in the hot, interior, low elevation zone. Plants are low-water-using; in fact, too much water can cause leaves to rot. The growth rate is quite slow, especially when grown as a miniature in a container, and it will take many years to achieve full size.

Grow in a soil type that has good drainage to minimize rot problems. Watch out for rodents! This is one that they seem to relish, and they can ravage a young plant overnight.

Agave applanata 'Cream Spike' showing its creamy yellow variegation

Agave asperrima Jacobi

ROUGH LEAF AGAVE

The broad leaves of *Agave asperrima* ssp. *potosiensis* are distinctive.

Synonym: *Agave scabra* Salm-Dyck. The name *asperrima* is based on the Latin *asper* meaning rough, referring to the sandpaper-like leaf surface.

FIELD NOTES

Agave asperrima is divided into four subspecies and has a wide distribution range, being found in many parts of the Chihuahuan Desert Region between 4000 and 7200 feet (1200–2100 meters) elevation. Some of the smaller plants are seen in the very arid region of southern Coahuila while some larger plants can be found further east and north in the more mesic parts of eastern Coahuila.

This species is encountered on nearly every road as one travels through the Chihuahuan Desert Region. Along with some fellow plant fanatics, I once went to the top of the Sierra Patagalana in southern Coahuila and saw some beautiful specimens in flower in the heat of summer. I have also seen some fantastic flowering specimens in the desert proper near San Lazaro Pass south of Monclova in Coahuila, and still others on Mexico Highway 30 south of Cuatrociénegas in Coahuila.

The plants near the top of the Sierra Patagalana have deeply folded leaves with vicious marginal teeth topping the large teats, and a long, needle-like terminal spine at the end of each leaf. The paniculate stalk is colorfully topped with red buds that open to reveal flowers that are mostly yellow and flushed with red at the tips.

The Festival de la Toltequidad takes place in the former mining town of Mineral de Pozos in the state of Guanajuato. Musicians from all over Mexico travel here to partake in the festival in the middle of July. Art and handicraft vendors set up booths around the main square while performers dress up in colorful costumes and dance, some even walking on stilts, while musicians form drum circles and explore various beats and rhythms. If you ever go to this festival, be sure to venture west of town to visit the ruins from a bygone era of silver mining that peaked in the nineteenth century. While wandering around the ruins, you should spot several plants of *Agave asperrima* ssp. *potosiensis*, which are distinct in that the rosettes appear fuller and the blue-gray leaves are broadest above the middle, and not below the middle. The margins have large, mammillate scallops with downward-pointing teeth, while the long, needle-like terminal spine is deeply grooved for most of its length. Plants are generally found in semi-open vegetation with larger shrubs and small trees.

DESCRIPTION

Unsurprisingly, with four distinct subspecies, *Agave asperrima* is quite variable. In general, the medium to large, individual rosettes are few-leaved and open, providing an appealing architectural form in xeric landscapes. Plants can produce many offsets around the base of the mother plant, forming large masses, so allow ample room for full development. The more xeric forms tend to be on the smaller end of the size range, while the more mesic forms are on the larger end of the size range with plants obtaining a size of 2–4 feet tall by 3–6 feet across (0.6–1.2 by 0.9–1.8 meters).

The leaves are usually blue-gray, grayish green, or pale green, blending beautifully with a desert landscape. Plants are easily recognized owing to their deeply guttered, 15–36 inch long by 4–6 inch wide (40–90 by 10–15 cm) leaves with the texture of medium-grit sandpaper. These leaves are deeply guttered to nearly folded lengthwise, resembling the bottom of a boat, with a sigmoid curve near the tip. The blades are narrow above the base, widening to their broadest point near the middle, and tapering to the long, sharp, needle-like, deeply grooved terminal spine. The edges are crenately wavy, each teat festooned with large and formidable teeth.

The branched, 12–20 foot (3.6–6.1 meter) tall, relatively open flower stalk has 8–14 side branches in the upper one half to one third, each with small, compact clusters of 2–3 inch (5–7.5 cm) long, bright yellow flowers, and frequently bright red flower buds, at the ends.

CULTURE

Agave asperrima is considered a hardy species, though the southern forms may not be as cold hardy as the northern forms. It is a zone 8a–11 plant, breezing through winter lows of the low teens F (−9 to −10 C), which can be grown outdoors in all low and mid-elevation southwestern U.S. zones and should be tried in warm microclimates in the high elevation zone.

The growth rate is moderately slow, taking several years to achieve a mature, flowering size. This is one of the more xeric species, and once established, plants will survive on 10 inches (25 cm) of annual rainfall. If any summer supplemental water is applied, be sure to allow the soil to dry before giving plants more water as they have a knack for rotting if the soil is kept too wet. Grow these only in full sun for the best form, as any amount of shade results in a more open rosette.

Flowering specimens of the more commonly seen, desert form of *Agave asperrima* growing in central Coahuila

The typical inflorescence and bright yellow flowers on *Agave asperrima*

Agave asperrima is quite soil tolerant, being found on both limestone hills and flat, silty ground throughout much of north-central Mexico.

LANDSCAPE VALUE

Agave asperrima is best used in full sun in the most xeric part of a desert landscape. The open form provides an unusual architectural shape, affording many exciting opportunities to create interesting and unique landscapes. Plants can be used as a focal point in a wildflower garden, and the soft gray-green color is perfect for mixing with rich-green-leaved perennials and small shrubs with colorful flowers. Some excellent choices include *Baileya multiradiata*, *Ericameria laricifolia*, *Penstemon* species, *Salvia greggii*, *Thymophylla pentachaeta*, and *Zinnia acerosa*. Mix in with larger desert shrubs such as *Buddleja marrubiifolia*, *Calli-*

andra californica, *Leucophyllum frutescens*, *Justicia californica*, and *Senna wislizenii*, and trees like *Cordia boissieri*, *Ebenopsis ebano*, and *Parkinsonia microphylla*.

Agave asperrima has hybridized with *Agave nickelsiae*, giving rise to *Agave* 'Sharkskin'.

TAXONOMIC NOTES

The taxonomic history of *Agave asperrima* is clouded with uncertainty. It was thought that two horticulturists, Salm-Dyck and Jacobi, had given the same plant two different names—*A. scabra* and *A. asperrima*, respectively—until 1992 research by Bernd Ullrich indicated that they had in fact described two distinct plants. The plant described by Salm-Dyck was actually what we now know as *Agave parryi*. Even though Salm-Dyck's name of *A. scabra* was applied earlier than Engelmann's *A. parryi*, and would have therefore had priority, the species name *scabra* had been used even earlier for another plant which has since been transferred to the genus *Manfreda*, so that the species name *scabra* could not be applied to any other plant. *Agave asperrima* Jacobi is therefore the legitimate name for the plants described in this entry, as well as the ones called *A. scabra* by Gentry.

With that out of the way, let's look at the distribution of the four subspecies of *Agave asperrima*. The first, subspecies *asperrima*, is found in the desert regions of Coahuila to adjacent northeastern Durango, northern Zacatecas, and Nuevo León. There are also a few localities recorded in southwestern Texas.

The second, known as *Agave asperrima* ssp. *maderensis*, is restricted to canyons in the Sierra de la Madera near Cuatrociénegas in central Coahuila. This form has smooth, green leaves with larger teeth.

The third is *Agave asperrima* ssp. *potosiensis*, which can be found growing on plains and hills in the semi-open tree-like vegetation in San Luis Potosí and Querétaro in central Mexico. This one is distinguished by its recurving, glaucous gray to nearly white leaves and more upright form.

The fourth is *Agave asperrima* ssp. *zarcensis*, found growing in grassland vegetation in northeastern Durango. This one is recognized by the denser rosettes with straight, mostly sword-shaped leaves.

Agave 'Blue Glow'

BLUE GLOW AGAVE

Agave 'Blue Glow', used as a container plant, can be a spectacular specimen.

The red and yellow edges on the bluish leaves glow when backlit by the early morning or late afternoon sun.

FIELD NOTES

Because *Agave* 'Blue Glow' is a manmade hybrid, it will not be found growing in nature. However, a tour of some nurseries and private gardens in the southwestern United States will reveal some beautiful specimens. Thought to be a cross between *A. ocahui* and *A. attenuata*, this Rancho Soledad release combines the best features of the two to give us a spectacular cultivar. It gets its hardiness, stiff leaves, and sharp terminal spine from *A. ocahui* while *A. attenuata* contributes the frosty blue sheen on the leaves.

DESCRIPTION

The gorgeous, solitary, rounded rosettes reach a size of about 1.5–2.5 feet tall by 2–3 feet across (45–75 by 60–90 cm). Glaucous blue-green, bayonet-shaped leaves are generally about 12–18 inches long and 1–1½ inches across (30–45 by 2.5–4 cm) at the widest point, which is just above the middle of the blade. Leaf margin is a narrow, continuous, cinnamon red and lemon-lime yellow edge with small, irregular projections that pass for teeth. When backlit, the colorful leaf edge comes alive, the translucent lemon yellow strip next to the glowing cinnamon red edge making an eye-catching combination. The continuous leaf margin gives way to a ½ inch (12 mm) long, dark reddish brown terminal spine that is deeply grooved for half its length.

The flowers are still a mystery. In spring of 2010, a plant thought to be 'Blue Glow', but with slightly different leaves, flowered in a Phoenix, Arizona, garden. The flowers were waxy, light green with purplish red stamens, unlike either *Agave attenuata* or *A. ocahui*.

CULTURE

Agave 'Blue Glow' is considered a zone 8b–11 plant. It has been proven hardy to at least the low 20s F (−5 to −6 C), and with *A. ocahui* as one of the parents it could be a few degrees hardier. *Agave* 'Blue Glow' makes a great landscape plant in areas that receive moderate frost, and can be used in much of the Pacific coast and Gulf coast states. Plants are hardy in all southwestern U.S. zones except for the high elevation zone and the extreme northern reaches of the cold, low elevation zone of Texas.

The growth rate is moderate, with plants taking several years to

The glowing red and yellow leaf edges of *Agave* 'Blue Glow' come alive when backlit.

achieve full size, making this an ideal plant for smaller landscapes and even large, decorative containers. Established plants are drought tolerant, though they will require some supplemental water once every seven to ten days from late spring through summer in the hot, interior, low elevation zone and in the mid-elevation zone in the southwestern United States. Plants grown in the coastal, low elevation zone can get by with less frequent supplemental irrigation.

For the most compact form, grow this one in full sun, or at least full sun for half the day. Place plants between a patio and the early morning or late afternoon sun to get the full effect of the glowing leaf edge. This hybrid is not particular about soil type as long as the drainage is adequate and roots are not sitting in standing water.

LANDSCAPE VALUE

Agave 'Blue Glow' makes a wonderful landscape plant in most regions of the southwestern United States, and can be used singly as a focal point or grouped for a spectacular display showing off the glowing red edges as the sun dips down low in the western sky. This one combines beautifully with colorful perennials and small shrubs such as *Calliandra eriophylla*, *Chrysactinia mexicana*, *Conoclinium dissectum*, *Dalea frutescens*, *Glandularia gooddingii*, *Penstemon* species, *Poliomintha maderensis*, *Salvia greggii*, *Tetraneuris acaulis*, and *Viguiera deltoidea*. Try growing it in a large, decorative container and keeping it close to a patio where you can enjoy the glowing red leaf edge.

Agave bovicornuta Gentry

COW'S HORNS AGAVE

Agave bovicornuta growing in east-central Sonora

The species name *bovicornuta* is derived from the Latin *bovi*, meaning cow, and *cornu*, meaning horned—alluding to the way the marginal teeth will curve both away from and towards the tip, resembling the horns on a cow and the Hook 'em Horns hand sign made popular by the University of Texas Longhorns.

FIELD NOTES

Agave bovicornuta is restricted to the rocky slopes in oak woodland and pine-oak forest in eastern and southern Sonora, southwestern Chihuahua, and northern Sinaloa in the Sierra Madre Occidental, Mexico, between 3000 and 6000 feet (900–1800 meters) elevation.

With some strenuous hiking and climbing, it is possible to see plants growing among car-sized boulders in the east-facing Las Piedras Canyon in the Sierra de Alamos in southern Sonora, Mexico. If you make the trek to southern Sonora and want to see them in flower, be sure to go in March and hire a local who should be able to lead you up the mountain on a path free of marijuana fields.

The easiest and safest spot to see a fine stand of these plants is on Mexico Highway 16 to Yécora in east-central Sonora. This population of *Agave bovicornuta* grows on the open slopes and roadcuts in the oak zone between KM post 251 and 255, with the elevation range from about 4650 to 5000 feet (1410–1525 meters) or a difference of only about 350 feet (110 meters). In June of 2006, I noticed that the area was extremely dry, and trees were leafless with some oaks even dying, but the agaves stood bright green against the brown and red landscape. Many of the plants appeared to be infested with *Caulotops barberi* (running bug). Another visit to the area in April 2010 revealed a large percentage of the plants to have been mutilated by a machete-wielding vandal.

DESCRIPTION

Agave bovicornuta is a medium-sized, non-offsetting plant that usually grows wider than it does tall, maxing out at about 2–3 feet tall by 3–4 feet across (0.6–0.9 by 0.9–1.2 meters), but frequently smaller. The highly ornamental, broadly lanceolate to spatulate leaves are deep green to light green or yellowish green, 18–24 inches long by 4–6 inches wide (45–60 by 10–15 cm), with a semi-tropical look that is not normally found in the desert proper.

The most highly sought after forms have very broadly spoon-shaped leaves with deliciously wicked teeth. These marginal teeth are of two sizes, with smaller teeth in between the larger ones, creating intricate bud prints that are highly visible and fun to stare at for hours on end. The teeth are a brilliant, glowing yellow to cinnamon reddish orange to chocolate brown on new leaves, turning dark chestnut brown on older leaves to create a festival of color that is a landscape designer's paradise.

At the tip of the leaf, the margins fold up to form a raised edge that continues into the ½–1½ inch (1.3–3.8 cm) long, openly grooved terminal spine. The spine is dark chestnut brown on new leaves, turning ash gray on older leaves.

When the plant has gathered enough energy, the 16–23 foot (5–7 meter) tall, narrowly branched flower stalk begins to emerge in autumn, grows slowly over winter, and then pops out with its many short side branches laden with 2¼–2½ inch (5.5–6.5 cm) long, bright yellow and green flowers clustered at the branch ends. Emergence of the flower stalk signals the end of the line for that plant.

The opposing teeth on *Agave bovicornuta*, resembling the horns of a cow

CULTURE

Agave bovicornuta is a zone 9b–11 plant that is generally hardy in the low elevation southwestern U.S. zone, except for the cold zone in Texas. Plants require some frost protection in the mid-elevation southwestern U.S. zone when overnight lows drop to the mid-20s F (−3 to −4 C) for an extended period. As long as the soil is not soggy in the winter, cow's horns agave can be grown as a landscape plant in frost-free areas of the world or even in places that experience short stretches into the mid-20s F, but is primarily a container plant in regions where the winter lows routinely dip to about 20 degrees F (−6 to −7 C). Protect plants from frost damage by covering with frost cloth or an old blanket from grandma's attic.

Although moderately drought tolerant, the plants will grow faster when given consistent supplemental water in the summer. Plants are best grown in filtered light in the hot, interior low elevation and mid-elevation zones. They can tolerate full sun in the cooler, coastal low elevation zone, and even in the mid-elevation zone if given sufficient supplemental water in the summer. Cow's horns agave makes a beautiful specimen when grown in full sun in the coastal regions of the southwestern United States.

As with most of the species, this one is not very particular about the type of soil it is in as long as it has good drainage.

LANDSCAPE VALUE

Place this gem under a small tree in a highly visible spot to best appreciate the intricate patterns created by the ornamental teeth. Mix this agave

ABOVE Colorful contrast of spines and leaves on *Agave bovicornuta*

RIGHT The paniculate inflorescence of *Agave bovicornuta* rising above the trees

with green, lush-looking plants under a ferny-leaved desert shade tree such as *Acacia berlandieri* or *Lysiloma watsonii* var. *thornberi* to create a subtropical effect. Some plants that are quite compatible include *Cycas revoluta, Dalea capitata, Dioon edule, Justicia spicigera, Poliomintha maderensis*, and *Salvia greggii*. Use up close or in a large decorative container to show off the rich green leaves and the very colorful, cool-looking teeth that produce interesting bud imprints.

Agave bovicornuta 'Heifer's Cream'

I found a partially variegated plant in a batch of seedlings, and through a series of tip mutilation, a fully variegated plant was developed. Mature size is unknown, but there is no reason to expect it to differ significantly from the species; it is just slower growing because of the extensive variegation. 'Heifer's Cream' should reach a full size of 2–3 feet tall by 3–4 feet across (0.6–0.9 by 0.9–1.2 meters). The leaves are broadly lanceolate, widest near the middle, and have decorative marginal teeth. The broad, central stripe of creamy, butter yellow offers a nice contrast to the rest of the bright green leaf color.

Plants are probably best grown in a large, decorative container in order to showcase the distinctive variegation. 'Heifer's Cream' is low-water-using, grows best in a soil with very good drainage, and will need light shade in hot, dry regions but will tolerate more sun in areas with mild climates. The growth rate is quite slow, owing to the large proportion of variegation, especially when grown in a container, and it will take many years to achieve full size.

Agave bovicornuta 'Holstein'

San Marcos Growers found a partially variegated plant in their block of *Agave bovicornuta* and, through a succession of coring, developed an attractive plant with a broad swath of bright, rich buttery yellow down the center of the normally bright green leaf. The San Marcos Growers information page indicates that 'Holstein' can take the full sun in coastal southern California. As with the species, this will need some shade in the low and mid-elevation, desert southwestern U.S. zones. The plants are moderately drought tolerant. They will sustain minor frost damage when winter lows dip into the mid-20s F for an extended period.

Randy Baldwin of San Marcos Growers first proposed the name 'Holstein' for this plant at the International Plant Propagators Western Conference meeting in San Diego on October 1, 2009.

Agave bovicornuta 'Reggae Time'

This glaucous, bluish-green-leaved form is an attractive alternative to the normally glossy, rich green leaves of *Agave bovicornuta*. The size and culture of 'Reggae Time' is the same as for the species.

Agave bracteosa S. Watson ex Engelmann

GREEN SPIDER AGAVE

Cliff-dwelling *Agave bracteosa* at San Lazaro Pass in Coahuila

The common name was coined because the plants resemble large, green spiders frozen on the perpendicular rock walls.

FIELD NOTES

Agave bracteosa is restricted to limestone cliffs in a few localities in Coahuila and Nuevo León in northeastern Mexico from 3000 to 5500 feet (900–1700 meters) elevation.

Clumps of this agave look like great big, green spiders plastered to the narrow ribbons of vertical, limestone cliffs of El Cañon de la Huasteca (Huasteca Canyon) south of Monterrey in Nuevo León. To get to Huasteca Canyon, one has to negotiate the sprawling, congested metropolis of Monterrey which is best done with a person who can converse in Spanish in order to obtain directions, as signs to the canyon are virtually nonexistent. As you travel the bumpy, dusty dirt road snaking its way through the towering slabs of limestone that were forced into sheer verticality by massive geologic forces, prepare to be awestruck by the magnificence and beauty of the scenery. Get there with plenty of daylight left so you can snap some pictures of the big green spiders frozen in time on the sharp limestone. Visit the canyon on a cold, stormy, winter day, and notice how the jagged, limestone spires tickle the underbellies of the low-hanging clouds.

If you are ready for some scrambling around on a steep slope full of thick vegetation, you can get up close and personal with these spectacular spider-like plants at San Lazaro Pass in the Sierra La Gavia on Mexico Highway 57 between Monclova and Saltillo in Coahuila. The mountains here are composed of limestone which is a favorite substrate of *Agave bracteosa*. The plants grow in small cracks in the solid limestone face on north- and northeast-facing cliffs, so try to arrive early on a crisp summer morning for maximum ambient light for your photos. As you can imagine, the climb up to the plants is not the easiest, but it is always rewarding.

DESCRIPTION

In its native habitat, *Agave bracteosa* is a small, offsetting species. The 1–1½ foot tall by 1½–2 foot diameter (30–45 by 45–60 cm) individual rosettes have a graceful urn-like shape formed by the upright leaves that grow up and curve out and down, looking like the drooping handlebar mustache commonly seen on cowboys of the Old West. In habitat, plants usually have just one or two small offsets, but in the garden they will produce numerous offspring and form a 3–6 foot (1.5–1.8 meter)

diameter mass of vegetation resembling a child's overstuffed toy box. The narrow, medium green, toothless, 18–24 inch long by 1 inch wide (45–60 by 2.5 cm) leaves grow upright and curve out and then down near the tip. Although the overall shape resembles an urn, the plant does not make a good water jug.

The 4–8 foot (1.2–2.4 meter) tall, unbranched flower stalk is so densely packed with white, 1 inch (2.5 cm) long flowers that it resembles a bottle brush. One particular plant that I had been growing in Tucson in a dilapidated, broken, half whiskey barrel finally put forth a meager, barely 2 foot (60 cm) tall flower stalk in the summer of 2009. Apparently, when the container falls apart, the soil erodes and the plant is never watered, it figures that life just isn't worth living anymore. On the bright side, I can fix the barrel and resume storing whiskey.

ABOVE Leaf detail revealing the toothless margins on *Agave bracteosa*

OPPOSITE The spicate inflorescence of *Agave bracteosa*, packed with white flowers

CULTURE

As long as the plants are kept dry during winter, *Agave bracteosa* is reliably hardy in zones 7b–11, to at least single digits F (–13 C). It can be grown in all but the coldest parts of the Pacific coast and Gulf states, and in the milder parts of the Atlantic coast at least as far north as North Carolina. Plants are readily grown in all southwestern U.S. zones.

The growth rate varies with the amount and frequency of supplemental water applied, but in general plants are moderate to slow growing. Although drought tolerant, the plants will appreciate an extra drink of water every seven to ten days during the hot summer months in the interior, low elevation parts of the desert southwestern United States and in other areas with low rainfall. Plants develop their most interesting forms when grown in filtered sun in the hot, dry, interior, low elevation desert and the hot, coastal zones. In middle elevation cities, plants will tolerate full sun, but will benefit from a little shade on extremely hot, dry summer days. Plants will thrive in the sunlight in the cooler coastal zone and the high elevation cities.

As with most of the species, this one is not very particular about the type of soil it is in as long as it has good drainage.

LANDSCAPE VALUE

Agave bracteosa looks great as a potted plant, and can be placed on patios, near entryways, or in other spots where the plant would be highly visible. In the ground, use this beauty under the shade of small desert trees, mix into cactus and succulent gardens, or plant in a wildflower garden to provide some interest when the wildflowers are dormant.

The soft, toothless leaves with no terminal spine make this a very user friendly plant no matter where you place it.

Agave bracteosa 'Monterrey Frost'

Although 'Monterrey Frost' has been around for over a decade, it is so slow growing that we do not have a good grasp on its eventual size. However, on a visit to the San Diego Botanical Garden in October 2009, I noted that their largest plant was about 1 foot tall by 1½ feet across (30 by 45 cm). The leaves are upright and gracefully arching, creating a superb urn-shaped rosette. Each leaf has snow white margins sandwiching the medium green center.

Tony Avent put this cultivar into tissue culture, making the plants more readily available to agave fanatics the world over.

'Monterrey Frost' is less hardy than the species, tolerating temperatures in the 15–20 degree F range (–7 to –9 C) without damage. Although hardy enough to be a landscape plant, this one is probably best grown in a large, decorative container in order to showcase the distinctive variegation. Plants seem to prefer light shade throughout the desert southwestern United States. It is a low-water-using cultivar that grows best in a soil with very good drainage. Owing to the high proportion of variegation, the growth rate is quite slow, especially when grown in a container, and it will take many years to achieve full size.

Agave bracteosa 'Monterrey Frost' growing in a decorative pot made by Phoenix, Arizona, potter Mike Cone

Agave cerulata Trelease

BAJA BLUE AGAVE

Agave cerulata growing near Laguna de Chapala in Baja California

The species name *cerulata* comes from the Latin *cerul*, meaning blue—a reference to the leaf color.

FIELD NOTES

Three of the four subspecies of *Agave cerulata* occur on the Baja California peninsula from near sea level to about 2000 feet (600 meters) elevation, while subspecies *dentiens* is found only on San Esteban Island. Subspecies *cerulata* is found on the peninsula as well as on Isla Ángel de la Guarda in the Sea of Cortez. I saw some beautiful plants of *A. cerulata* ssp. *cerulata* near Laguna de Chapala just off of Mexico Highway 1 in Baja California Norte, and if you happen to visit this area, look for the ghostly white plants that stand out among the incredibly red-spined *Ferocactus gracilis*. To see some exceptional specimens of *A. cerulata* ssp. *nelsonii*, take one of the four-wheel-drive dirt roads that head north from Mexico Highway 1 toward the southern end of the Sierra San Pedro Mártir, a mountain range in northern Baja California. This distinctive subspecies has broad, sword-shaped leaves and a very symmetrical rosette, and in overall appearance resembles what I would imagine a cross between *A. cerulata* ssp. *cerulata* and *A. shawii* ssp. *goldmaniana* would look like.

A glance at the key in *Agaves of Continental North America* shows that ssp. *cerulata* and ssp. *dentiens* are grouped together for their yellowish to light glaucous, long acuminate leaves, and ssp. *nelsonii* and ssp. *subcerulata* are together because of their light gray to bluish glaucous, short acuminate leaves. While ssp. *cerulata* is probably the more commonly found subspecies in cultivation, ssp. *nelsonii* is found infrequently in cultivation. These two are quite easily distinguished from each other by their leaves and rosettes. Leaves of ssp. *cerulata* tend to be yellowish green to light glaucous gray, long and narrow, broadest near the base with a long, gradual taper to the tip, with the rosettes having a more open appearance. Leaves of ssp. *nelsonii* tend to be gray to bluish, rarely green, and broadest from the base to above the middle and then with a broad taper to the tip, with the rosettes having a denser, symmetrical form.

DESCRIPTION

While individual rosettes of *Agave cerulata* fit in the small category, reaching 1½–1³/₅ feet tall by 1³/₅–2½ feet wide (45–50 by 50–75 cm), it is an offsetting species and can form large, dense clumps 3–5 feet (0.9–1.5 meters) across. Leaves are variable, from long triangular to lanceolate, colored light yellowish green to blue-gray to nearly white, with small,

A solitary specimen of *Agave cerulata* ssp. *nelsonii*, showing the symmetrical rosette

weak teeth on nearly smooth margins to large, lethal teeth on prominent teats, all with a brown ring around them at the base. The slender, needle-like, 1–2 inch (2.5–5 cm) long, terminal spine is decurrent to the upper teeth and colored brown on new leaves, turning grayish on older ones.

Late spring to early summer is the time for *Agave cerulata* to send up its slender, branched, 6–13 foot (2–7 meter) tall flower stalk with few, 2 inch (5 cm) long, light yellow flowers on each side branch.

An excellent combination of an *Agave cerulata* plant with alabaster white leaves and *Ferocactus gracilis*, with bright cherry red spines

CULTURE

With its four subspecies, *Agave cerulata* has variable hardiness—but subspecies *cerulata* and subspecies *dentiens* have been proven hardy to at least the high teens F (−7 to −8 C) and can be considered at least zone 8b–11 plants. They should be great landscape plants in the mild winter parts of California as long as the soil is not too moist during winter. These can be grown without threat of frost damage in the cool, coastal and hot, interior low elevation and mid-elevation southwestern U.S. zones.

The growth rate is slow, with the plants taking several years to flower and eventually form large clusters. Once established, they are quite drought tolerant, rarely needing supplemental water even in the heat of summer; in fact, they have a tendency to rot if watered too much.

Even though plants will tolerate full sun in the low and mid-elevation zones, they will benefit from having some companion plants to help keep the soil cooler. Plants in native rocky clay soil in Tucson have been growing and surviving on total neglect since 1985, though they have yet to flower. Soil should have excellent drainage and should be kept dry to minimize rotting of the roots.

LANDSCAPE VALUE

Agave cerulata is one of the better choices for use in the hotter, drier parts of a natural desert landscape. It makes a great addition to a wildflower garden, and mixes well with hardy, desert-adapted perennials and small shrubs with colorful flowers. Some excellent choices include *Baileya multiradiata, Chrysactinia mexicana, Penstemon* species, *Psilostrophe cooperi, Salvia greggii,* and *Zinnia acerosa.* Mix in with hardy desert shrubs *Anisacanthus quadrifidus, Calliandra eriophylla, Justicia californica,* and *Leucophyllum zygophyllum.*

Agave chrysantha Peebles

GOLDEN FLOWER AGAVE

A handsome specimen of *Agave chrysantha* growing in central Arizona

The Latin *chrys* means gold, while *anth* means flower, and this combination refers to the very showy, golden yellow flowers.

FIELD NOTES

Agave chrysantha is found mostly in central Arizona between 2300 and 6900 feet (700–2100 meters) elevation. During the Memorial Day holiday in 2009, my wife, Carol, and I saw some spectacular specimens, with their tall stalks and clusters of golden yellow flowers gracing the skyline, while driving along Arizona State Route 87 north from Phoenix past Payson and along Arizona State Route 260 east of Camp Verde. Another good spot in central Arizona for glimpsing spectacular specimens of *A. chrysantha* is on the drive from Route 87 to the Barnhardt Trail parking area in the Mazatzal Mountains.

A population can also be found growing in the Santa Catalina Mountains just north of Tucson. Plants are in full glorious golden yellow flower during the summer, and it is best to drive up the mountain early in the day to scout out the best plants in time to see them in perfect late afternoon lighting as the sun sinks low on the horizon.

DESCRIPTION

Under cultivation, *Agave chrysantha* tends to tip the scales on the medium to large side, with the occasional plant creeping into the extra large category, eventually reaching about 1½–3 feet tall by 2½–6 feet across (0.5–1 by 0.8–1.8 meters). The rosettes are a symmetrical hemisphere of narrow, pale blue to green or yellowish green, lanceolate to broadly lanceolate, with deeply guttered leaves and two different-sized teeth. The smaller teeth are found near the leaf base and between the larger ones. Leaves are widest near the middle, and long tapering to the tip, usually about 12–30 inches long by 3–4 inches wide (40–75 by 8–10 cm). The slender, 1–3 inch (2.5–7.5 cm) long, terminal spine is decurrent to the upper teeth and brown on new leaves, turning grayish on older ones. Plants are usually solitary, though under cultivation they will occasionally throw out an offset or two.

Come summer, *Agave chrysantha* bursts forth with a 13–23 foot (4–7 meter) tall, branched flower stalk with several side branches, each loaded with stunning, 2 inch (5 cm) long, golden yellow flowers that make the sky come alive with color.

CULTURE

Agave chrysantha is hardy to at least single digits F (−13 C), can be considered a zone 7b–11 plant, and makes a great landscape plant along the Pacific and Gulf coast states and along the Atlantic coast at least to North Carolina. It can be grown without threat of frost damage in the low and mid-elevation southwestern U.S. zones, and should be tried in the high elevation zone as well.

The growth rate is slow, with the plants taking several years to achieve flowering size and age. They thrive in full sun in the mid- to high elevation zones or very light shade in the hot, interior, low elevation zone in natural desert landscape. Once established, the plants are quite drought tolerant, only needing minimal supplemental water in the heat of summer. I have seen plants in a rocky clay soil in a mid-town Tucson landscape that receive a thorough soaking once every fourteen days in the summer and once a month or less often in the winter. Those growing in the hot, interior, low elevation zone would appreciate a good thorough soaking more frequently in the summer, maybe once every seven to ten days, while in the cool, coastal, low elevation zone, once every two to three weeks ought to be sufficient. Plants grow fine in most soil types as long as watering is adjusted accordingly and the soil is not kept soggy.

LANDSCAPE VALUE

Agave chrysantha is one of the best landscape species for use in hotter parts of the desert southwestern United States, and should be equally adapted to any desert region that experiences winter lows down to the mid-20s F (−3 to −4 C). Try using the plant as focal points in a wildflower garden or mixing with rich green-leaved perennials and small shrubs with colorful flowers. Some excellent choices include *Berlandiera lyrata, Dalea frutescens, Ericameria laricifolia, Glandularia gooddingii, Penstemon* species, *Salvia greggii, Scutellaria suffrutescens,* and *Tetraneuris acaulis.* Mix in with hardy desert shrubs *Anisacanthus quadrifidus, Buddleja marrubiifolia, Justicia californica, Larrea divaricata, Leucophyllum zygophyllum, Lycium* species, and *Simmondsia chinensis.*

OPPOSITE The tall flower stalk of *Agave chrysantha,* with golden yellow flower buds ready to burst

ABOVE *Agave chrysantha* with its golden yellow flowers in full, glorious color

Agave colorata Gentry

MESCAL CENIZA

The longer-leaved form of *Agave colorata* found near Guaymas, Sonora

The plants of *Agave colorata* can be used in the making of mescal, an alcoholic drink.

Agave colorata is primarily found from near sea level to about 1000 feet (300 meters) elevation near the coast and in thorn forest vegetation in southern Sonora and northern Sinaloa, Mexico. There are two distinct forms. The more commonly cultivated one, with shorter, spoon-shaped leaves, is more southerly, with some very nice specimens found between Obrégon and Navajoa in Sonora. The other form has longer, more sword-shaped leaves and is found in Nacapule Canyon outside of San Carlos and near Guaymas, Sonora.

DESCRIPTION

Although there are two distinct forms of *Agave colorata*, the smaller one produces offsets, and is more commonly grown than the larger, non-offsetting form. The smaller one reaches about 12–18 inches tall by 12–18 inches across (30–45 cm tall and wide) and produces several pups around the base. The short, powdery blue, nearly spoon-shaped leaves are resplendent with distinctive crossbanding, and pronounced mammillate edges with large, formidable, dark brown teeth and a stout terminal spine. Both surfaces of the 12 inch long by 4–6 inch wide (30 by 12–18 cm) leaves are very slightly rough to the touch.

The other form, rarely seen in cultivation, is a medium-sized plant, growing 2½–3 feet tall by 3–4 feet across (0.75–0.9 by 0.9–1.2 meters), with long, broad, sword-shaped, blue-gray leaves and frequently crossbanded. The leaves are 18–24 inches long by 4–6 inches wide (45–60 by 12–18 cm) with the margins not as deeply scalloped, and while the teeth are not quite as prominent as on the more commonly cultivated form, the terminal spine is just as lethal.

After several years, a short, 6–12 foot (2–4 meter) tall flower stalk emerges in early spring, and has several side branches clustered in the upper one fourth of the shaft. Each side branch is adorned with clusters of 2–2¾ inch (5–7 cm) long, greenish brown to greenish yellow flowers in spring and early summer. On some forms the buds are a striking deep red and contrast nicely with the open flowers.

CULTURE

Agave colorata is hardy to the high teens F (−7 to −8 C), is considered a zone 8b–11 plant, and can be grown as a landscape plant throughout the

mild winter parts of the Pacific coast states as long as the soil is kept dry. It also makes a great landscape plant in the low and mid-elevation southwestern U.S. zones, though it may be marginal in the northern part of the cold, low elevation zone of Texas.

Growth rate varies from moderate to slow, depending upon frequency of supplemental watering during the growing season, and will take several years to attain mature size. The most attractive plants in the low and mid-elevation zones are those grown in full sun and not watered too frequently. These tend to develop the most compact, dense rosettes and the best frosty blue leaf color with more pronounced crossbanding.

This drought-tolerant species will grow best if given some supplemental water during the hottest part of summer. However, it is best to cut back on the frequency of watering in the autumn and keep the soil dry in winter. It is not very particular about the type of soil it grows in, as long as the drainage is good.

LANDSCAPE VALUE

Use this tough, sun-loving species with cactus and succulents as well as seasonal plants such as wildflowers, low-growing perennials or small shrubs. An awesome landscape could be made with a grouping of *Agave colorata* scattered among the small shrubs *Poliomintha maderensis*, *Salvia greggii*, and *Scutellaria suffrutescens*, the pink-flowered *Penstemon parryi*, the scarlet-flowered *Penstemon eatonii*, and the yellow-flowered *Baileya multiradiata*.

Agave deserti Engelmann

DESERT AGAVE

Agave deserti var. *simplex* growing in the Silverbell Mountains west of Tucson, Arizona

The Latin word *desert* means solitary or lonely, and some populations are found in very sparsely vegetated areas.

This hardcore Sonoran Desert native is easily spotted in the hills along Interstate 8 as you drive east from San Diego as well as in the desert near Anza-Borrego and Palm Desert. These offsetting type plants are *Agave deserti* var. *deserti*, which can develop into large colonies 10–15 feet (3–4.5 meters) across. In May 2009, while hiking along the California Riding and Hiking Trail in Anza-Borrego Desert State Park, I saw innumerable plants dotting the landscape, many with their tall stalks laden with clusters of bright yellow flowers.

Agave deserti var. *simplex* is typically seen as a solitary rosette, with some beautiful plants occurring in the Silverbell Mountains just west of Tucson and in Organ Pipe National Monument along the Arizona-Mexico border. The elevation ranges from about 1000 to 5000 feet (300–1500 meters).

Agave deserti var. *pringlei* is found in the Sierra Juárez and Sierra San Pedro Mártir the Mexican state of Baja California Norte, from about 1950 to 6000 feet (600–1825 meters) elevation.

DESCRIPTION

Depending on the variety, plants are either solitary or clustering, with individual rosettes reaching about 1–2 feet tall by about 1½–2½ feet across (30–70 by 45–80 cm) and falling into the small size category. Thick and rigid leaves are light green to bluish gray, often seen with prominent crossbanding. Generally shaped like the large bayonet frequently affixed to the rifle of a World War I footsoldier, the 10–16 inch long by 2–3 inch wide (25–70 by 6–8 cm) blades are widest near the middle, with a long taper to the tip. The margins are regularly armed with slender teeth, while the stout, 1–2 inch (2.5–5 cm) long terminal spine is light or dark brown, reddish brown on young leaves, and light to dark grayish on older leaves.

Plants of variety *simplex* develop compact, solitary rosettes about 1½ feet tall by 2 feet wide (45 by 60 cm). Individual leaves are stout, powdery gray or light green, with wavy to crenate margins and large, brown to gray teeth that curve back towards the base. The heavy, thick, terminal spine is dark brown on new leaves to grayish on older leaves, 1½ inches (3.75 cm) long, broadly grooved above, and decurrent to the second or third pair of teeth which are able to inflict major pain.

A perfect rosette of
Agave deserti var. *deserti*
in Anza-Borrego Desert
State Park in southern
California

Variety *deserti* is a clumper, making 4–5 foot (1.2–1.5 meter) diameter mounds of tightly clustered rosettes. Individual rosettes are a bit larger than those of var. *simplex*, reaching about 2 feet tall by 2½ feet across (60 by 75 cm). Light gray to bluish gray leaves are widest at mid-blade before tapering to the 1½ inch (3.75 cm) long, light brown to grayish, openly grooved terminal spine. The leaf margins are armed with evenly spaced, loosely attached teeth that point out or curve back toward the base.

Variety *pringlei* is the largest of the three varieties, with individual rosettes reaching 2½ feet tall by 3 feet across (75 by 90 cm). Around her base, the mother rosette pops out little baby clones which eventually grow up, developing into large colonies. Green to whitish green leaves are deeply concave, narrowly triangular lanceolate, and widest near the base before gradually narrowing to the 1½ inch (3.75 cm) long terminal spine. The margins have small, evenly spaced teeth. The terminal spine is reddish brown on new leaves to grayish on older leaves, with a short, narrow groove above and decurrent to the upper teeth or to near the middle of the blade.

The branched flower stalk can grow to 8–13 feet (2.5–4 meters) tall, with six to fifteen side branches, each festooned with clusters of 2 inch (5 cm) long, bright yellow flowers at the ends. In Anza-Borrego Desert State Park in southern California, some plants of *Agave deserti* ssp. *deserti* have large, fleshy bracts surrounding the flower clusters prior to the side branches becoming fully erect. The flower stalks begin to emerge in spring, with full flowering occurring in late spring or early summer.

CULTURE

Although hardiness may vary depending on the variety, *Agave deserti* is generally hardy to at least the mid teens F (–8 C) if kept dry through the winter. In 2002 Mary Irish showed that plants grown in Littleton, Colorado, were subjected to –20 degrees F (–29 C) and suffered no damage, while plants growing in Raleigh, North Carolina, were killed at 9 degrees F (–13 C). She speculated that those in North Carolina were subjected to a wetter winter than those in Colorado, but they may have been different varieties which may have affected their hardiness. Plants should be reliably hardy in zones 8b–11, able to be grown throughout much of the western United States, across the southern states, and into the southeastern part of the country. Plants can be grown in all the low and mid-elevation zones in the southwestern United States except for the northernmost part of the cold, low elevation zone of Texas.

These are slow growing plants that will last for several years in the landscape before deciding to push forth their flower stalk. For the best-looking plants, grow only in full sun. The mantra for successfully growing all varieties is *dry, dry, dry. Agave deserti* occurs in areas with annual rainfall averaging less than 5 inches (13 cm), so once plants are established they are unlikely to need supplemental water. Along with keeping plants dry, the soil should have excellent drainage to reduce the risk of rotting the roots.

Did I mention that plants should be kept dry and not given too much water?

LANDSCAPE VALUE

Plants look spectacular when used in full sun and grouped with large rocks, and their smaller size and powdery blue leaves combine well with native shrubs, cactus, and succulents. Try using *Abutilon* species, *Baileya multiradiata, Ferocactus cylindraceus, Fouquieria splendens, Glandularia gooddingii,* and *Penstemon parryi* for a truly native look.

Agave deserti is seldom used in landscapes, as it can die out from overwatering. However, if you can get a plant established in the right spot, it is tough and can be an attractive specimen.

TAXONOMIC NOTES

In *Flora of North America*, James Reveal and Wendy Hodgson stated that three varieties of *Agave deserti* occur in the drier parts of western Arizona and southern California, the extreme northwestern part of Sonora, Mexico, and northern Baja California, Mexico. The one most often found for sale is *A. deserti* var. *simplex*. This variety forms a solitary rosette and is found in arid parts of western Arizona, adjacent southern California, and northwestern Sonora.

Occasionally plants of *Agave deserti* var. *deserti* are seen for sale. This clumping form is found in the dry areas of southern California and northern Baja California.

Rarely offered is *Agave deserti* var. *pringlei*. Another clumping form, it is found growing in northern Baja California alongside *A. deserti* var. *deserti*. The two occasionally mix genes, making identification difficult.

OPPOSITE TOP LEFT The enlarged bracts sometimes seen on inflorescences of *Agave deserti* var. *deserti*, in Anza-Borrego Desert State Park

TOP CENTER Bright, lemon yellow flowers of *Agave deserti* var. *deserti* in Anza-Borrego Desert State Park

TOP RIGHT The orange-yellow flowers of *Agave deserti* var. *simplex* in the Silverbell Mountains west of Tucson, Arizona

BOTTOM *Agave deserti* var. *simplex* growing in a xeric yet colorful setting at Tohono Chul Park in Tucson, Arizona

Agave filifera Salm-Dyck

THREAD-EDGE AGAVE

Agave filifera growing on Cerro El Zamorano in Querétaro

The Latin *filum* means thread, which is apropos considering that the species has many thin, white fibers along the leaf edges.

FIELD NOTES

Having a limited distribution in central Mexico, *Agave filifera* can sometimes be difficult to find. Few plants can be seen growing on large slabs of rock mixed in with some oaks and prickly pears near the top of the Cerro El Zamorano in the state of Querétaro in central Mexico at around 8000–8500 feet (2500–2600 meters). To get to the top of Cerro El Zamorano, start early from the city of Querétaro, and head towards the tallest mountain to the northeast. After traveling along the flat road, you will eventually turn north and start climbing the long, bumpy dirt road that winds its way up and up some more, finally peaking at 10,761 feet (3280 meters) elevation.

DESCRIPTION

This small species is a clumper, producing few offsets to form small clusters up to 3 feet (1 meter) across. The individual rosettes are not very large, maxing out at about 8–12 inches tall by 15–24 inches across (20–30 by 38–60 cm). Leaves are dark green, narrow, straight or slightly curved, lance-shaped and widest near the middle, each lovingly hand-painted by Mother Nature with white bud prints on both the top and bottom sides, and measuring 6–12 inches long by ¾–1½ inches wide (15–30 by 2–4 cm). It has no marginal teeth, instead having thin, curly, white fibers along the edges. One of the more intriguing aspects of this species is the way the leaves will turn a brilliant shade of deep red or purplish red when stressed by excess sun, too little water, or a combination of both. The short, grayish terminal spine is flat on top and rounded below.

The 6–8 foot tall (2–2.5 meter), spicate flower stalk emerges in late spring and summer, with the upper half densely covered with 1–1½ inch (25–38 mm) long, reddish flowers.

CULTURE

Agave filifera has been proven hardy to at least the high teens F (−7 to −8 C) in Tucson, and reportedly has survived 9 degrees F (−13 C) in Las Vegas. It is reliably hardy in zones 8a–11, and is a good landscape plant in all but the coldest areas of the Pacific coast states and throughout the Gulf coast states as long as the soil is kept dry. *Agave filifera* can be used in the low and mid-elevation zones in the southwestern United States,

though it might need winter protection in the northern reaches of the cold, low elevation zone of Texas. Wean your plant of excess water in the fall and keep it on the dry side during winter to increase hardiness.

The growth rate is moderately fast if given some supplemental water during the warm season. Once established, these plants are very-low-water using and will provide a bit of leaf color if drought-stressed. Plants will respond to supplemental summer water by greening up and growing more rapidly. In the hot, interior low elevation zone, a thorough soaking once every seven to ten days ought to be sufficient, while in the mid-elevation zone once every two weeks should suffice. Plants grow well in full sun in the cool, coastal, low elevation and mid-elevation zones, but seem to like a little afternoon shade in the very hot, interior, low elevation zone.

Agave filifera is not particular about the soil type as long as drainage is adequate. In nature, plants can be found growing on virtually solid rock slabs with little cracks where a thin layer of soil could develop and the wayward seed might fall and sprout.

LANDSCAPE VALUE

Agave filifera is a great little plant to mix with cactus, other succulents, perennial wildflowers, and small shrubs that provide seasonal color. Weave masses of *Baileya multiradiata*, *Glandularia gooddingii*, *Penstemon parryi*, or *Tetraneuris acaulis* in with a stand of *Agave filifera* to create seasonally showy flower displays. The plants will also provide a spark of interest when the leaves turn reddish purple with drought or cold.

TAXONOMIC NOTES

Some agavologists consider *Agave multifilifera* and *A. schidigera* to be subspecies of *A. filifera*, which would substantially widen the distribution. However, they are horticulturally if not botanically distinct and so are treated as separate species here, as Gentry had done.

A small cluster of *Agave filifera* growing in a crevice of a rock slab on Cerro El Zamorano

Agave geminiflora (Tagliabue) Ker-Gawler

TWIN-FLOWER AGAVE

The green and reddish purple leaves of this *Agave geminiflora* plant add color to the landscape.

The species name, derived from the Latin *gemin* (twin) and *flor* (flower), was coined to reflect the characteristic of paired flowers on one pedicel.

FIELD NOTES

Agave geminiflora is restricted to the Mexican states of Jalisco and Nayarit, and is found growing in association with pines and oak woodland from about 3000 to 7000 feet (900 to 2150 meters) elevation where the area receives about 40 inches (100 cm) of annual rainfall.

DESCRIPTION

The solitary rosette consists of hundreds of long, thin, flexible, leaves and forms a dense, symmetrical, beautifully sculptured, small to medium-sized plant, 2–3 feet tall by 2–3 feet across (60–90 by 60–90 cm). Occasionally a plant in cultivation will produce offsets that can be removed and planted elsewhere. The medium to dark green, user-friendly leaves reach 15–24 inches long by about a quarter inch across (38–60 by 0.6 cm), and frequently turn purplish red near the tips during times of cold or drought. They are toothless along the margin, instead almost always having thin, curly, white fibers. These flexible leaves end in a small, weak terminal spine and do not make very good jousting weapons.

Two-toned, 2 inch (5 cm) long flowers are greenish yellow on the inside of the tepals, purplish red on the outside, and densely cover much of the unbranched, 13–20 foot (4–6 meter) tall flower stalk.

CULTURE

Plants are hardy to at least the low 20s F (−4 to −6 C), as long this low temperature is short lived and the plants have been weaned from excess water starting in the autumn. This is generally considered to be a solid zone 9a–11 plant, and can be used as a landscape plant in the mild winter parts of the Pacific coast and Gulf coast states. Plants will last without damage through most winters in the low and mid-elevation zones, except in the cold, low elevation zone of Texas.

The growth rate is moderately fast, and depending on the amount of supplemental water applied, nice specimens can be attained in a relatively short time. This gem can be grown in a variety of exposures, ranging from part shade to filtered sun, full sun, and even reflected sun; the more sun a plant receives, the smaller and denser it will be. It will suffer in the hot, interior, low elevation zone when planted up against a south- or west-facing wall, unless it is planted under the light shade of a wispy desert tree.

Although *Agave geminiflora* is from an area receiving 40 inches (100 cm) of annual rainfall, it is moderately drought tolerant in the mid-elevation zone. Plants will require supplemental water during the heat of summer in the low, interior zone, especially if planted in full sun. Plants do not seem to be picky about the soil type, and will grow as well in a heavier, slower-draining clay soil as they will in a sandy or rocky soil with good drainage, as long as the amount of supplemental water is adjusted for the type of soil.

LANDSCAPE VALUE

Plant in masses and weave colorful, low-growing perennials and small shrubs in between for an eye-catching effect. In the hot, interior, low elevation and mid-elevation zones try using *Baileya multiradiata*, *Chrysactinia mexicana*, *Ericameria laricifolia*, various *Penstemon* species, *Poliomintha maderensis*, *Salvia greggii*, *Scutellaria suffrutescens*, *Tetraneuris acaulis*, and *Zauschneria californica*. In the cooler coastal, low elevation zone, some nice complementary plants would include *Halimium umbellatum*, *Lavandula angustifolia*, *Phlox nana*, *Salvia greggii*, and *Trichostema lanatum*. Mix with a variety of cactus and other succulents in a low-water-use garden. Group several together under the shade of a desert tree. The thin, flexible leaves provide a unique sculptural quality in a Southwestern-style landscape.

OPPOSITE *Agave geminiflora* nearing peak bloom in a Phoenix, Arizona, landscape

ABOVE LEFT The thin leaves of a particularly filiferous *Agave geminiflora* plant

ABOVE A well-grown specimen of *Agave geminiflora* tucked in a mass of *Lantana* 'New Gold'

Agave gentryi Ullrich

GENTRY AGAVE, MAGUEY, MAGUEY VERDE

A spectacular specimen of *Agave gentryi* on Cerro Potosí in central Nuevo León

Bernd Ullrich paid the ultimate compliment to Howard Scott Gentry by naming this magnificent species in his honor.

FIELD NOTES

Agave gentryi has a widespread distribution in northeastern Mexico, but only at higher elevations, usually between 7000 and 9000 feet (2130–2750 meters). It can be found in the mountains of Coahuila, Nuevo León, San Luis Potosí, Tamaulipas, and Zacatecas, and seems to be highly variable with at least two distinct forms as well as possible intergrades with *A. americana* ssp. *protamericana*, *A. asperrima*, and *A. montana*.

I once saw plants growing on a treeless, west-facing slope at about 7200 feet (2200 meters) at the western end of the Sierra Patagalana in southern Coahuila. On several plants, the branched flower stalks were poking majestically skyward, showing the characteristic thick, succulent bracts along their stalks. One plant in particular was going out in a blaze of glory, the normally green leaves turning orange-red to deep red due to the loss of green chlorophyll as it succumbed to inevitable death. There were some fine specimens of *Agave asperrima* growing nearby, and a few plants of *A. gentryi* showed deeply guttered leaves—an indication of some hanky panky having gone on between the two species.

An easy way to see some nice *Agave gentryi* is to go near the entrance of the tourist hot spot of Real de Catorce in San Luis Potosí. Travel the long, bumpy, cobblestone road, badly in need of repair, up into the mountains; near the top are large green specimens on the slopes both above and below the road. Once a bustling mining town, Real de Catorce is now a thriving tourist destination with access through the mile-long Ogarrio tunnel. This tunnel is only wide enough for a single lane of vehicles, so you might have to wait in line to drive through. This is a fun stop; be sure to have cash at hand as there are street vendors selling practically every imaginable useless trinket known to man.

The most spectacular specimens I have seen were on Cerro El Potosí in Nuevo León. These massive plants reached 4–5 feet tall by 5–6 feet across (1.2–1.5 by 1.5–1.8 meters); some even had two or three rosettes that size and took up space 12–15 feet (3.6–4.6 meters) across. The light green leaves were thick and extra wide, the edges armed with fierce teeth, ending in a vicious terminal spine. Not only were the plants impressive, but the flower stalk looked downright phallic, the thick, erect shaft topped by a large, bulbous knob of fleshy bracts that protect the unopened flower buds from potential freeze damage. On one

visit, I noticed that leaves on one flowering plant were nearly translucent while turning brilliant orange-red—and on a return visit, another flowering plant stood out from the others, its leaves glowing apple green and banana yellow with a flush of orange-red. Both appeared to be calling out a warning to the surrounding plants as life ebbed away from these magnificent specimens.

In the botanically rich mountains beginning south of Monterrey and extending all the way to Tamaulipas, things get really interesting. *Agave gentryi* is quite variable here and could very well be mixing genes with *A. montana* and *A. asperrima*. Some plants are more open with fewer, deeply folded leaves while others are denser with more leaves that are flatter and more characteristic of *A. montana*, yet retaining the offsetting nature of *A. gentryi*.

DESCRIPTION

In general, *Agave gentryi* is a medium, large, or extra large species, ranging in size from 3–5 feet tall by 3–6 feet across (0.9–1.5 by 0.9–1.8 meters). The light, yellowish green to deep, rich green leaves are either broad from the base to above the middle before quickly tapering to the sharp tip, or long triangular and widest at the base before gradually narrowing to the tip. They measure anywhere from 2–4 feet long and 6–10 inches wide (60–120 by 15–25 cm) at the base, with small to large marginal teeth

that create exceptional bud imprints, ending in the 2–3 inch (5–7.5 cm) long, stout terminal spine.

When the plant matures, the thick inflorescence emerges in late summer or autumn and then stops for the winter, the fleshy, imbricate bracts forming a thick bulbous knob covering the tip. The stalk resumes bolting the following spring to reveal the massive flowering section laden with large, yellow flowers clustered at the ends of short side branches. The stalk eventually reaches 15–18 feet (4.5–5.5 meters) tall, and is topped by the Christmas tree arrangement of side branches, each holding clusters of numerous, 3–4 inch (7.5–10 cm) long, yellow flowers.

Although more research is needed, there appear to be three distinct forms, none of which have been designated as varieties. One, from Cerro El Potosí in west-central Nuevo León, is the most massive, reaching 4–5 feet tall and 5–6 feet across (1.2–1.5 by 1.5–1.8 meters). Although Bernd Ullrich's original description indicates the plants do not produce offsets, the plants on Cerro El Potosí can produce several offsets and make large clusters. Individual leaves are light green and very broad and thick, measuring 36–48 inches long by 8–10 inches wide (90–120 by 20–25 cm). They are widest from the base to above the middle, and then taper to the thick and heavy terminal spine which could be used effectively in acupuncture or to pierce light body armor without snapping. This one has the most massive flowering stalk, measuring 7–8 inches thick and reaching 15–18 feet (4.5–5.5 meters) tall. The 3–4 inch flowers are clustered at the ends of short side branches that emerge from behind the large, fleshy bracts.

A second form is found in the Sierra Patagalana and near Carneros Pass of southern Coahuila, as well as in the Sierra Catorce in San Luis Potosí. These large plants tend to be solitary, reaching about 3–4 feet tall and 3½–5 feet across (0.9–1.2 by 1–1.5 meters). Leaves are 30–36 inches long by 6–8 inches wide (75–90 by 15–20 cm), medium to dark green, broadest from the base to above the middle, and then tapering to the tip. Marginal teeth are small, yet will rip into the flesh of fingers and hands if the handler is inattentive. The terminal spine is shorter than those on the plants from Cerro El Potosí.

A third form is by far the most widespread and variable, being found in the Sierra Madre Oriental of central Nuevo León. Generally offsetting, these plants vary in size and leaf density, growing to about 3–5 feet tall by 3–6 feet across (0.9–1.5 by 0.9–1.8 meters). The dark green leaves are 24–36 inches long by 6–8 inches wide (60–90 by 15–20 cm), and

OPPOSITE LEFT A flowering *Agave gentryi* plant on Cerro El Potosí, with overlapping bracts covering the shaft

TOP RIGHT In April, the flower clusters of *Agave gentryi* are just beginning to emerge from the protection of the bracts.

BOTTOM RIGHT A fruiting *Agave gentryi* specimen with deeply guttered leaves and an open panicle, showing possible introgression with nearby *A. asperrima*

either broad from the base to mid-blade before tapering to the tip, or long triangular, broadest at the base and long tapering to the tip. Teeth are fewer, smaller, and further apart, yet the leaves have the same stout, 2–3 inch (5–7.5 cm) long terminal spine as the other form.

CULTURE

Being a high montane species, *Agave gentryi* is generally considered very hardy, and can be reliably grown in zones 8a–11 as long as the soil is dry in winter. This one can be planted in the ground in the drier parts of the Pacific coast and Gulf coast states, and up the Atlantic coast to North Carolina where some forms are hardy and others struggle through the winter. *Agave gentryi* can be used throughout the low and mid-elevation southwestern U.S. zones and in warm microclimates of the high elevation zone.

This species is no speed demon and will take several years to achieve significant size. As with many other *Agave* species, the water needs will vary depending on sun exposure, climate and soil type. Because this one hails from areas that receive anywhere from 16 to 40 inches (40–100 cm) of annual rainfall, the plants will benefit from some supplemental water in areas receiving less. These spectacular plants can tolerate full sun in areas that do not experience extreme summer heat with temperatures exceeding 100 degrees F (38 C) for most of the summer. They do prefer some afternoon shade in the hot, interior, low and mid-elevation zones of the southwestern United States.

Agave gentryi is generally found growing on limestone, but not necessarily on raw, exposed limestone like *A. bracteosa* does. Make sure that the soil has very good drainage so no standing water puddles around the base of the plant.

LANDSCAPE VALUE

Use this hefty giant as a great focal point in any landscape, or place in the shade of pines, oaks, mesquites, or acacias in the hot, interior, low elevation zone or mid-elevation zone to give them some relief from the high summer temperatures and very low humidity. Mix with larger cactus and succulents or toss several in the middle of a mass of colorful small shrubs and flowering perennials for a dynamic, ever-changing landscape. Some ideal companion flowering plants could include *Anisacanthus quadrifidus, Calylophus hartwegii, Dalea versicolor* var. *sessilis, Justicia spicigera, Poliomintha maderensis, Salvia greggii,* and *Zinnia grandiflora*.

The interesting imprints left in the leaves by the large teeth are quite attractive when viewed close up. Just be careful not to poke an eye out with the lethal terminal spine while getting up close and personal.

TAXONOMIC NOTES

The history of this species is a bit confusing, but with a fitting ending. Howard Scott Gentry discussed *Agave macroculmis*, citing several localities in northeastern Mexico. He also cited a drawing by Tódaro of a plant, growing in Palermo, Italy, that was designated as the type specimen. The drawing does not show the very large, fleshy bracts that hide the flower stalk and bunch up at the tip to form a huge knob that protects the unopened flower buds during the winter cold, as is seen on plants in habitat in Mexico. Gentry dismissed this as a result of the mild climate in Palermo compared to the freezing temperatures experienced in the mountains of northern Mexico. Bernd Ullrich recognized this difference and realized that the plant drawn by Tódaro actually represented another species, *A. atrovirens*, relegating the name *A. macroculmis* to synonym status. It then became necessary to apply a new name to the plants from further north, and in 1990 Ullrich paid homage to the late Gentry and named these plants *A. gentryi*.

Agave gentryi 'Jaws' can be a spectacular potted specimen

CULTIVAR

Agave gentryi 'Jaws'

In the late 1990s, Yucca Do Nursery in Texas selected a form with exceptionally large teeth that leave quite an impression on both sides of the leaves, and dubbed it 'Jaws'. This cultivar will reach 3–4 feet tall by 5–6 feet across (0.9–1.2 by 1.5–1.8 meters) and is slow to produce offsets. Highly prized for its cold hardiness, glossy, rich green leaves and huge teeth, 'Jaws' has created quite a stir in the agave world.

Plants should be given some shade and extra water during the summer months in hot, dry regions. It is a bit slower growing than some of the other seed-grown forms, and will take several years to achieve its maximum size. This is a good thing, though, as the plants will adapt nicely to being grown in a large, decorative container, allowing for close-up viewing of the really wicked teeth. Cold hardiness is generally not a problem and it can be grown in all southwestern U.S. zones as well as zones 7b-11 worldwide.

Agave havardiana Trelease

HAVARD AGAVE

A stout specimen of *Agave havardiana*

William Trelease honored the army officer/physician/botanist Valery Havard by naming this stately plant for him.

FIELD NOTES

On the way back from a Mexico expedition one summer, three other plant freaks and I were meandering along the two-lane highways through the mountains of western Texas when we spotted the robust rosettes of *Agave havardiana* in full flower. If you travel through western Texas, be aware that most of the property is fenced off and, unlike in Mexico where one can usually pop across the barbed wire fence for a peek at the plants, entry onto private ranch land is frowned upon in Texas—so bring a tripod and telephoto lens to capture some good shots from a distance. While in the area, be sure to make the drive on U.S. Route 67 to Marfa, Texas, to see the Marfa ghost lights southeast of town. *Agave havardiana* occurs between 4000 and 6500 feet (1200–2000 meters) elevation in western Texas, and in Chihuahua and Coahuila in north-central Mexico.

DESCRIPTION

Agave havardiana is a solitary, medium to large plant, reaching about 1½–2½ feet tall and 3–5 feet across (0.5–0.8 by 1–1.6 meters). The 12–24 inch long and 6 inch wide (30–60 by 15–20 cm), blue-gray leaves are quite stout and rigid, and if you get careless around them, they will make you pay! The prominent teeth are quite decorative and leave visible imprints on the surrounding leaves. The 2 inch (5 cm) long, dark brown to black terminal spine is grooved above and rounded below. The spine can be quite lethal and care should be taken when handling the plants. The 6½–13 foot (2–4 meter) tall, branched flower stalk rises well above the plant and has twelve to twenty side branches, each heavily laden with 3 inch (7.5 cm) long, yellow flowers at the tip.

CULTURE

As this species occurs in the northern Chihuahuan Desert, one would expect it to be perfectly hardy—and it is, having survived −20 degrees F (−29 C) in Colorado without damage. Although that is the extreme, *Agave havardiana* is reliably hardy to 0 degrees F (−18 C) and should make a great landscape plant in the drier areas along the Pacific coast, through the Gulf coast states and up the Atlantic coast at least to North

Carolina. It is generally considered a zone 7a–11 plant, and is easily grown in all southwestern U.S. zones without damage.

With its slow growth rate, *Agave havardiana* is no speed demon, requiring several years to make an impressive specimen. Once established, plants should be watered infrequently so they will develop the densest rosettes possible. Although plants are drought tolerant, they might require some supplemental water during the summer months in the hot, interior, low elevation zone. Plants are best grown in full sun where they will develop the most dense, compact form with the best blue leaf color.

Make sure that the soil has good drainage to prevent the rotting of roots and eventually the death of the plant. Plants are frequently found growing in association with an extensive cover of perennial grasses at slightly higher elevations in western Texas, where the soil temperature is a bit cooler than in the hot, interior, low elevation zone. With this in mind, plant perennial wildflowers and low-growing grasses to help cool the soil if you live in the low or mid-elevation zone of the desert southwestern United States, or in any place else where summer temperatures routinely exceed 100 degrees F (38 C).

LANDSCAPE VALUE

Try using *Agave havardiana* as a bold focal point in a desert grassland landscape or a perennial garden. Having ephemerals providing seasonal ground cover should help to moderate the soil temperature in hot, desert areas. Use some flowering perennials or small shrubs to provide bursts of seasonal color. In the hot, interior low elevation and mid-elevation zones try using *Chrysactinia mexicana*, *Penstemon* species, *Poliomintha maderensis*, or *Salvia greggii*.

ABOVE A flower cluster of *Agave havardiana*

OPPOSITE *Agave havardiana* in peak bloom in the Davis Mountains of western Texas

Agave horrida Lemaire ex Jacobi

WICKED AGAVE

A nice *Agave horrida* rosette with sword-shaped leaves and colorful teeth

Apparently Charles Lemaire fancied this a horrible-looking agave—while others find the bizarre and wicked teeth on some of the plants to be fascinating.

FIELD NOTES

There are two subspecies of *Agave horrida*: subspecies *horrida*, occurring in central Mexico, and ssp. *perotensis*, which grows in western Veracruz and adjacent eastern Puebla.

The two-lane highway that takes you to a nice population of *Agave horrida* ssp. *horrida*, near Pinal de Amoles in the state of Querétaro, snakes through some mountainous terrain, necessitating a top speed of about twenty miles per hour lest you wind up hurtling off the road as others have (evidenced by the number of crosses set up by the roadside). Plants populate the east-facing slope, so plan to arrive early enough to get good light or take a tripod and use a slow shutter speed. Look for the ones with incredibly gnarly teeth and take some close-up shots to show impressive bud prints burned into the leaves. If you make the trip in summer, you should see the plants' tall, unbranched flower stalks loaded with greenish yellow flowers.

In the hills not far from the town of Perote in Veracruz, one can see fine stands of *Agave horrida* ssp. *perotensis*. While there, be on the lookout for the stately *Nolina parviflora* with its thick, shaggy head of spreading to drooping, dark green leaves. Subspecies *perotensis* differs in its darker green, more numerous leaves, slightly larger and denser rosette, and slightly larger inflorescence. It is hardier to frost than ssp. *horrida*.

Plants are found growing between 7000 and 8500 feet elevation (2100–2600 meters) in Morelos, Puebla, and Querétaro in central Mexico.

DESCRIPTION

Agave horrida forms solitary, compact, and small to medium-sized rosettes reaching 1–2 feet tall by 1½–3 feet across (30–60 by 45–90 cm), each eighty to one hundred leaves. The thick, rigid, bright emerald green to dark olive green leaves are elliptic-lanceolate, 7–15 inches long by 1½–3 inches wide (18–38 by 4–7.5 cm), and look like the bronze Centurion sword used by soldiers in the Middle Ages to stab their enemies. Small to large, straight or wickedly curved to sinuous, chocolate brown to grayish white teeth grow out from the continuous, white margin, making beautiful bud prints on the tender, succulent flesh of the surrounding

leaves. The 1–2 inch (2.5–5 cm) long terminal spine is a continuation of the horny margin, and is straight or sinuous, grooved or lightly flattened above, and partially rounded below.

The 6½–16 foot (2–5 meter) tall, spicate flower stalk holds thousands of 1½ inch (4 cm) long, greenish yellow, yellowish, purplish green or dark reddish purple flowers grouped in twos or threes directly on the stalk.

CULTURE

As this species is relatively new to southwestern U.S. horticulture, not much is known about its eventual size and frost hardiness. Since sometime in the 1990s, San Marcos Growers have been growing a plant they believe is *Agave horrida,* though the identification is still in question—especially as the website indicates that the plant survived the 1990 freeze in a Goleta, California, garden when temperatures dropped to the low 20s F (−5 to −6 C), which seems a bit unusual for a species from frost-free areas of the south-central Mexican states of Morelos, Querétaro, and Puebla. My experience has been that the plants of ssp. *horrida* need some protection once overnight lows drop to near freezing, while those of ssp. *perotensis* show no damage when temperatures hit the low 20s F (−5 to −6 C). If you are growing ssp. *horrida*, be sure to protect your plants if the nighttime temperature looks like it will drop to 30 degrees F (−1 C) or lower. Consider ssp. *horrida* to be a zone 10a–11 plant, hardy enough for landscape use in frost-free zones of California and the coastal, low elevation southwestern U.S. zone, while ssp. *perotensis* can be used in parts of the Pacific coast states, Florida, and the Atlantic coast states that experience some frost as well as the hot, interior low elevation zone and warmer regions of the mid-elevation southwestern U.S. zone.

The growth rate is slow to moderate, allowing for an ample number of years to enjoy the wickedly wonderful teeth on the leaf edges. Although plants hail from an area with a bit more annual rainfall than most of the southwestern United States receives, *Agave horrida* requires relatively low amounts of water. They will, however, grow a bit faster if given consistent supplemental water from late spring through the end of summer as long as they are not kept soggy. Plants can be grown in full sun in the coastal, low elevation zone. If you are willing to protect plants in the hot, interior, low elevation zone and the mid-elevation zone, make sure that they have some shade, especially during the brutally hot summer.

Agave horrida is frequently found growing on dry, rocky slopes, and relishes a soil with excellent drainage.

OPPOSITE LEFT *Agave horrida* growing on a rock slab near Pinal de Amoles in Querétaro, Mexico

TOP RIGHT White teeth and terminal spine set against bright green leaves on *Agave horrida*

BOTTOM RIGHT The spicate inflorescence of *Agave horrida*, just beginning to open its flowers

LANDSCAPE VALUE

Use *Agave horrida* in a cactus and succulent garden or mix with small, flowering shrubs and perennials in frost-free regions. Put it in a nice, decorative pot and keep it near an oft-used patio or entryway to show off the rich green leaves and interesting marginal teeth. Small plants with the most bizarre teeth are quite decorative, and make excellent potted plants.

TAXONOMIC NOTES

In 1990, while researching the true identity of the plant that Gentry listed as *Agave obscura* Schiede, Bernd Ullrich found that botanist Miguel Cházaro Basáñez had actually determined Schiede's plant to be the same as *A. xalapensis* Roezl ex Jacobi. However, the name *A. obscura* was published before *A. xalapensis* and had priority, rendering Gentry's use of *A. obscura* incorrect. This in turn meant that the plant Gentry regarded as *A. obscura* Schiede needed a new name. Because Gentry, Ullrich and other agave botanists were of the opinion that *A. horrida* Lemaire and the plant formerly known as *A. obscura* Schiede were very closely related, Ullrich renamed the latter as *A. horrida* Lemaire ex Jacobi ssp. *perotensis* Ullrich.

There is a spot to the south of the city of Tehuacán, Puebla, on the road to Oaxaca City, which has a population of plants that appear to be *Agave horrida* ssp. *perotensis*. If you find this population, notice how different the young plants look from the adult plants nearby. The young plants resemble little ones of those going by the names of *Agave* 'Sierra Mixteca' and *Agave* 'FO76'.

Agave isthmensis García-Mendoza & Palma Cruz

ISTHMUS AGAVE

Agave isthmensis rosettes with blue leaves and black terminal spines

A sizable colony of
Agave isthmensis
growing on the rocks
near Santiago Laollaga
in southeastern Oaxaca

Abisaí García-Mendoza and Felipe Palma Cruz used this agave's occurrence on the Isthmus of Tehuantepec in southern Mexico as the inspiration for the species name.

FIELD NOTES

This miniature marvel exists in three known localities, of which two are relatively accessible. All localities are on the Isthmus of Tehuantepec (hence the species name *isthmensis*), which is in southernmost Mexico, straddling the states of Oaxaca and Chiapas.

The coastal form is on a hillside just west of Salina Cruz, Oaxaca, which is within spitting distance of the Pacific Ocean, while one of the inland forms occurs on an east-facing slope north of the town of Laollaga in Oaxaca. Plants near Salina Cruz can be found growing tucked in among grasses and boulders, trying to stay out of the midday sun which can be brutal, even that close to the ocean. These cute little plants are quite variable, making dwarf rosettes of about 10–12 inches (25–30 cm) across and sparingly producing offsets to form small clusters. The best forms have powdery blue leaves, black teeth, and black spines. The relatively large, handsome teeth make impressive bud imprints on the surrounding leaves.

Anyone familiar with the plant sold as *Agave verschaffeltii* var. *minima*, *A. potatorum* var. *verschaffeltii* 'Compacta', or *A. potatorum* var. *verschaffeltii* will notice its resemblance to the inland form of *A. isthmensis*. The name *A. verschaffeltii* var. *minima*, as used in horticulture, should not be confused with *A. verschaffeltii* as described by Lemaire in 1868, which has been relegated to synonymy with *A. potatorum*. It is a much larger plant that does not produce as copious numbers of offsets as does the inland form of *A. isthmensis*. The plants of *A. isthemsis* near Salina Cruz are larger and produce fewer offsets than those to the north of Santiago Laollaga.

Plants are found within the elevation range of 50–2870 feet (15–875 meters).

DESCRIPTION

This delightful dwarf has been in cultivation for quite some time, being sold as a miniature form of *Agave potatorum*. However, in 1993 the botanists Abisaí García-Mendoza and Felípe Palma Cruz recognized *A. isthmensis* as a distinct species, separate from *A. potatorum* based on the smaller flowers and overall size. Some of the smallest rosettes reach

Agave isthmensis from the population near Santiago Laollaga

maturity at just 4–5 inches tall and 6–8 inches across (10–12 by 15–20 cm) while some of the larger ones top out at about 8–12 inches tall and 10–15 inches across (20–30 by 15–36 cm). Some of the plants near Santiago Laollaga produce copious quantities of offsets and form colonies that are strikingly large for such a diminutive dwarf.

The powdery blue or gray-blue leaves are short and wide, 2–6 inches long and 1–3 inches wide (5–15 by 2.5–8 cm), and obovate to spoon-shaped, though they do not make very good utensils with which to eat your morning oatmeal while out camping. They are slightly rough to the touch, with the widest point being above the middle of the blade. The prominent, reddish brown or black teeth sit atop large, mammillate projections and leave deep impressions on the surrounding leaves. The short terminal spine is reddish brown to black on fresh leaves, aging to a distinguished gray on older leaves.

The 5–7 foot (1.5–2.2 meter) tall, thin, branched flower stalk starts to appear in summer, with flowers opening in late summer and capsules beginning to ripen in fall. The stalk bears fifteen to twenty-five short branches, each with several 2 inch (5 cm) long, yellow flowers clustered at the tip.

CULTURE

As this agave hails from the southern Mexican states of Oaxaca and Chiapas, it is not surprising that it will not tolerate much frost. In Tucson, I routinely cover even my larger plants when winter lows dip below 30 degrees F (–1 C). Plants should not suffer any frost damage in zones 9b–11, the mild winter parts of California and Florida, or the hot, interior low elevation southwestern U.S. zone. They will need some frost protection even in warm microclimates in the mid-elevation zone.

The plants are relatively slow growing, taking several years to achieve flowering size and to form clusters of rosettes. These are low-water-using, but will reward you with a thicker, more pumped-up specimen if given consistent supplemental water from late spring through the end of summer. Plants can be grown in full sun in the coastal, low elevation zone, and although they will tolerate full sun in the mid-elevation zone, they appreciate a bit of midday shade in the summer. Locate plants under the shade of a finely textured tree—or try using that old beach umbrella to provide some afternoon shade in the hot, interior low elevation zone. Plant in soil with very good drainage to avoid any possibility of rot.

LANDSCAPE VALUE

Because of its miniature stature, cool bud imprints, and frost sensitivity, *Agave isthmensis* is best grown as a potted plant except in the cooler climate of coastal southern California where it can be used as a landscape plant. Take advantage of the decorative nature by placing a nice specimen near a patio or in an area which you will walk by on a daily basis.

TAXONOMIC NOTES

Although this beauty resembles a dwarf form of *Agave potatorum*, there are also some distinct differences. The plants that make up the inland population of *A. isthmensis* are much smaller, but form bigger clusters than the form that is found a stone's throw from the Gulf of Tehuantepec along southern Oaxaca.

Agave 'Kichijokan'

HAPPY CROWN AGAVE, LUCKY CROWN AGAVE

A well-grown plant of *Agave* 'Kichijokan' in a southern California garden

The common names are loose translations of the Chinese characters applied to this plant. It is also sold as *Agave* 'Kitsusyokan', *A. potatorum* 'Kichiokan', *A. potatorum* 'Kichijokan', *A. verschaffeltii* 'Kichiokan', *A. verschaffeltii* 'Kichijokan', and *A.* 'Kissho Kan'.

FIELD NOTES

Agave 'Kichijokan' is a bit of a taxonomic conundrum, as there is no known collection data, leaving its origin shrouded in mystery so that growers and collectors haphazardly apply to it the names *A. potatorum* and *A. verschaffeltii*. In fact, the cultivar name has also been a confusing matter. In the United States, at least three cultivar names—'Kichiokan', 'Kichijokan', and 'Kissho Kan'—have been applied to this particular plant, causing confusion among collectors. Recently, several people who read *kanji* characters and speak Japanese have helped to interpret the characters originally used for this cultivar, and they have indicated that the characters can be interpreted in more than one way. As the word 'Kichijokan' is one interpretation of the *kanji* characters, and it is well established in the trade, it seems prudent to maintain it as the cultivar name for this particular plant.

The leaves look very much like those of the closely related *Agave isthmensis*, *A. potatorum* or *A. pygmaea*, or even like a very dwarf form of *A. parryi* var. *truncata*. Although leaf characteristics can be helpful, they are not always definitive when determining species. Inflorescence structure and flower dimensions are usually more critical in determining species affinities. In July of 2010, a picture of a flowering specimen growing in Florida was posted on an internet forum, showing few, greenish yellow, wide spreading flowers on long, thin side branches—characteristics that show affinity with *A. isthmensis*, *A. potatorum* and *A. pygmae*, but not with *A. parryi* var. *truncata* which can therefore be ruled out. The owner of the plant was contacted and flowers were sent to Tucson. The flower measurements place it in between *A. pygmaea* and *A. isthmensis*, further muddying the picture and leaving me wanting more flowers to measure. From a batch of seedling *A. isthmensis* germinated in 2009, two plants have grown up to strongly resemble *A.* 'Kichijokan', throwing more uncertainty into the equation. Without a botanical voucher for the original collection, the evidence is not conclusive enough for a definitive answer and the name for this beautiful plant should remain as is.

DESCRIPTION

The beautiful powder blue, spoon-shaped leaves of *Agave* 'Kichijokan' spiral around the central point, forming a spectacular, perfectly formed rosette. This cultivar develops a fantastic, uniformly symmetrical rosette to about 1–1¾ feet tall and 1–2 feet across (30–53 cm by 45–60 cm). Over time the plant can form small clusters as offsets are produced from underground shoots. These offsets are easily removed to keep the clean look of a single rosette if so desired. As the new leaves emerge, the dark reddish to chestnut brown teeth and spines contrast beautifully with the overall powdery blue color. The large, down-curved teeth make deep impressions on the young leaves, creating intricate patterns of shadow and light when the sun hits the plant at the right time of day. The terminal spine can be straight to squiggly, about 1 inch (2.5 cm) long, dark reddish brown-black on new leaves, aging to gray on old leaves, and connected to the first one or two set of teeth. The flower stalk is tall with widely spaced, very slender side branches, each holding several greenish yellow flowers.

CULTURE

Agave 'Kichijokan' is a bit sensitive to frost, showing some leaf damage when winter lows drop down into the high 20s F (–2 C). To be on the safe side, this should be considered a zone 10a–11 plant, and should probably be given some frost protection when the forecast is for 30 degrees F (–1 C) or lower. It can be grown in the ground only in frost-free areas of California and Florida; otherwise, keep it as a potted plant so it can be moved into a greenhouse for the winter.

The plants have a slow to moderately fast growth rate, depending on conditions. With high-quality cactus soil, light shade and sufficient water during the growing season, they can reach a nearly mature size in five to six years while those grown hard will take nearly twice that long. When grown in full sun, they will have a much tighter rosette that will look more like a dense, multiple-petaled rose flower than the more open rosette produced by plants grown in some shade. Although somewhat drought tolerant, they will respond to supplemental water with a faster growth rate. My container-grown plants in Tucson have survived our hot summers in clay pots even when watered inconsistently. In the hot, interior, low elevation zone, this cultivar does best with some midday shade during the hottest part of the year. When grown in the mid-elevation zone or any area with mild summer temperatures below 100 degrees F (38 C), the plants can take full sun as long as they receive supplemental water in the summer.

Grow this one in a loose soil that drains quickly. If growing in a heavier soil, adjust the frequency of watering to prevent it from becoming soggy. When grown in a container, use a high-quality cactus mix, even adding coarse sand to increase drainage.

Packrats are drawn to the thick, succulent leaves like paperclips to a magnet. When growing your prized specimen in a pot, be sure to put it up on a stand that these rodents are unable to negotiate; otherwise, you will find large chunks of leaves eaten when they discover your plant.

LANDSCAPE VALUE

In the coastal, low elevation zone or zones 10a–11, these can be planted in the ground and used as small specimens. They look great when mixed with small perennials and low shrubs so that they are not hidden by larger plants. Try using *Calylophus hartwegii*, *Conoclinium dissectum*, *Glandularia gooddingii*, *Penstemon* species, *Thymophylla pentachaeta*, and *Zinnia grandiflora*. *Agave* 'Kichijokan' makes a great container plant no matter where you live, and should be given a place front and center on an oft-used patio or front entry.

Agave 'Kichijokan' is a great container plant.

Agave 'Kissho Kan'

HAPPY CROWN AGAVE, LUCKY CROWN AGAVE

With its creamy, butter yellow variegation, *Agave* 'Kissho Kan' is a striking container plant.

The common names are loose translations of the Chinese characters applied to this plant.

FIELD NOTES

In his *Nishiki Succulent Handbook*, published in 1999, Tony Sato depicted several variegated forms of a plant which he lists as *Agave verschaffeltii* (a synonym for *A. potatorum*), including figure 1292 which shows the plant known as *A.* 'Kissho Kan'. All of the plants pictured as *A. verschaffeltii* have the Japanese name 'Kitsusyokan' which, according to some interpretations, means awkward. Tony Avent indicated to me that he found a publication dated 1996 with the cultivar name 'Kissho Kan' used for this form with creamy butter yellow leaf margins. Because that predates Sato's book, 'Kissho Kan' has priority over 'Kitsusyokan'.

DESCRIPTION

The rosette of *Agave* 'Kissho Kan' is dense and symmetrical in shape, growing to about 1–1¾ feet tall and 1–2 feet across (30–53 cm by 45–60 cm). As the plant ages, it produces offsets from underground shoots. These offsets are easily removed to keep the clean look of a single rosette if so desired. The spoon-shaped leaves are powdery blue with creamy, butter yellow variegation along the margins. The teeth and terminal spines are dark reddish to chestnut brown on new leaves, turning charcoal gray as the leaves age. The terminal spines can be straight to squiggly, about 1 inch (2.5 cm) long, and connected to the first one or two sets of teeth. The flower stalk has not been seen.

CULTURE

Agave 'Kissho Kan' is frost sensitive, showing leaf damage when winter lows drop into the high 20s F (−2 C). To be on the safe side, this should be considered a zone 10a–11 plant, and should be given frost protection when the forecast is for 30 degrees F (−1 C) or lower. It can be grown in the ground only in frost-free areas of California and Florida; otherwise, keep it in a pot so that it can be moved into a greenhouse for the winter.

The plants have a slow growth rate, taking several years to reach full size. When grown in full sun, they will have a much tighter rosette that will look more like a densely, multiple-petaled rose flower than the more open rosette produced by a plant grown in some shade. Although somewhat drought tolerant, they will respond to supplemental water with a faster growth rate. My container-grown plants in Tucson have survived our hot summers in clay pots when receiving water twice a week. In areas that experience summer temperatures over 90 F (32 C), provide midday shade for your plant during the hottest part of the year, and you will be rewarded with a magnificent specimen.

Grow this one in a loose soil that drains quickly. When grown in a container, use a high-quality cactus mix, even adding coarse sand to increase drainage.

Packrats are notorious for chewing large chunks out of leaves in the middle of the rosette, so be sure to put your plant up on a stand that these rodents are unable to negotiate.

LANDSCAPE VALUE

In the coastal, low elevation zone or zones 10a–11, these can be planted in the ground and used as small specimens. They look great when mixed with small, flowering perennials; try combining with *Calylophus hartwegii*, *Conoclinium dissectum*, *Glandularia gooddingii*, *Penstemon* species, *Thymophylla pentachaeta*, and *Zinnia grandiflora*. With its compact size, *Agave* 'Kissho Kan' makes an excellent container plant and should be placed in a spot that is highly visible.

This cultivar was first seen in the horticulture trade in the southwestern United States in the late 1990s, and has been a popular plant since. It has taken the trade by storm and its popularity has far surpassed that of *Agave* 'Kichijokan'.

Agave macroacantha Zuccarini

LARGE SPINE AGAVE

The blue leaves of *Agave macroacantha* combine nicely with the violet flowers of *Glandularia aristigera* (frequently sold as *Verbena tenuisecta*).

Joseph Zuccarini used the long terminal spine as inspiration when combining *macr*, Greek for large or long, with *acanth*, Greek for spine, in the species name.

FIELD NOTES

Agave macroacantha is restricted to the area around Tehuacán in southern Puebla and northern Oaxaca. Possibly the most attractive plants I have ever seen were growing out in the open on exposed dry, chalky, desert soil with the occasional exception found nestled among small trees on rocky, limestone outcrops. This beauty usually forms a perfect rosette of powdery blue leaves with black teeth along the edges and a stout, thick, black terminal spine. On an excursion into northern Oaxaca, I spotted one plant with glowing candy apple red teeth.

Plants are found growing with cactus and other arid-loving plants between 3800 and 4500 feet (1150–1370 meters) elevation.

DESCRIPTION

Individual rosettes of *Agave macroacantha* are small, reaching 10–16 inches tall by 10–18 inches across (25–40 by 25–45 cm). Plants will produce offsets and form medium-sized clusters to 2–3 feet across (60–90 cm). Narrow, dagger-like, powdery blue to blue-gray or blue-green leaves measure 9–14 inches long and about 1–1½ inches wide (25–35 by 2.5–3.5 cm) with small, curved black teeth along the edges. The dark chestnut brown to black terminal spine is usually about 1–1½ inch (2.5–4 cm) long, though spines as long as 3–3½ inches (7.5–9 cm) can be found on some plants.

The 6–7 foot (2 meter) tall, branched flower stalk emerges in late spring and has ten to fourteen side branches, each with clusters of 2 inch (5 cm) long, green flowers with purple-flushed tips.

CULTURE

Some forms of this southern Mexican species have proven to be hardier than others. Mary Irish reported that plants in the Sierra Foothills of California showed no damage when temperatures reached 17 degrees F (–8 C). My own plants, exposed to the open sky in Tucson, have shown minor leaf damage when winter lows hit the low 20s F (–5 to –6 C), while others, surrounded by some small shrubs and with a little bit of protection from a sparsely leaved tree, showed no damage. It should be reliably hardy in zones 9b–11, needing some protection on cold nights in zone

ABOVE A colony of good-sized *Agave macroacantha* plants in northern Oaxaca

LEFT An unusual specimen of *Agave macroacantha* with candy apple red teeth in habitat in northern Oaxaca

9a. It makes a good landscape plant in mild winter parts of California and Florida, in the hot, interior low elevation zone, and with some overhead protection in the milder parts of the mid-elevation southwestern U.S. zone.

Agave macroacantha is relatively slow growing, taking several years to reach flowering size. Plants can tolerate full sun in the cooler coastal, low elevation zone, but benefit from the shade of open-canopied desert trees in the hot, interior, low elevation and mid-elevation southwestern U.S. zones.

The blue- and blue-gray-leaved forms are from very arid areas, and once established the plants should be kept dry to prevent any potential rot. The blue-green-leaved form is from slightly more moist areas, and will tolerate extra water, especially in the hot, dry interior low elevation zone. These should be planted in soil with very good drainage.

LANDSCAPE VALUE

Agave macroacantha can be planted in the ground in the frost-free areas of the cool, coastal zone in southern California, and can be used in a desert or xeric garden mixed with flowering small shrubs and perennials, or mixed effectively with other cactus and succulents. Try planting some soft pink- or deep purple-flowered perennials to highlight and complement the blue-gray leaves.

Agave marmorata Roezl

MARBLE LEAF AGAVE

The blue-gray leaves, with prominent crossbanding, of the desert form of *Agave marmorata*

Marmor is Latin for marble. According to Gentry, the word was used by Benedkit Roezl to describe the leaves' "marble-like hue." Gentry noted three local names for this species: pisomel (apparently a corruption of the Nahuatl name pitzometl), huiscole, and maguey curandero. Curandero means healer, indicating that the plant may have been used medicinally.

FIELD NOTES

Agave marmorata is a variable plant depending on the habitat in which it is growing. The strikingly handsome desert form with beautifully banded, marbled gray leaves is found growing with *Neobuxbaumia tetetzo* in the arid region around Tehuacán in southern Puebla. This is perhaps my favorite form as the plants appear to grow too heavy so that, unable to support their massive weight, they tip over so much that the apex is growing nearly parallel to the ground. The banding of blue-gray and light green is highlighted as the leaves unfurl from around the central cone, looking like a Jack-in-the-pulpit flower.

Further south and east as you travel Mexico Highway 190 from Oaxaca to the Isthmus of Tehuantepec, look up above the roadcuts for the gigantic, green-leaved form that lives in more forested habitat. Frequently, these plants have floppy leaves that lack the distinctive crossbanding that characterizes the desert form. If you travel this narrow, two-lane highway in November, you will be treated to a rainbow display of shades of red, yellow and orange as the deciduous trees lose their leaves in preparation for the dry season.

The species is generally found between 4400 and 6000 feet (1350–1800 meters) elevation in Puebla and Oaxaca.

DESCRIPTION

Two distinct forms of *Agave marmorata* can be found in the southern Mexican states of Puebla and Oaxaca. Both produce large solitary rosettes, reaching about 3½–4 feet tall and about 4–6½ feet across (1.3 by 1.3–2 meters). They differ mainly in habitat and leaf color: one occurs in mesic habitat and has light green to dark green leaves, sometimes with faint crossbanding, while the other is found in more xeric habitat, with deeply folded, rough-textured, blue-gray leaves that are conspicuously marked with distinctive crossbanding. It is this second form that is most sought after by agavephiles; with 40–50 inch long by 7–12 inch wide (100–135 by 20–30 cm) leaves, complete with spectacular color

and crossbanding and topped by large teeth on huge mammillate cusps which leave deep impressions on surrounding leaves, the plants are highly decorative. The conical, ³/₅–1¹/₅ inch (1.5–3 cm) long, dark chestnut brown to black terminal spine is unobtrusive yet quite sharp and painful when jabbed into fingers or legs.

As the weather starts to cool and the days get shorter, the tall flower stalk rises 15–20 feet (5–6.5 meters) above the plant and has twenty to twenty-five side branches in the upper half of the shaft. Each side branch is densely packed with clusters of 1¹/₂–2 inch (4–5 cm) long, golden yellow flowers at the tips.

The blue-gray-leaved form of *Agave marmorata* resembles both *A. colorata* and *A. zebra*. To distinguish among the three, see "Comparing Look-Alikes."

CULTURE

As *Agave marmorata* hails from the southern Mexican states of Puebla and Oaxaca, its inability to tolerate extreme frost is not surprising. Gentry reported that small to medium-sized plants were killed both in his garden in Murrieta, California, and at the Desert Botanical Garden in Phoenix, Arizona, when winter lows reached between 20 and 25 degrees F (–4 to –6 C). My large plant with blue-gray leaves, growing in a pot in Tucson, gets covered when the temperature is expected to drop to the mid- to high 20s F (–2 to –4 C), though it has withstood 28 degrees F –2 C) for a brief time without damage. These can be grown in zones 9b–11, in mild winter parts of California and Florida, in the coastal, low elevation zone, and in warm spots in the hot, interior, low elevation zone.

The slow growth rate means that it will take several years to become an impressive specimen. On the upside, though, the plant will last a long time before it flowers and dies. The xeric form is best grown in full sun where plants will develop the best blue leaf color and maximum crossbanding. The blue-gray-leaved form is from a very arid area and, once established, plants should be kept dry to prevent any potential rot. The green-leaved form is from areas with a bit more moisture and thrives with some shade and extra water, especially in the hot, dry, interior low elevation zone.

The form with blue-gray leaves needs soil with very good drainage to keep excess water away from the roots. While the green-leaved form is not quite as picky about the soil type, it still should have adequate drainage; alternatively, adjust the watering according to the soil type.

The leaves unfurling from the central cone of *Agave marmorata* resemble the flowers of Jack-in-the-pulpit

LANDSCAPE VALUE

Agave marmorata can be planted in the ground in the frost-free areas of the cool, coastal zone in southern California, and can be used as a bold focal point in a desert or xeric garden. Try planting some blue- or soft-pink-flowered perennials and small shrubs to highlight and complement the blue-gray leaves. In San Diego and Los Angeles, try *Aethionema* ×*warleyense*, *Agastache cana*, *Ageratum houstonianum*, *Amsonia tabernaemontana*, *Armeria maritima*, *Diascia* 'Coral Belle', or *Penstemon pseudospectabilis*. In the Phoenix area, this agave should be tried in warm spots. If you give it a go, mix in *Calliandra eriophylla*, *Penstemon parryi*, or *Salvia greggii* for the pinkish flower contrast to the marble blue foliage of the agave. *Agave marmorata* could possibly be used in warmer spots in Tucson if it is covered with a blanket or frost cloth when temperatures are expected to drop below freezing.

Agave mitis Martius

APPLE GREEN AGAVE

A pale-green-leaved plant of *Agave mitis* growing on a rock roadcut in northern Querétaro

Synonym: *Agave celsii* Hooker. The Latin *miti* means mild or harmless—which botanist Karl Friedrich von Martius apparently felt was an appropriate description for this agave with unthreatening teeth.

FIELD NOTES

Agave mitis is found on steep, shaded, east-facing cliffs and roadcuts in semi-tropical to tropical habitats of eastern Mexico between 4000 and 6500 feet (1230–2000 meters) elevation. In order to get optimal photos of these shy, shade-loving inhabitants of vertical surfaces, I have used a tripod and cable release to eliminate camera shake due to the slow shutter speed necessary to allow in maximum light. The open rosettes of rich, jade green leaves stand out against the brown dirt of roadcuts, but can be somewhat obscured by dense vegetation. On the road to the cloud forest near Goméz Farías in Tamaulipas, I have seen nice specimens with their purplish red flowers on slender stalks just begging to be photographed.

DESCRIPTION

Agave mitis is an offsetting type, with new plants developing by means of axillary branching. The development of exceptionally large clusters in habitat is frequently limited by the topography in which they are found. However, the formation of large massive clusters up to 6–8 feet (1.8–2.5 meters) across can occur in cultivation. Individual rosettes are small to medium in size, typically 1–1½ feet tall by 1½–3 feet across (30–45 by 45–90 cm). The bright, Granny Smith apple green to darker jade green or rarely glaucous light green leaves are a long oval shape, 12–24 inches long by 3–5 inches across (30–60 by 7–13 cm) at the broadest spot, which is usually above the middle. The edges are clothed with small, weak, evenly and closely spaced teeth. The terminal spine is somewhat weak and less than 1 inch (2.5 cm) long.

The short, spicate inflorescence reaches 5–8 feet (1.5–2.5 meters) tall, and is densely crowded with 1½–2⅓ inch (4–6 cm) long, usually purplish red (but sometimes greenish or yellowish) flowers in the upper one third to one half of the stalk.

CULTURE

My plants in Tucson have been subjected to temperatures in the high teens F (−7 to −8 C) several times, albeit only for short durations, without any damage. This is somewhat surprising as *Agave mitis* hails from a more subtropical climate. It can be considered a zone 8b–11 plant and

can be reliably grown in many areas of the Pacific coast and Gulf coast states, and in the cool, coastal and hot, interior low elevation and mid-elevation southwestern U.S. zones.

The growth rate is relatively slow, and plants will take several years before flowering. *Agave mitis* is one of the more mesic species and bene-fits from supplemental water from spring until the end of summer, except during monsoon season if the rains come consistently. As it is native to densely forested hillsides in subtropical eastern Mexico, you would be correct in assuming that *Agave mitis* is happiest with some shade in the hotter parts of the desert southwestern United States and other regions that routinely experience summer temperatures over 100 F (38 C). In the hot, interior, low and mid-elevation zones, place plants under the shade of trees or on the east side of a building to prevent them from sunburn-ing, or try a daily slathering of SPF 70 sunscreen. Plants can tolerate full sun along the coast in southern California.

Plants are not too particular about soil, though they will look health-ier and grow better if the soil has some organic matter. Adding a layer of compost or organic mulch will help the soil to retain moisture while also keeping it cooler, which the roots greatly appreciate.

LANDSCAPE VALUE

Agave mitis is best used in the shade of a tree, and looks great when planted with colorful perennials and small shrubs. In the interior, low elevation and mid-elevation zones, group several together under a can-opy-forming tree, such as *Lysiloma watsonii* ssp. *thornberi* or *Proso-pis velutina*, to create a lush, semi-tropical feel close to your house. Try planting with *A. bovicornuta* and *Dioon edule* along with shade-tolerant perennials such as *Aquilegia chrysantha*, and *Heuchera sanguinea* to liven up an entryway. Along the cooler, coastal zone, plants are more tolerant of the full sun but will still benefit from the shade of a canopy-forming tree; a nice choice would be *Albizia julibrissin* or *Chorisia speciosa*. Some excellent flowering perennials or small shrubs would include *Agastache* species, *Ageratum corymbosum*, *Salvia* species, and *Teucrium fruticans*.

TAXONOMIC NOTES

In 1982 Gentry used Hooker's name of *Agave celsii* for this species, but eleven years later Ullrich dug into the literature and determined that Martius's name of *Agave mitis* was the correct one.

OPPOSITE This *Agave mitis* specimen in peak bloom was growing along the road to the Reserva de la Biosfera El Cielo in Tamaulipas.

ABOVE The long, showy, purplish red stamens of *Agave mitis*

Agave mitis 'Multicolor'

Tony Avent first saw this one at Succulenta Nursery in Holland, and then later at several nurseries in Thailand.

Plants of this interesting cultivar are known to get at least 1–1½ feet tall and 1½–2 feet across (30–45 by 45–60 cm), and possibly a little larger with ideal conditions. The glaucous blue leaves are decorated with a creamy border on each edge along with small, black teeth that look like tiny ornaments dotting the margins. The short terminal spine is black on new leaves before aging to a deep chestnut brown on older leaves.

The flower stalk is unknown at this time, but there is no reason to expect it to differ from the 5–8 foot (1.5–2.5 meter) tall, spicate stalk with 2 inch (5 cm) long purplish red flowers of typical *Agave mitis*.

Plants should be given some shade and extra water during the summer in hot, dry regions. It is a bit slower growing than the typical form, and will take several years to achieve its maximum size. This slow growth is a good thing, though, as the plants will adapt nicely to being grown in a large container, allowing for close-up viewing of the really decorative variegation. Cold hardiness is generally not a problem in zones 8b–11.

Agave montana Villarreal

MOUNTAIN AGAVE

Perfectly formed rosettes of *Agave montana* growing on the slopes of Cerro La Laja in Querétaro

Botanist José Angel Villarreal used the Spanish word for mountain, not a reference to the state of Montana, in the name of this awesome species.

FIELD NOTES

This species, described in 1996, has only been found above 8500 feet (2600 meters) in the northeastern Mexican states of Tamaulipas and Nuevo León, with a disjunct population occurring in Querétaro. To see these dense, perfect rosettes of neatly stacked leaves spiraling around the center of the plant, I traveled up and up and up and then up some more along bumpy, rutted dirt roads that wind their way into and past the pine forest above the town of Miquihuana in southern Tamaulipas. Some of the best-looking plants are found scattered among the tall pines and in association with the recently described, tall, trunk-forming *Nolina hibernica* whose trunks are swathed in a thicket of leaves that swirl about them as if perpetually blown by the wind. I also visited another population near the top of Cerro La Laja in Querétaro, which required driving on (surprise!) a long, bumpy dirt road.

Plants start to shoot their thick, telephone-pole-like flower stalk in the summer and fall, reaching their full height before winter, but waiting until the weather warms in the spring to poke their short, stubby side branches out of the knob of densely congested bracts. Once fully open, the compact, Christmas-tree-shaped cluster of side branches holds numerous, long, yellow flowers.

DESCRIPTION

Agave montana is a solitary, non-offsetting species that forms an extremely dense rosette of very broad, uniform leaves, giving the plant the look of a gigantic artichoke. These invincible-looking plants top out at 3–4 feet tall and 4–5 feet across (0.75–1.25 by 1.25–1.5 meters), with about a hundred flat, bright green to dark green, 12–20 inch long by 6–7 inch wide (30–50 by 15–17 cm), broadly dagger-shaped leaves that are spirally stacked in twelve to sixteen layers. I can just imagine the plant as some type of throwing weapon conceived and used by giant aliens after visiting medieval England. Some of the most striking forms above Miquihuana and on Cerro La Laja have silvery blue frosting on the leaves, which really shows off the bud prints. The leaves are broad from the base to past the middle, at which point they taper to a stout, reddish brown, 1–2 inch (2.5–5 cm) long, lethal, terminal spine that could be used in acupuncture treatments. Large, hooked teeth are a beautiful

OPPOSITE TOP A specimen of *Agave montana*, with dark green leaves overlaid with a striking frosty silver coating

BOTTOM LEFT This *Agave montana* plant has exceptionally nice teeth and corresponding deep bud prints.

BOTTOM RIGHT The dense, congested panicle, with flaming, dark red buds and electric yellow flowers of *Agave montana*

cinnamon reddish brown on new leaves before turning grayish as the leaves age.

When the plant reaches flowering age, the inflorescence begins to emerge, and the plant looks like a giant artichoke with a gigantic asparagus shoot poking straight up from the heart. The phallic shaft is about 6–10 inches (15–25 cm) thick and obscured by the imbricately layered bracts. When mature, the branched inflorescence is 12–15 feet (3.6–4.5 meters) tall, with twenty to thirty very short side branches densely clustered in the top one third. Brilliant yellow, 2.5–2.75 inch (6–7 cm) long flowers are tightly packed at the ends of the side branches. As all of the energy is used up, the flowering plants will look as if they have been set on fire, turning spectacular shades of purple, red, orange and yellow.

CULTURE

The fact that these plants are found above 8500 feet (2600 meters) elevation in the mountains of Mexico does not necessarily mean that they can be grown at or above that elevation in the higher latitudes in the United States. However, it is an indication that plants will probably grow better in areas with cooler summer temperatures. They have proven hardy to at least 5 degrees F (−15 degrees C) and can be grown as landscape plants in zones 7b–11, the Pacific coast and Gulf coast states, all low and mid-elevation southwestern U.S. zones, and warmer spots in the high elevation zone.

Because of the moderately slow growth rate, there is no danger of these plants reaching flowering size too quickly. In fact, it will take several years to achieve a decent-sized specimen. Coming from very high altitudes in northeastern Mexico, this is one of the more mesic species, preferring some supplemental water in the summer. Plants seem to prefer some shade in the hot, interior, low elevation and mid-elevation zones, but should do fine in full sun in the cooler coastal, low elevation zone.

Plants naturally grow in areas with large rocks and boulders mixed with soil rich in organic matter and covered with a thick layer of pine needles. In areas with alkaline, desert soil low in organic matter, it is wise to amend the soil almost as if you are planting a vegetable garden. The plants will also benefit from a cover of seasonal perennials and low-growing, summer-active grasses to help keep the soil cool.

Being a high elevation species growing with pine trees, this one really benefits from some shade in the mid and hot, interior, low elevation

ABOVE A dying *Agave montana* plant turning orange, red, and purplish as the last of its reserves go to the inflorescence

RIGHT A very young *Agave montana* plant growing in the rocks in the Sierra Peña Nevada in Tamaulipas

desert zones. In Tucson, I have seen some plants develop light-colored patches on the leaves, which is likely the result of some sort of physiological stress.

LANDSCAPE VALUE

Use *Agave montana* by itself as a big, bold focal point in the garden or, if you have the space, group several plants in a wildflower garden or in a meadow with low-growing grasses and under shade trees. In the cooler coastal, low elevation zone, try planting with gray-leaved plants such as *Artemisia californica*, *Artemisia* 'Powis Castle', *Ericameria nauseosa* (*Chrysothamnus nauseosus*), *Lavandula angustifolia*, and *Perovskia atriplicifolia* for an interesting contrast.

In the hot, interior low elevation and mid-elevation zones, plant under the shade of a lacy-leaved desert tree such as *Lysiloma watsonii* ssp. *thornberi* and use some companion plants such as *Ageratum corymbosum*, *Aquilegia chrysantha*, *Dioon edule*, *Oenothera stubbei*, and *Poliomintha maderensis* to create a lush, rich green landscape that will also burst forth with colorful flowers.

Some great companion plants in the high elevation zone would include *Agastache* species and hybrids, *Aquilegia chrysantha*, *Campanula rotundifolia*, *Heuchera sanguinea*, *Penstemon strictus*, and *Poliomintha maderensis* for their seasonally colorful flowers.

TAXONOMIC NOTES

The name *Agave montana* cannot be found in *Agaves of Continental North America* because it was unknown until 1996, when José Angel Villarreal wrote the original description for this beautiful new species.

Agave multifilifera Gentry

SHAGGY HEAD AGAVE, CHAHUIQUI

Agave multifilifera plants on the rocky slopes at Cascada de Basaseachi in Chihuahua

Howard Scott Gentry noticed that this species had many more marginal threads than plain old *Agave filifera* and dubbed it *A. multifilifera*. The common name evokes jealousy among those of us who are follically challenged.

Traveling off the beaten path in the high mountains of Sonora, Chihuahua, and Sinaloa is necessary in order to find *Agave multifilifera*. It's an all-day hike from the base of Sierra de Alamos up to the top where plants are known to grow, and then back down. This hike is best done in late spring or early summer before the summer rains hit and when the days are long enough for sufficient time to make the trek up and back in one day. Be sure to hire a local to guide you up the safest route as there are marijuana fields scattered about on the mountain.

While strolling along the paved path that leads to the head of the Cascada de Basaseachi (Basaseachi Falls), I have seen plants on the slopes above the trail. Be extra careful if you scramble around on the slopes as they are usually covered with pine needles and quite slippery. If you go there and find plants in bloom, be sure to snap some photos of the impressive, unbranched flower stalk teeming with yellow and green flowers infused with rusty reddish orange or deep reddish purple.

Agave multifilifera is found growing with pines and oaks from 4600 to 7200 feet (1400–2200 meters) elevation.

Agave multifilifera is a solitary, non-offsetting species that forms a more or less rounded shape to about 1½–3 feet tall by 2–4 feet across (0.5–1 by 0.6–1.2 meters). The narrow, 15–24 inch long by $^2/_5$–1 inch wide (40–60 by 1–2.5 cm) stiff, dark green leaves lack teeth; instead, there are numerous, white, curly fibers that peel away from the margin, giving the appearance of a head full of curly hair. Exquisite white bud prints, appearing to be carefully painted on each leaf by somebody with way too much time on their hands, combine with the curly white marginal threads to provide a visual feast on even very young plants. Unlike the flexible leaves of *A. geminiflora*, these have no give and the ½ inch (1.3 cm) long, sharp terminal spine can inflict much pain to the unsuspecting legs of passersby.

After ten to twenty years, come spring or early summer, the narrow, spike-like, life-ending inflorescence emerges from the center. This 15–20

foot (5–6 meter) tall stalk is covered with numerous 1½ inch (4 cm) long, waxy, yellow and green flowers flushed with either rusty reddish orange or deep reddish purple.

CULTURE

Agave multifilifera has been through minimum temperatures in the mid-teens F (−7 to −8 C) unscathed, and although the low temperature was not recorded, it has been grown successfully in Sierra Vista, Arizona (zone 8b), of the high elevation zone without damage. These can be grown in zones 8b–11, throughout most of the Pacific coast states and in most of the Gulf coast states. The plants can be used outdoors in the cool, coastal and hot, interior low elevation and mid-elevation zones in the southwestern United States, and even in some well-protected locales in the high elevation zone.

They have a moderately slow growth rate, as exhibited by two plants that recently flowered in Tucson after having been in the ground for at least fifteen years. Provide minimal supplemental water for the densest, most compact form. Place plants in full sun in the coastal and mid-elevation zones, and very light shade in the hot, interior low elevation zone. Avoid too much shade, which will cause them to stretch out.

This one does not like wet feet and should be grown in a soil that has very good drainage. Other than that, it is not too picky about the amount of organic matter in the soil.

LANDSCAPE VALUE

For the densest, most attractive form, grow in as much sun as possible and keep the supplemental water to a minimum. The slower it is grown, the tighter and more attractive the rosette will be.

Even though it is not an exceptionally large species, *Agave multifilifera* can still be used as a focal point in a cactus and succulent garden, or mass-planted and mixed with low-growing shrubs and seasonal flowering perennials to create an ever-changing landscape. In the low and mid-elevation southwestern U.S. zones, try combining with *Calliandra eriophylla*, *Chrysactinia mexicana*, *Dalea frutescens*, *Ericameria laricifolia*, *Glandularia gooddingii*, *Justicia californica*, *Penstemon* species, *Poliomintha maderensis*, and *Salvia greggii*.

The dense rosette of narrow leaves, with their numerous marginal fibers, makes for a striking specimen plant either in a large pot or in the ground.

OPPOSITE A flowering plant of *Agave multifilifera* at Cascada de Basaseachi

ABOVE The greenish flower of *Agave multifilifera*, with dark red filaments topped with butter yellow anthers

TAXONOMIC NOTES

In 1992, Bernd Ullrich stated, "*Agave schidigera, Agave filifera* and *Agave multifilifera* are, in the writer's opinion, three nearly allied taxa, hard to differentiate as species*," and reduced *A. schidigera* and *A. multifilifera* to subspecies of *A. filifera*. He indicated that in the mid-1860s Jacobi and Koch, two prominent agave monographers, held opposing viewpoints on whether *A. schidigera* and *A. filifera* should be considered one or two species. This is an ongoing taxonomic argument between classic lumpers and splitters, not only regarding agaves but in the plant world in general. In reducing *A. schidigera* to subspecies status, Ullrich sided with Koch, and by extrapolation applied the same rank to *A. multifilifera*. My personal experience, both in the field and in growing them horticulturally, leads me to take the opposite tack and leave them as three separate species. Besides, the genus *Agave* is young and still evolving, and if they are not already isolated as species, they will be in a few thousand years, so why make taxonomy more difficult for future botanists?

OPPOSITE An open plant of *Agave multifilifera* growing on a northeast-facing slope at Cascada de Basaseachi

BELOW A dense rosette of *Agave multifilifera* growing in a Tucson, Arizona, landscape

Agave nickelsiae Gosselin ex Roland Gosselin
NICKELS' AGAVE

Agave nickelsiae is distinguished by its dark olive green leaves and black terminal spines.

Synonyms: *Agave ferdinandi-regis* Berger, *Agave victoriae-reginae* T. Moore var. *laxior* Berger. Roland Gosselin named this plant in honor of Anna B. Nickels, the intrepid plant collector from Laredo, Texas.

FIELD NOTES

The distribution of *Agave nickelsiae* is restricted to southeastern Coahuila, northeast of Saltillo, Mexico. I have seen plants growing on a dry, south-sloping limestone hill between 4600 and 4900 feet (1400–1500 meters) elevation. *Agave asperrima* and *A. lechuguilla* also grow there and both have hybridized with *Agave nickelsiae*. In fact, plants similar to the cultivar *A.* 'Sharkskin' (*A. asperrima × A. nickelsiae*) can be found growing on the same slope.

DESCRIPTION

Rosettes are solitary or clustering, growing to about 2 feet tall by 2½–3 feet across (60 cm by 75–90 cm). The dark green leaves are 10–15 inches long by 2–3 inches wide (25–40 cm by 5.5–7.5 cm), adorned with decorative white bud prints, and lacking teeth along the edges, instead having a continuous white margin. The black terminal spine is up to 1 inch (2.5 cm) long, with two smaller spines at the base. Occasionally a plant will have an additional spine along the leaf keel to act as a backup in case the main spine misses its mark. In summer, a 10–20 foot (3–6 meter) tall, spicate inflorescence, packed with 1½ inch (4 cm) long yellowish green flowers, pokes skyward.

CULTURE

Plants are known to have withstood winter lows down into single digits F (−12 to −13 C) in Rhode Island and North Carolina without damage, and can be considered hardy in zones 7b–11. They can be grown throughout much of the Pacific coast and Gulf coast states, and in other regions worldwide where the winter lows do not drop below the 8–10 degrees F (−12 to −13 C) range. They are easily grown in the low and mid-elevation U.S. southwestern zones without fear of frost damage.

This is one of the slowest growing species, taking up to twenty or twenty-five years to reach flowering size, but then you are rewarded with a tall stalk of yellowish-green flowers flushed with purplish red. Once established, plants are quite drought tolerant, but those growing in the hot, low elevation zone will look better if the root zone is given a thorough soaking once every ten to fourteen days. Plants in the mid-elevation zone will relish a thorough soaking once every fourteen to twenty-one days when temperatures creep up above 90 degrees F (32 C) during the day. In areas that receive over 15 inches (38 cm) of annual rainfall, place the plants on a slope or in a raised bed.

Established plants of *Agave nickelsiae* can tolerate full sun in all zones except in the hot, interior, low desert and hotter parts of the mid-elevation zone where they will appreciate a bit of afternoon shade in the summer. Young plants especially will benefit from summer shade in the low and mid-elevation zones and regions throughout the world that routinely experience summer highs over 100 degrees F (38 C).

LANDSCAPE VALUE

With its bold white markings on the dark green leaves and black terminal spine, a mature specimen of *Agave nickelsiae* is an unforgettable sight. Tuck several of these in with seasonally flowering perennials to give colorful interest at various times of the year. Try using *Baileya multiradiata*, *Calylophus hartwegii*, *Chrysactinia mexicana*, *Dalea capitata*, *Ericameria laricifolia*, *Glandularia gooddingii*, *Poliomintha maderensis*, and *Salvia greggii* to provide an array of flowers.

TAXONOMIC NOTES

In 2011, a team of Mexican botanists, including M. Socorro González-Elizondo, revised the *Agave victoriae-reginae* complex, splitting it into three species. They determined that *A. nickelsiae* is the correct name for the plant that has long been called *A. ferdinandi-regis* (= *Agave victoriae-reginae* forma *nickelsii* Trelease and *Agave victoriae-reginae* var. *laxior* Berger).

Agave ocahui Gentry

OCAHUI

A dense specimen of *Agave ocahui* growing in the Sierra Baviso in northern Sonora

Three *Agave ocahui* plants
in various stages of flower
development in the
Sierra Baviso in northern
Sonora

The word *ocahui* is used by people indigenous to where this plant grows and means fiber or cordage, referring to the use of the leaf fibers for making rope.

FIELD NOTES

Even with two varieties, *Agave ocahui* is known to occur in only a few spots in north-central and northeastern Sonora, Mexico. One of the most accessible places in which to see *Agave ocahui* var. *ocahui* is the Sierra Baviso, home to a wonderful semi-tropical canyon full of majestic blue palms. The entrance is fenced off, so it is necessary to park just off the road and hike back to the agaves. It is a lengthy but flat hike past the palm canyon and on to the more xeric, open, exposed, west-facing slopes. Climb up and meander about on the slopes to seek out the most beautiful specimens with tight, dense, sun-drenched rosettes. If you head there as the heat cranks up and spring turns to summer, chances are you can catch a few of these beauties in full flower. *Agave ocahui* var. *longifolia* can be spotted growing with *Lysiloma*, *Nolina matapensis*, and *Quercus* species in the Sierra Matape on the road northeast of Mazatán as you head east of Hermosillo, Sonora.

Plants are found between 1500 and 4500 feet (450–1375 meters) elevation in Sonora.

DESCRIPTION

In its natural habitat, this solitary species only reaches 1–2 feet tall by 1–2 feet wide (30–60 by 30–60 cm), while under cultivation the plants can get a little larger, topping out at about 2–3 feet tall and 2–3 feet wide (60–90 by 60–90 cm). In either case, they form perfect spheres or hemispheres of numerous, narrow, dagger-like, medium to dark green leaves that lack marginal teeth. Instead of teeth, the leaves have a continuous, thin, reddish-brown to gray border. The terminal spine is short, yet sharp, drawing blood whenever it is poked into the skin. The leaves are narrow and resemble a letter opener, with the shape described as linear-lanceolate, widest near mid-blade and then tapering to the tip, measuring 10–20 inches long by ½–1 inch wide (25–50 by 1.5–2.5 cm).

A ten- to twenty-year wait yields a 10–15 foot (3–4.5 meter) tall spike-like inflorescence jam-packed with 1–1½ inch (2.5–4 cm) long, deep golden yellow flowers that are abuzz with bees seeking nectar. As the plants flower and die, the leaves will sometimes lose their chlorophyll, resulting in a circus of color.

CULTURE

Agave ocahui has been subjected to winter lows of high teens F (–7 to –8 C) in the Tucson basin without suffering any frost damage. Plants have also been subjected to a winter low of 6 degrees F (–14 C) in North Carolina without suffering damage. They can be grown in zones 8a–11, in nearly all dry parts of the Pacific coast states, the Gulf coast states, and partway up the Atlantic coast as long as the soil is kept dry through the winter. They are hardy landscape plants in all low and mid-elevation southwestern U.S. zones except for the coldest regions of northern Texas.

The growth rate is moderate, taking anywhere from ten to twenty years for a plant to achieve flowering size. Once it does, it goes out with a colorful bang. Although quite drought tolerant once established, plants will thank you with a healthy green color if given a good, thorough soaking once every seven to ten days during the dry summer heat in the interior low elevation zone. Plants will also benefit from consistent thorough soakings starting in late April or early May and continuing until the summer monsoons hit in the mid-elevation zone. To get the most compact form, grow the plants in full sun in all zones, though they will appreciate a bit of reprieve from the May-to-July heat in the hot, interior low elevation zone.

Plants are not too fussy about the type of soil they are in as long as the watering schedule is adjusted accordingly.

LANDSCAPE VALUE

Agave ocahui looks great when grouped in mass plantings of three or more. Place a grouping as a focal point or mix in with cactus and other succulents. Try weaving small shrubs and flowering perennials in with a mass planting to give exceptional seasonal color. In the interior, low elevation and mid-elevation zones try using *Baileya multiradiata*, *Calylophus hartwegii*, *Chrysactinia mexicana*, *Dalea capitata*, *Ericameria laricifolia*, *Glandularia gooddingii*, *Poliomintha maderensis*, and *Salvia greggii* for their showy flower displays.

Create an otherworldly look by mixing these little round balls in with large boulders and other spiky plants.

OPPOSITE TOP LEFT A section of *Agave ocahui* inflorescence in peak bloom

TOP RIGHT A well-grown *Agave ocahui* plant in full sun in a Tucson, Arizona, landscape

BOTTOM A flowering specimen losing its chlorophyll while in the final stages of flowering

Agave ovatifolia Starr & Villarreal
WHALE'S TONGUE AGAVE

A ripply leaved *Agave ovatifolia* specimen growing in the Sierra Lampazos of central Nuevo León

In 2002, José Angel Villarreal and I combined the Latin *ovat*, meaning egg-shaped, with the Latin *foli*, meaning leaf, to describe the extremely wide, ovate-shaped leaves. The common name was coined by my friend Pat McNamara who, upon seeing a picture of the plant, exclaimed, "Those leaves look like a whale's tongue!"

FIELD NOTES

This plant was undescribed when it was first brought into horticulture by renowned Texas planstman Lynn Lowrey in the mid-1980s from a private ranch in the Sierra Lampazos in Nuevo León. (This ranch is now in the process of being transformed into a travel destination with cabins for rent and a large dining/gathering hall.) It was not until 2002, after retracing Lowrey's path, that José Angel Villarreal and I were able to officially provide the species name for the plant that quickly set the agave world on fire.

To get a glimpse of these majestic beasts, one must first secure permission from the ranch owner, and then proceed twelve miles on a bumpy, dirt road that snakes its way across the desert, eventually heading into the mountains. As you are climbing up and winding around the mountainous curves, keep an eye open for the first sight of plants growing out of the roadcuts across the way. From there, watch for a super-large plant, informally dubbed El Rey, that is 4 feet tall and over 6 feet across (1.2 by 1.8 meters). Keep climbing another two miles, past the cabins to the plateau at the top, where you will be greeted by a fabulous display of whale's tongue agaves growing among slate gray, limestone boulders.

Two agave populations in Nuevo León are tentatively identified as *Agave ovatifolia*. One can be found growing in the countryside along a dirt road south of Monterrey-Saltillo, while the other is found growing in the mountains further south of Monterrey along—you guessed it—a long, bumpy dirt road. Photographs of plants with inflorescences but unopened flowers reveal an identical structure with the large, fleshy bracts subtending the side branches and smaller bracts subtending groups of flowers within each cluster that terminates the side branch. However, until a proper herbarium voucher with flowers and leaves for comparison is collected from one or both localities, we will hold true to botanical protocol and leave them as *A.* aff. *ovatifolia*.

As attractive as those plants are, none are as spectacular as the plants in the Sierra Lampazos. The Sierra Lampazos plants occur between 3000 and 4000 feet (900–1200 meters) elevation, while the other two populations are found between 7000 and 8000 feet (2130–2440 meters).

DESCRIPTION

This massive monster can eventually reach about 3–4 feet tall by 4–6 feet across (1–1.2 by 1.2–2 meters), never failing to evoke a "wow!" from anyone who sees a mature specimen. In nature, this is a solitary species, rarely producing an offset or two in cultivation. The broadly ovate, silvery blue, blue-gray or dark gray-green leaves are quite distinctive, measuring 18–24 inches long by 9–11 inches across (45–60 by 23–28 cm) at the widest point with a distinctive, longitudinal cup shape on the upper surface, somewhat reminiscent of what I imagine a whale's tongue must look like. If the biblical Jonah were alive, we could ask him if the leaves really do look like a whale's tongue. Some of the most interesting forms are valleculate, which means that they have multiple ridges and valleys on the underside of the leaves, just begging to have their picture taken. The leaf margin is straight to very slightly undulate, with small to medium-sized teeth along the leaf edge. The larger teeth are in the upper half of the leaf, greatly diminished toward the base. Small teeth measure about ¼–½ inch (0.6–1.2 cm) long and are evenly spaced, either spreading out or pointing back towards the base, while the thin yet sharp terminal spine is about ¾–1 inch (2–2.5 cm) long, black or rarely yellowish tan on new leaves, gray and brown on older leaves, and usually decurrent to the first one or two pairs of teeth.

The thick-shafted, paniculate flowering stalk emerges from the center of the plant in spring, and is densely covered with large bracts. The stalk eventually reaches 10–15 feet (3–4.5 meters) tall with about fifteen to twenty side branches, each extending out from the thick, fleshy bracts laden with dense clusters of large, greenish yellow flowers at the ends.

CULTURE

Agave ovatifolia has been grown successfully in Dallas, Texas, and Raleigh, North Carolina, where it has experienced winter lows of 5 degrees F (–15 C) without damage. They are considered zone 7b–11 plants and are cold hardy enough to grow in the Pacific coast states, the Gulf coast states, and up the Atlantic coast as far north as North Carolina. They make great landscape plants in all low and mid-elevation southwestern U.S. zones, and should be tried in the high elevation zone as well.

Plants have a relatively fast growth rate, having the potential to reach 3–5 feet (1–1.6 meters) across four to seven years after being planted in the ground. These are found growing in areas that receive a bit more

A mass of *Agave ovatifolia* growing on limestone, where the broad leaves capture rainwater

rainfall than most parts of the desert southwestern United States, and will respond to extra summer water in the hot, interior, low elevation and mid-elevation desert regions of the southwestern United States. Thoroughly soak the root zone once every one to two weeks in those zones, and once every two to three weeks in the high elevation and coastal zones. The key, as with most other xeric species, is to let the soil dry between supplemental watering.

Do not let the powdery silver-blue leaves of *Agave ovatifolia* fool you into placing plants in the wrong location. They relish a bit of shade, especially in the hot, interior, low and mid-elevation southwestern U.S. zones. They can be used in full sun in areas with more mild summer temperatures and/or higher summer humidity.

In its native habitat, plants of *Agave ovatifolia* are found growing on porous, limestone soil, and will appreciate receiving a similar type of soil in the landscape. Keep them away from heavy clay soil or one with a shallow layer of solid caliche.

LANDSCAPE VALUE

Use whale's tongue agave as a specimen accent or focal point in a landscape full of drought-tolerant plants. It has a spectacular form that commands attention, so give it a special spot and supplement with low-

The silvery blue leaves of *Agave ovatifolia* make a nice backdrop for the pink flowers of *Penstemon parryi*.

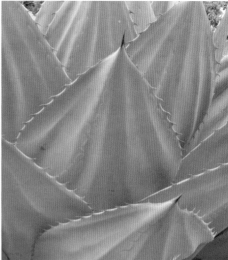

ABOVE LEFT *Agave* aff. *ovatifolia* growing in the mountains south of Monterrey in Nuevo León

ABOVE A specimen of *Agave ovatifolia* with nicely valleculate leaves

LEFT The thick shaft emerging from a magnificent specimen of *Agave ovatifolia*

ABOVE The top of an *Agave ovatifolia* inflorescence, with its large, fleshy bracts protecting the developing flowers

RIGHT *Agave ovatifolia* with its tall inflorescence

OPPOSITE A young *Agave ovatifolia* 'Flipper' plant looks handsome in a decorative container.

growing, flowering perennials and small shrubs in a fun-filled, colorful landscape. In the interior, low elevation and mid-elevation zones try using *Chrysactinia mexicana*, *Dalea frutescens*, *Ericameria laricifolia*, *Glandularia gooddingii*, *Salvia greggii*, and *Zinnia grandiflora* for their colorful flowers and rich green foliage, and *Penstemon parryi* or *Penstemon superbus* for their spectacular spring display of pinkish and coral flowers that contrast with the silvery blue foliage of whale's tongue agave.

In the cooler, coastal, low elevation zone and the high elevation zone, try plants such as *Agastache* species and hybrids, *Aquilegia chrysantha*, *Caryopteris* ×*clandonensis*, *Nepeta* species, and *Perovskia atriplicifolia*.

The wide, deeply cupped, silvery blue leaves resembling a huge whale's tongue create a look that is truly unique in the agave world.

Agave ovatifolia 'Flipper'

'Flipper' is a variegated form with a broad, longitudinal stripe the color of banana cream pie filling running down the center of the otherwise dark gray-green leaf. This cultivar has not been around long enough to determine its eventual size, so if you plant it in the ground, make sure to give it ample room in case it reaches the same size as the non-variegated form.

In a batch of seedlings, Tony Avent found a yellow-streaked plant which he sent to a tissue culture lab to stabilize the variegation. The best plant was selected, and Tony named it 'Flipper'.

Plants of 'Flipper' should be identical in care to the species, though the growth rate is a bit slower, probably because of the amount of variegation in the plant. The plants are hardy to at least 15 degrees F (−9 C), and the growth rate is moderate to slow. Place in full sun except where summer temperatures climb over 100 degrees F (38 C) for most of the summer. Plants grow best in a fast-draining soil, and with some supplemental water in the summer as long as the soil is not waterlogged.

Agave palmeri Engelmann

PALMER AGAVE

Agave palmeri on State Route 83 in southeastern Arizona

Botanist George Engelmann named this species for the British-born botanist Edward Palmer who traveled and collected extensively in the southwestern United States and in Mexico.

FIELD NOTES

Drive nearly anywhere in southeastern Arizona and you will likely encounter one of the many forms of *Agave palmeri*. Some excellent specimens can be found growing in among the large, rounded boulders in the otherworldly landscape of Texas Canyon east of Tucson along Interstate 10. Another easy spot is near the top of the pass along the winding, twisty Arizona State Route 83 as it snakes its way from Vail to Sonoita. Also, some fantastic specimens are seen along Route 80 as you wind your way through the Mule Mountains northwest of the historic mining town of Bisbee, and then as you continue on to the border city of Douglas in the southeastern corner of Arizona. Visit the Chiricahua Mountains in southeastern Arizona and look for an area where *A. palmeri* and *A. parryi* grow together and even have a little fun mixing genes, resulting in some interesting offspring.

This wide-ranging species can be found between 3000 and 6000 feet (900–1800 meters) elevation in southeastern Arizona, southwestern New Mexico, northwestern Chihuahua, and northern Sonora.

DESCRIPTION

A variable plant with solitary rosettes ranging from 1½ to 3 feet tall and 2½ to 4 feet across (45–90 by 75–120 cm), some *Agave palmeri* populations have plants that are smaller and more compact, while others have plants that are larger and more open. Pale blue to light or dark green to yellowish green leaves are shaped like the sword favored by professional sword-swallowers at carnivals. These can be anywhere from 14–30 inches long by 2½–4 inches wide (35–75 by 6–10 cm) near mid-blade, deeply channeled above, with nearly straight or wavy margins topped by slender, evenly spaced black to grayish teeth. The 1–2½ inch (2.5–6.3 cm) long terminal spine is grooved on top and dark brown to black on new leaves, going gray on older leaves.

Come early summer, a 10–16 foot (3–5 meter) tall, paniculate inflorescence reaches for the sky. Pale greenish yellow to waxy white, 2 inch (5 cm) long flowers are red in bud and clustered at the ends of the eight to twelve short lateral branches, which are in the upper one third of the main shaft.

A bluish-leaved plant of *Agave palmeri* in the grasslands of southeastern Arizona

CULTURE

Having a widespread distribution in the grasslands of southeastern Arizona, southwestern New Mexico, and northeastern Sonora and northwestern Chihuahua in Mexico, *Agave palmeri* is hardy to at least 9 degrees F (−12 C) and can be considered a zone 7b–11 plant. The higher elevation forms can be used outdoors throughout most of the Pacific coast states, along the Gulf coast and up the Atlantic coast as far as North Carolina as long as the soil is kept dry during the winter. *Agave palmeri* can be used in all southwestern U.S. zones, with the possible exception of the coldest parts of the cold, low elevation zone of northern Texas.

Growth rate varies dramatically with temperature and with the amount of water the plant receives during the growing season. Established plants will survive on 12–15 inches (30–38 cm) of annual rainfall in the mid-elevation zone of the southwestern United States, but will not grow very much. However, when given some supplemental water during the summer months, plants will grow a little more quickly.

Place plants in full sun in the mid- and high elevation zones as well as the cool, coastal, low elevation zone. Plants in the hot, interior, low elevation zone relish a bit of relief from the burning desert sun when temperatures creep up to over 100 degrees F (38 C) and the night temperatures stay in the mid- to high 80s (>30 C) or more. This one is not too picky about the soil, as long as the drainage is adequate.

LANDSCAPE VALUE

Agave palmeri is best used in full sun, and mixed with xerophytic wildflowers, small perennials, and small shrubs with colorful flowers. Some excellent choices include *Baileya multiradiata*, *Berlandiera lyrata*, *Chrysactinia mexicana*, *Glandularia gooddingii*, *Penstemon* species, *Salvia greggii*, and *Tetraneuris acaulis*. Mass plant in a xeric landscape with hardcore desert plants such as the shrubs *Buddleja marrubiifolia*, *Larrea divaricata*, *Leucophyllum frutescens*, and *Simmondsia chinensis*, and trees like *Bauhinia lunarioides*, *Eysenhardtia orthocarpa*, *Havardia pallens*, or *Parkinsonia microphylla*.

Agave parrasana Berger

CABBAGE HEAD AGAVE

Agave parrasana, with a perfect sphere of leaves with a dusting of silvery blue that shows deep bud prints

This species was first collected by Carl Albert Purpus near the town of Parras, Coahuila, in Mexico.

FIELD NOTES

Agave parrasana is found only at high elevations, between 4500 and 8000 feet (1400–2480 meters), in a few, remote, limestone mountains in central and southern Coahuila, Mexico. One summer I traveled with several other plant enthusiasts to the top of the Sierra Patagalana in hope of seeing these marvelous plants. To get there, we traveled in high clearance vehicles for seven bumpy miles on the narrow dirt track to the pass at about 7200 feet (2200 meters) elevation. Once there, we unfolded ourselves from vehicles and headed up the slope to wander among some fantastically beautiful specimens and seek out the most attractive plant for photographing. This was nearly impossible as each plant was frosty, silvery blue with handsome teeth creating impressive bud imprints, encouraging us to declare that each one we found was even more attractive than the last.

DESCRIPTION

In its native habitat, *Agave parrasana* is a small plant, with leaves held upright so the tight, rounded rosette looks like a head of cabbage. Typically, this is a non-offsetting species with each rosette reaching about 1–1½ feet tall and 1½–2½ feet across (30–45 by 45–75 cm); however, under cultivation some plants will produce suckers and form small clumps. Thick, rigid, blue-gray to gray-green, 8–12 inch long by 4–5 inch wide (20–30 by 10–12 cm) leaves are frequently irregularly covered with a silvery coating, creating an attractively mottled appearance. The gnarly teeth are straight or frequently curving, the largest near the leaf tip, getting smaller towards the base, and make very impressive bud imprints. The stout, 1–1½ inch (2.5–3.8 cm) long terminal spine is colored dark chestnut brown on young leaves before aging to grayish on the older leaves, and is decurrent to the upper teeth.

The 10–13 foot (3–4 meter) tall flower stalk is adorned with twelve to fifteen side branches all clustered in the upper one third of the stalk and subtended by large, fleshy bracts. Each side branch is laden with numerous, 2 inch (5 cm) long flowers that are reddish or purplish in bud, opening yellow to create a riot of color. *Agave parrasana* is one of the few species whose stalk begins to shoot in the fall, stops for the winter and resumes when the weather warms, with the flowers produced in late spring or early summer.

ABOVE LEFT Leaf detail of *Agave parrasana*, showing the deep bud prints formed by the teeth of the leaves

ABOVE The inflorescence of *Agave parrasana* showcases colorful flowers.

LEFT Silvery blue leaves of *Agave parrasana* with yellow-flowered *Chrysactinia mexicana*

CULTURE

Agave parrasana can tolerate temperatures to at least 10 degrees F (–12 C) without wincing, and some forms can even withstand 6 degrees F (–14 C) without damage. It can be grown in zones 7b–11 and should make a gorgeous landscape plant in the drier parts of the Pacific coast states. Plants have been successfully grown in the low and mid-elevation southwestern U.S. zones, and should be tried in the high elevation zone although they might need to be protected if the winter temperatures get too low.

Due to the slow growth rate, these beauties take a while to develop into mature specimens with the classic artichoke form. Although plants are drought tolerant, they will benefit from some supplemental water in the heat of summer, especially in the hot, interior, low elevation zone. Older, more established plants need water less frequently than do younger, newly planted ones. While *Agave parasanna* will grow fine in full sun in the cool, coastal, mid- and high elevation zones, they really benefit from a bit of shade in the hot, interior, low elevation zone.

As with many other species of *Agave*, this one is not too particular about the soil type as long as the roots do not sit in waterlogged soil. Adjust the watering frequency according to the drainage and the plants should grow fine.

Agave parrasana seems to be particularly susceptible to indoor burn

A blue-gray-leaved *Agave parrasana* with its classic cabbage head look

or edema, a condition where large patches of tissue die and turn brown when plants are subjected to a drastic change in growing conditions, especially from high light to low light.

LANDSCAPE VALUE

Plants make wonderful potted specimens as well as spectacular landscape plants. Because seed-grown plants exhibit a wide range of variation, you might want to collect several and mass them together in a xeriscape, cactus and succulent garden, or comingle with seasonally flowering perennials, groundcovers, or low shrubs to create year-round interest in your garden. Some great companion plants include *Baileya multiradiata*, *Berlandiera lyrata*, *Chrysactinia mexicana*, *Glandularia gooddingii*, *Penstemon* species, *Salvia greggii*, *Scutellaria suffrutescens*, and *Tetraneuris acaulis*.

Look for the forms with the really frosty blue leaves and the gnarliest teeth, which create the most awesome bud imprint patterns on the leaves.

CULTIVARS

Agave parrasana 'Fireball'

'Fireball' is a variegated selection first found by agave collector Mike Mahan. The leaves on this compact rosette have narrow yellow margins that are more conspicuous on the front side of the leaf than on the back side.

Agave parrasana 'Meat Claw'

'Meat Claw' is a form found in a block of plants at Mountain States Wholesale Nursery in Phoenix, Arizona, by the Yucca Do duo of Carl Shoenfeld and Wade Roitsch. It was selected for the extremely large, curved, jagged teeth resembling exposed claws on a mad cat. These large, claw-like teeth make intricate bud prints that can give even the most casual agave collector hours of viewing pleasure while knocking back shots of tequila.

The care and culture of 'Meat Claw' is identical to that of the species. The plants are hardy to about 10 degrees F (−12 C), and the growth rate is moderate to slow. Place in full sun except where summer temperatures climb over 100 degrees F (38 C) for days on end. Plants grow best in a fast-draining soil, and with some supplemental water in the summer as long as the soil is not waterlogged.

Agave parryi Engelmann

PARRY AGAVE

Agave parryi tucked in among yellow-flowered *Thymophylla pentachaeta* at the Desert Botanical Garden in Phoenix, Arizona

George Engelmann named this one in honor of the British-born, American-trained botanist Charles Parry.

DESCRIPTION

All *Agave parryi* are offsetting types, with individual, compact rosettes achieving a size of 1–2 feet tall and 2–3 feet across (30–60 by 60–90 cm). Each mature, freely suckering rosette is packed with over a hundred closely overlapping, glaucous gray to light green leaves on mature plants. Individual leaves are thick and rigid, 10–24 inches long by 2–5 inches wide (25–60 by 5–12 cm); their outline looks like a rocket from a 1970s cartoon—wide at the base, bulging near the middle, and tapering gradually to the tip. The leaf blade is flat above and rounded below, with small teeth about ½–1 inch (1.3–2.5 cm) apart on a straight margin, the largest teeth above the middle. The sharp, ³/₅–1²/₅ inch (1.5–3 cm) terminal spine is dark brown to black on new leaves, aging to gray on older leaves, decurrent to the first or second pair of teeth.

In the summer months, a branched flower stalk rises 10–20 feet (3–6 meters) above the plant, providing a perfect perch for birds. The side branches are packed with numerous 2½–3 inch (6–7.5 cm) long flowers that can be a striking pinkish red in bud, eventually opening a brilliant golden yellow.

CULTURE

While hardiness will vary from variety to variety, this is generally considered one of the hardier agaves, able to tolerate winter lows down to at least 10 degrees F (−12 C); for more specific information, see the varieties' individual entries. All varieties have a moderately slow growth rate, and will take several years to achieve flowering size. These develop the best form when grown in full sun, but will tolerate a little bit of shade also. Plants relish an extra large drink of water every ten to twenty days from spring until autumn, depending on the daytime temperature in the summer and amount of rainfall received. None are picky about the type of soil as long as the drainage is adequate and soil is not kept soggy.

LANDSCAPE VALUE

All varieties of *Agave parryi* have striking forms. They can be used as stand-alone plants, mixed with low-growing grasses to re-create a natural landscape, or used with flowering perennials and small shrubs for a mix of form, color, and texture. The spectacular, densely leaved rosettes are great attention-getters and should be used as a focal point in a low-water-use or natural landscape. Try placing several in a grouping with large boulders or in a cactus and succulent garden. Some perfect grasses would include *Aristida purpurea*, *Bouteloua* species, and *Muhlenbergia porter*; some nice small shrubs and perennials would be *Baileya multiradiata*, *Calliandra eriophylla*, *Chrysactinia mexicana*, *Ericameria laricifolia*, *Penstemon* species, *Poliomintha maderensis*, *Salvia greggii*, *Scutellaria suffrutescens*, and *Viguiera stenoloba*.

TAXONOMIC NOTES

Agave parryi has a widespread distribution, with plants found as far north as north-central Arizona, spreading southeast to southeastern Arizona, the mountains of western Chihuahua, and western Durango, and extending into southeastern New Mexico and extreme western Texas. With this widespread distribution comes a corresponding amount of variability.

This variability has been recognized by botanists and the current thinking by agave taxonomists is that *Agave parryi* consists of two subspecies: *A. parryi* ssp. *neomexicana* and *A. parryi* ssp. *parryi*. *Agave parryi* ssp. *parryi* is further divided into four varieties; var. *couesii*, var. *huachucensis*, var. *parryi*, and var. *truncata*.

The distinctions between the varieties are somewhat ambiguous. As Gentry noted, var. *couesii* is separable "by its smaller flowers" and "its smaller leaves", while var. *huachucensis* is "more robust, the leaves larger" and "the panicle broader with larger flowers", and var. *truncata* "is distinguished by its very small leaves with acute to truncate apex." Bernd Ullrich stated that ssp. *neomexicana* has leaves that "tend to be somewhat more narrow, the inflorescence shorter, and the branches fewer". In *Flora of North America*, Reveal and Hodgson stated that "although the varieties are weakly differentiated, it appears that there is some geographic separation between them."

Agave parryi Engelmann var. *couesii*
(Engelmann ex Trelease) Kearney & Peebles

COUES AGAVE

Agave parryi var. *couesii* near the town of Jerome, Arizona

This form of *Agave parryi* was named for the ornithologist Elliott Coues.

FIELD NOTES

Agave parryi var. *couesii* is found between 3600 and 6900 feet (1100–2100 meters) elevation in mesquite-acacia grassland and oak-juniper woodland in the mountains of central Arizona. Take a drive in late spring or early summer to Jerome, Arizona, and check out the *A. parryi* var. *couesii* that should be blooming. On a trip to central Arizona over the Memorial Day holiday, I noticed that plants on the slopes just below Jerome were in full, glorious flower, while those about four miles east were in bright red bud with no open flowers. These very attractive plants with symmetrical rosettes were tucked in among grasses and boulders on open slopes that were dotted with mesquite and acacias, or nestled in the grasses among oaks and junipers. While many were solitary, allowing their perfect form to shine, some had one or two small offsets, and occasionally there were large colonies up to 6–7 feet (1.8–2 meters) across.

OPPOSITE The blue-gray-leaved rosette of *Agave parryi* var. *couesii*

LEFT The yellow flowers of *Agave parryi* var. *couesii*

ABOVE The red buds of *Agave parryi* var. *couesii*, growing about four miles east of Jerome, Arizona

DESCRIPTION

The plants in flower in central Arizona topped out at about 1½ feet tall by 1½–2½ feet across (45 by 45–76 cm). Blue-gray or gray-green, the linear-ovate leaves are generally shaped like the bayonet that Civil War soldiers would put on the ends of their rifles. One look at the 10–14 inch long by 2–3 inch wide (25–35 by 5–7.5 cm) leaves and you can imagine the damage that could be done to the careless gardener, let alone an enemy gardener. While the marginal teeth are variable, some plants having relatively small and straight teeth while others have larger, slightly curved teeth, the 1 inch (2.5 cm) long terminal spine is stout, and waiting to skewer the leg or arm of the careless gardener.

Late spring and early summer sees the rise of the broadly paniculate flower stalk reaching to the sky. The panicle can be quite colorful with deep red unopened flower buds and bright yellow open flowers.

CULTURE

This variety is hardy to at least 0 degrees F (–18 C), and can be grown in the ground without frost damage in zones 7a–11, throughout the Pacific coast states, the southern and southeastern states, and up the Atlantic coast at least as far north as North Carolina as long as the soil is not soggy in winter. This makes a great landscape specimen in all southwestern U.S. zones and other hot, dry, desert climates that are subject to mild winter frosts. Plants are best used in full sun in the coastal, low elevation, mid-, and high elevation zones, but should have some filtered light in the interior, low elevation zone. Provide them with periodic supplemental water from spring until summer rains hit.

Agave parryi Engelmann var. *huachucensis* (Baker) Little ex Benson

HUACHUCA AGAVE

A colony of *Agave parryi* var. *huachucensis* in the Huachuca Mountains of southeastern Arizona

Cyrus Guernsey Pringle was the first to collect this plant in 1884, in the Huachuca Mountains of southeastern Arizona.

FIELD NOTES

Agave parryi var. *huachucensis* is found in oak woodland and occasionally pine forest from 5000 to 7200 feet (1550–2200 meters) elevation in the mountains of southeastern Arizona and northeastern Sonora, Mexico, on the border with Chihuahua. A nice hike up Sunnyside Canyon in the Huachuca Mountains of southeastern Arizona will lead you to some nice-looking plants sunning themselves on south-facing slopes. These very attractive plants with symmetrical rosettes are frequently tucked in among grasses and boulders on open slopes or scattered among the pines.

DESCRIPTION

This variety can develop some of the largest rosettes of all the *Agave parryi*, reaching 1½–2 feet tall by 2½–3 feet across (45–60 by 75–90 cm). Leaves are yellowish green to bluish gray-green, ovate-lanceolate, 12–24 inches long by 4–8 inches wide (30–60 by 10–20 cm), with small, mostly straight teeth along the margin. Comparing the leaves of var. *huachucensis* to those of var. *couesii*, one can see that they are quite a bit wider in the middle, tapering quickly to the lethal, 1 inch (2.5 cm) long, black terminal spine. The accident-prone gardener should wear full body armor when working around these plants.

When the weather heats up, the mature specimen will shoot forth its asparagus-like spear, and when fully formed, the broad panicle harbors twenty or more side branches, each loaded with golden yellow flowers.

CULTURE

Variety *huachucensis* is hardy to at least 10 degrees F (−9 C), able to be grown in the ground without frost damage in zones 8a–11, throughout the Pacific coast states, the southern and southeastern states, and up the Atlantic coast at least as far north as North Carolina as long as the soil is kept dry in winter. If need be, plant on a slope to keep excess water away from the base of the plant. This is a fantastic landscape plant for all southwestern U.S. zones and other hot, dry, desert climates that are subject to mild winter frosts. Plants are best used in full sun and will periodically need a thorough soaking of the root zone when the weather turns warm, from spring until summer rains hit. *Agave parryi* var. *huachucensis* can develop into some of the more spectacular, uniformly symmetrical rosettes in a dry garden landscape.

ABOVE A solitary rosette of *Agave parryi* var. *huachucensis* perched atop a rocky outcrop in the Huachuca Mountains

LEFT *Agave parryi* var. *huachucensis* at the Arizona-Sonora Desert Museum near Tucson, Arizona

Agave parryi Engelmann **ssp. *neomexicana***
(Wooten & Standley) Ullrich

NEW MEXICO AGAVE

Agave parryi ssp. *neomexicana* in the Sacramento Mountains of southern New Mexico

This is New Mexico's contribution to the *Agave parryi* complex as determined by Germany's latest agavologist, Bernd Ullrich, in 1992.

FIELD NOTES

Drive over to the Guadalupe Mountains and visit the National Park and Carlsbad Caverns, and then take a side trip to find perfectly formed, hemispherical rosettes of *Agave parryi* ssp. *neomexicana* growing among the grasses near McKittrick Canyon. Head that way in early summer to catch plants in flower, or in early May to witness the Mescalero Apache Mescal Roast which is part of the coming of age ceremony for young Apache girls.

Over a Memorial Day weekend, I traveled along U.S. Route 82 east of Mayhill, New Mexico, to see the occasional plant of *Agave parryi* ssp. *neomexicana* growing among junipers in the Sacramento Mountains. As I continued further east down into the rolling hills, I was rewarded with copious quantities of agaves mostly behind barbed wire fences. If you make this trip, be sure to spend the night in Roswell, New Mexico, for a chance to see UFOs and little green aliens.

These plants grow in rocky or gravelly soil in grassland and desert scrub between 5250 and 7000 feet (1600–2100 meters) elevation.

DESCRIPTION

Agave parryi ssp. *neomexicana* is a small species, topping out at 1–1½ feet tall by 1¼–2½ feet across (30–45 by 40–60 cm), and forming symmetrical, flattened rosettes of light grayish blue, sword-shaped leaves, measuring 8–18 inches by 2–5 inches (20–45 by 5–12 cm), with a long, narrow taper to the tip. Marginal teeth are small, the ones near the leaf tip measuring about ½ inch (1.25 cm) and then getting smaller near the base of the leaf. The 1–1½ inch (2.5–3.8 cm) long terminal spine is dark brown to black, somewhat slender yet quite rigid and painful when run through soft flesh.

Plants of *Agave parryi* ssp. *neomexicana* are about the same size as those of *A. parryi* var. *couesii*, and the two might be difficult to tell apart.

Late spring and early summer is the time for the tall, branched flower stalk to reach for the sky. The inflorescence can be quite colorful with red or orange-red flower buds and open flowers of a brilliant golden yellow.

CULTURE

Agave parryi ssp. *neomexicana* has survived winter lows to at least 0 degrees F (–18 C), is hardy in zones 7a–11, and is a nice landscape plant in the drier parts of the Pacific coast states, throughout the southern states, into the southeast, and up the Atlantic coast to North Carolina. This makes an attractive landscape plant in all southwestern U.S. zones and in other dry regions that experience mild to no winter frost. Plants are best used in full sun. Water periodically when the weather turns warm, from spring until summer rains hit.

CULTIVAR

Agave parryi ssp. *neomexicana* 'Sunspot'

Agave parryi ssp. *neomexicana* 'Sunspot' is about the same size as the species—or maybe just a smidgen smaller, reaching about 12 inches by 15–20 inches (30 by 40–50 cm). It is distinguished by its broad creamy yellow variegation along the edges on the upper surface of each leaf that contrast nicely with the blue-gray central portion and underside of the leaf. According to David Salman at High Country Gardens Nursery, *A. parryi* ssp. *neomexicana* 'Sunspot' is cold hardy in zones 6–11, meaning it can tolerate winter lows of –5 to –10 degrees F (–20 to –23 C). The plant makes a nice potted specimen in any zone and a great landscape plant wherever regular *A. parryi* ssp. *neomexicana* can be grown. Plants in the ground tend to produce numerous offsets, forming large clumps.

OPPOSITE A solitary rosette of *Agave parryi* ssp. *neomexicana* growing along U.S. Route 82 east of Mayhill in southern New Mexico

ABOVE The fiery red buds of *Agave parryi* ssp. *neomexicana*

Agave parryi Engelmann **var.** *parryi*

PARRY AGAVE, MESCAL

Agave parryi var. *parryi* in the Parque Nacional Cumbres de Majalca

Historically, *Agave parryi* was a valuable resource for the Apache tribes.

FIELD NOTES

This variety of *Agave parryi* is found in gravelly or rocky soil in grass-lands, desert scrub, oak woodland, and pinyon-juniper vegetation from 4000 to 9200 feet (1200–2800 meters) elevation in Arizona, New Mexico, and northwestern Mexico.

One of the most famous localities for *Agave parryi* is in the Parque Nacional Cumbres de Majalca in northwestern Chihuahua, where you will find plants from the same colony of which Gentry took a picture in June 1971. These plants show impressive, dense, ball-like clusters with one hundred or more closely imbricate leaves which make this one of the most highly desirable ornamentals in the southwestern United States. Spend some time walking around on the slopes and hills, and notice the variation in form, from those nearly perfect spheres to those that are more open and flat-topped. Visit the Parque Nacional in June or July, with the hopes of catching them in full glorious flower!

DESCRIPTION

Agave parryi var. *parryi* is a generally rounded, ball-like plant to about 1½–2 feet tall by 2–3 feet across (45–60 by 60–75 cm), with numerous, short, blue-gray to gray-green, nearly egg-shaped leaves that each have an obtuse angle (hope you remember your high school math) at the tip. The 10–16 inch by 3½–5 inch (25–40 by 8–12 cm) leaves are broadest from the base to about two thirds the length, and then rounded before finally being terminated by a sharp, 1 inch (2.5 cm) long terminal spine.

The tall, branched flower stalk reaches for the sky in summer and holds twenty or more side branches, each packed with clusters of yellow flowers. As with other varieties, the flower buds on many plants will be red to orange-red, giving the Christmas-tree-shaped panicle a colorful appearance.

CULTURE

Agave parryi var. *parryi* is hardy to at least 10 degrees F (–9 C), survives in zones 8a–11 and can be planted out in the ground in the drier parts of the Pacific coast states, much of the south and southeastern states, and even up the Atlantic coast to North Carolina. This is a great landscape plant in all southwestern U.S. zones and in other hot, dry regions with little or no winter frost. Plants are best used in full sun or very light shade. Water periodically when the weather turns warm, from spring until summer rains hit.

CULTIVARS

Agave parryi 'J. C. Raulston'

Tony Avent says that, for the relatively humid and wet climate of North Carolina, the clone dubbed *Agave parryi* 'J. C. Raulston' has been the most reliable of all *A. parryi*. On his Web site, Tony states that plants came from a 1979 trip that Raulston took to California's Strybing Arboretum. Strybing acquired the plant from California professor Jack Napton in 1971, but prior to that the record runs dry. In North Carolina it will reach a size of 2 feet by 3 feet (60–90 cm) and is slow to offset, which makes it an ideal candidate for use as a nearly solitary, bold accent plant.

Agave parryi 'Sierra Estrella'

Mountain States Wholesale Nursery selected a form they dubbed 'Sierra Estrella', from a batch of plants grown from seed that originated in Chihuahua. 'Sierra Estrella' is distinguished by having a more rounded form and a maximum size of roughly 2 feet by 2 feet (60 by 60 cm). Plants have proven hardy to −20 degrees F (−29 C), and seem to relish very light shade in the hot, interior, low elevation zone.

Agave parryi var. *parryi* on a dry slope in the Parque Nacional Cumbres de Majalca

ABOVE A large colony of spherical *Agave parryi* var. *parryi* rosettes in the Parque Nacional Cumbres de Majalca

LEFT *Agave parryi* var. *parryi* with its symmetrical, rounded shape

Agave parryi Engelmann **var. *truncata***
Gentry

DWARF ARTICHOKE AGAVE

A plant showing the tight ball and very short truncated leaves which gave rise to this *Agave parryi* variety's name of *truncata*

Howard Scott Gentry separated this form from the others based on its truncate leaves with the very rounded, obtuse apex.

FIELD NOTES

Agave parryi var. *truncata* is known only from a couple of localities near the Durango-Zacatecas border in Mexico at altitudes between 7500 and 9000 feet (2300–2750 meters). If you are up for a long hike, try finding them in the Sierra Chapultepec, about twenty-five miles northwest of Fresnillo in Zacatecas. My friends Brian Kemble and Rob Nixon took me to see the plants here; we parked along Mexico Highway 45, and then set out for the long hike up to the oaks and pines near the top of the distant peaks. Once there, we had to look carefully for the plants as they are sometimes hidden behind boulders or under trees, while others are easily spotted thanks to the large clusters formed. Poke around and look for the most attractive form as there is some variability in the plants found here.

Easier to reach is the type locality in the Sierra Sombrerete on the Durango-Zacatecas border. Taking Mexico Highway 45 heading northwest from Fresnillo, you come to the town of San Martin where you will find a road leading up into the Sierra. Follow that road up to the top, and before you descend toward the mining operation, you can stop not far from a nice colony of plants. Again, they are growing with oaks, pines, and junipers, but should be easy to find. Try going in the summer to catch sight of some flowering specimens.

DESCRIPTION

Variety *truncata* is supposed to be distinguished by its small, broad leaves with acute to truncate apices, but Gentry's 1982 description and field observation both reveal a wide range of variability. It is a small plant, generally reaching 1–2 feet tall by 1½–2½ feet across (30–60 by 45–75 cm), with those in cultivation tipping the scales on the larger end of the range. Leaves are a nice blue-gray color, frequently short and broad with an obtuse or rarely acute angle at the apex.

CULTURE

Plants might suffer minor leaf damage when the thermometer hits the high single digits F (−12 to −13 C). It is reliably hardy in zones 8a–11, and makes a stately landscape plant in the drier parts of the Pacific coast states and the southern states, even into North Carolina. Certain forms

ABOVE A large specimen of *Agave parryi* var. *truncata* in the Sierra Chapultepec in northern Zacatecas

RIGHT The blue-gray leaves of *Agave parryi* var. *truncata* 'Huntington' mix nicely with the rose-purple flowers of *Dalea versicolor* var. *sessilis* in a xeric Tucson, Arizona, landscape.

of this variety are spectacular specimens in the low and mid-elevation southwestern U.S. zones. This one is worth trying in warmer microclimates in the high elevation zone. Plants are best used in full sun in the coastal and the mid-elevation southwestern U.S. zones, but should be given some filtered light during the middle of the hot, summer days in the interior, low elevation zone. In hot desert areas, thoroughly soak the root zone once every seven to fourteen days, starting in the spring until summer rains hit.

CULTIVAR

Agave parryi var. truncata 'Huntington'

By far the most popular clone of *Agave parryi* var. *truncata* being grown today is the one that Gentry pictured on page 544 of *Agaves of Continental North America* in 1982. This form has been grown at the Huntington Botanical Garden since he first brought the plant back from Mexico in June 1951. It has informally been called the 'Huntington' form and should officially be given a cultivar name. To that end, an official declaration for this widely popular form is made here.

Agave parryi var. *truncata* 'Huntington' can be distinguished by its broad, blue-gray leaves, bluntly rounded at the tip, that measure 8–10 inches long by 5–6 inches wide (20–25 by 12–15 cm), very tightly upright in the upper half of the plant to upright-spreading in the lower half. The leaf edges are dotted with widely spaced, very small, brownish red to gray marginal teeth. The terminal spine is distinctly wavy, dark brownish red-black on new leaves, gray on older leaves, and 1¼ inch (3 cm) long. The incurved, overlapping leaves give the plant an attractive ball-like form resembling a large artichoke.

Agave parviflora Torrey

SMALL FLOWER AGAVE

Agave parviflora growing on a west-facing roadcut along the Ruby Road to Peña Blanca Lake in southern Arizona

Perhaps the smallest flowers in the genus belong to this one, as illustrated by the species name *parviflora*, a combination of the Latin *parv*, meaning small, and *flor* for flower.

FIELD NOTES

The distribution of this little gem is somewhat restricted, occurring along the Ruby road to Peña Blanca Lake, in the Las Guijas Mountains, not far from Sasabe in southwestern Arizona, near Patagonia in Arizona, and in a couple of places in northeastern Sonora. While driving on the Ruby Road, I have seen some very attractive specimens on the roadcuts and tucked in among the grasses. If you get out and hike around, watch out for snakes that also like to hide in the tall grass.

Two other subspecies occur only in Sonora. One, *Agave parviflora* ssp. *flexiflora*, differs from the type in having downward flexed flowers, as the name implies, and is found in a handful of localities in northeastern Sonora. The other is a newly discovered subspecies which is proposed as *A. parviflora* ssp. *densiflora*. It differs from the typical form in having a larger rosette, occasionally reaching 12 inches (30 cm) across, with larger leaves and flowers packed more tightly together on the stalk. This subspecies is found in only three localities in the Municipio de Yécora in east-central Sonora. The elevation range for *A. parviflora* is from 2900 to 5500 feet (900–1675 meters).

DESCRIPTION

Agave parviflora is a diminutive species that falls within the extra small category, maxing out at about 4–6 inches high by 5–12 inches across (10–15 by 12–30 cm). Plants will occasionally produce offsets and can make clumps to 15–18 inches (40–45 cm) across, with the rare, ancient clump reaching 24 inches (60 cm) across. The dark green leaves are short and narrow, oblong-linear, and widest at or slightly above the middle, conspicuously marked with white bud prints on both surfaces. They are only 2½–4 inches long by ⅓–⅖ inch wide (6.3–10 by 0.7–1 cm), with the margins minutely toothed and adorned with conspicuous, curly, white fibers, while the terminal spine is small and weak, and colored brown to grayish white.

A 3–6 foot (0.9–1.8 meter) tall spicate flower stalk appears in summer, with the upper half of the shaft loosely covered with small, pale yellow flowers each under 1 inch (2.5 cm) long.

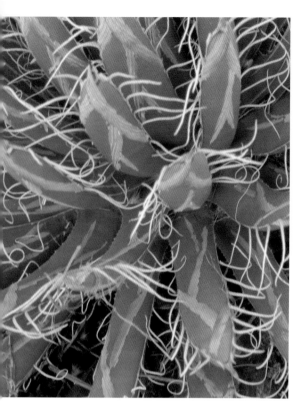

CULTURE

Plants can tolerate winter lows to at least 15 degrees F (−9 C) without damage and can be grown in zones 8b–11, in most of the drier parts of the Pacific coast states as well as the southern and southeastern states, and are marginally hardy as far north as North Carolina. They can be grown in all southwestern U.S. zones except for the very wet and cold parts of the cold, low elevation zone in Texas.

The growth rate is fast, and plants can reach flowering size in under a decade when grown with some extra water in the summer. Watering can be a bit tricky since the plants do not grow well if given too much water, but need enough to make it through summer in areas with numerous days with temperatures over 100 F (38 C). In Tucson landscapes, plants that appear to receive minimal supplemental summer water often look quite happy growing in soil that has been covered with a rock or gravel mulch that helps to cool the soil and prevent it from rapidly drying out. They naturally grow in rocky soil, which should be mimicked in the garden. Make sure the roots do not get too hot and too wet as that can lead to rot.

Plants in habitat grow hidden among grasses and shrubs, and are probably best used in at least *some* shade in the hot, interior low elevation and mid-elevation zones. They can tolerate a fair amount of sun in the cool, coastal and high elevation zones, or wherever the summer temperatures do not routinely climb over 100 degrees (38 C) F. A coarse soil with small volcanic or granitic rocks might be beneficial in growing good specimens.

LANDSCAPE VALUE

With its curly white marginal fibers and detailed white markings on the leaves, *Agave parviflora* makes a very cute little container plant, especially in a decorative pot. It also works well tucked in among boulders with cactus and other succulents, and small, flowering perennials or small grasses. Some ideal small companion plants would include *Baileya multiradiata*, *Bouteloua gracilis*, *Melampodium leucanthum*, *Tetraneuris acaulis*, and *Thymophylla pentachaeta*.

Agave pelona Gentry

BALD AGAVE

Mature *Agave pelona* growing on solid limestone in the Sierra El Viejo in Sonora

Howard Scott Gentry used the Spanish word *pelón*, or bald, as the basis for the name of this toothless, hairless species.

According to Gentry in 1982, *Agave pelona* occurs in four localities in Sonora, Mexico. However, I checked the specimens from the Sierra Seri locality and found that those plants were originally incorrectly identified; Dr. Richard Felger corrected the error and identified them as *A. chrysoglossa*. The *A. pelona* plants at Cerro Aquituni are the only ones that are not fenced off, while the two other localities are fenced.

The most famous locality is in the Sierra El Viejo, which is a bighorn sheep reserve, and special permission is needed to visit the area. My friend Rob obtained permission to visit the ranch, so he and I made plans to take a trip to see the area. Once at the ranch, we had to drive along a nasty, deeply rutted four-wheel-drive dirt road to get near the habitat. The plants here occur on steep, rocky slopes composed of sharp, flesh-eating limestone, necessitating one to be outfitted with full body armor and an excellent pair of rugged hiking boots to prevent damage to tender skin. However, the narrow, spicate flower stalks covered with large, cherry red to deep wine red flowers are an incredible sight and worth the effort! Plants do not bloom on a regular basis, and seem to be keyed to a really good rainy season, so catching them in flower is a hit or miss proposition. They are documented to occur between 1500 and 4000 feet (450–1200 meters) elevation.

DESCRIPTION

Agave pelona forms solitary, compact rosettes to about 1¼–2 feet tall by 2–2½ feet across (38–60 by 60–75 cm), full of narrow, dagger-like, dark green leaves that frequently color up with dark reddish purple near the edges when stressed by drought, cold, sun, or just plain old age. Leaves measure anywhere from 12–20 inches long and ⅘–2 inches wide (30–50 by 2–5 cm), are toothless along the margin, instead having a smooth, white border, and terminate in one of the most impressive, 1½–2¾ inch (4–7 cm) long, sewing-needle-like spines in the genus.

In nature, a spectacular 6–10 foot (2–3 meter) tall spike loaded with 2 inch (5 cm) long, dark wine red, bell-shaped flowers will appear in late spring if the conditions are right. Apparently there must be sufficient rainfall in order for these to flower, but when there is, a hillside in full flower can be impressive.

ABOVE A section of an *Agave pelona* inflorescence, with showy wine red flowers

OPPOSITE *Agave pelona* in peak bloom at the Arizona-Sonora Desert Museum near Tucson

CULTURE

Agave pelona plants can tolerate winter lows into at least the mid-teens F (−8 C) without sustaining damage, and can be grown outdoors in zones 8b–11 as long as they are kept bone dry in the winter in the more humid regions. Try this one as a landscape plant in the dry parts of California. Plants are hardy enough to be grown in the low and mid-elevation southwestern U.S. zones, except for the cold, low elevation zone of Texas.

Plants have a slow growth rate and might take fifteen to twenty years to achieve mature, flowering size. These are extremely drought tolerant and supplemental water should be kept to a bare minimum. In the hot, interior, low elevation and mid-elevation zones, a good thorough soaking of the root zone once a month as weather heats up and thoughts turn to shorts and tank tops ought to be plenty for established plants. Then, when the summer rains hit, stop supplying supplemental water and let nature take over. In the cool, coastal zone, where winter rain is the norm, established plants ought to be fine on rainfall or with a good thorough soaking a couple of times through the summer. Grow this xeric species in full, blazing sun in the low and mid-elevation southwestern U.S. zones.

In nature plants grow on steep slopes and cliffs composed of pure limestone, so in cultivation they ought to be grown in thin, gritty soil with excellent drainage. If you can build a massive, steep, limestone outcrop, they will relish growing on that, and it will be the most awesome landscape in your neighborhood!

In areas where winter moisture and/or humidity are high, watch for root rot and fungal diseases on the leaves.

LANDSCAPE VALUE

Because *Agave pelona* can be found growing with *Bursera microphylla*, *Echinocereus* species, and *Fouquieria splendens*, it certainly can be combined with these and similar plants in a creative landscape. Some other recommended companion plants include *Calliandra eriophylla*, *Dasylirion wheeleri*, *Encelia farinosa*, *Ferocactus* species, *Glandularia gooddingii*, *Penstemon* species, and *Viquiera deltoidea*.

The toothless leaves, with their propensity to develop a rich purple or reddish purple color when stressed, and the long, needle-like terminal spine make this a truly unique species. After many years, the patient gardener will be rewarded with an incredible flower display.

A young plant of *Agave pelona*, showing the rich green leaves with dark reddish purple on the edge

TAXONOMIC NOTES

Howard Scott Gentry himself stated that "this beautiful and distinct, endemic xerophyte has no close relative," yet he included *Agave pelona* in the group Marginatae based primarily on the continuous white, detachable margin. Other members of this group include *A. horrida, A. horrida* ssp. *perotensis, A. titanota, A. victoriae-reginae,* and *A. xylonacantha.*

Agave petrophila García-Mendoza & Martinez

ROCK-LOVING AGAVE

A grouping of *Agave petrophila* on a forested slope above the El Boquerón Canyon in Oaxaca

The Mexican botanists Abisaí García-Mendoza and Esteban Martínez Salas appropriately named this one for its rock-loving habit. The Greek *petr* means rock, and *philo* means loving.

FIELD NOTES

For the most part, plants of this recently described species grow where only a bird or Spiderman can reach them as they inhabit precipitous, vertical rock walls in narrow canyons. Occasionally it is possible to get up close to a couple of the lower-growing ones or find a nice cluster growing on a slope above the rock wall. The plants make rounded spheres of numerous, narrow leaves that stand straight out from the center even though gravity should be pulling them earthward as it seems to do to nearly everything else.

Seeing these plants cling to perpendicular rock walls in the El Boquerón Canyon of Oaxaca, Mexico, is a breathtaking sight that makes one gaze in wonder at their resilience as they sink their roots into minute cracks and fissures of seemingly solid rock. Plants are found in only two localities, one in southern Oaxaca and the other in Guerrero between 2800 and 4250 feet (850–1300 meters) elevation.

DESCRIPTION

Agave petrophila plants make rounded spheres of numerous, narrow leaves, the rosettes reaching 1½–2 feet by 1½–2½ feet (45–60 by 45–75 cm), and look a bit like *A. stricta*. Typically the rosettes produce few offsets, but in habitat the clumps are not huge as they are somewhat restricted by the lack of soil on the steep, vertical walls. Light glaucous green, linear-lanceolate leaves measure 15–24 inches long by $^1/_5$–$^2/_5$ inches wide (40–60 by 0.4–0.9 cm), and resemble a flattened shish-kebob skewer, widest at the base and narrowing gradually to the tip. Leaf edges are finely denticulate with tiny, nearly invisible teeth that are able to inflict paper cuts if handled carelessly. The dark reddish brown terminal spine is small, but still sharp and capable of lodging in unsuspecting fingertips.

The narrow, unbranched flower stalk is about 6–6½ feet (1.8–2 meters) tall and densely covered with 1 inch (2.5 cm) long, bell-shaped, greenish yellow flowers tinged dark reddish at the tips, with long, showy, purplish red stamens.

CULTURE

Agave petrophila hangs out in narrow, steep-walled canyons in a couple of spots in Oaxaca and Guerrero in southern Mexico. These canyons rarely if ever experience frost. With that in mind, I have yet to leave any

ABOVE Mature *Agave petrophila* growing on a slab of rock in the El Boquerón Canyon in Oaxaca

LEFT The spicate inflorescence of *Agave petrophila* jutting out overhead

plants outside during winter for fear that they will turn into a gelatinous pile of mush; in fact, plants have visibly shivered when I walked by them with a glass of ice water, even in the summer heat. Because of that chilling response, plants are probably best grown in containers in all elevation zones of the southwestern United States. This one could possibly be used as a landscape plant in frost-free parts of California and Florida, in the coastal, low elevation southwestern U.S. zone, or in zones 10b–11.

Plants take their sweet time growing, which is a good thing when you are trying to keep them confined to a decorative container and do not want them to outgrow the pot. In spite of growing in narrow, moist canyons, *Agave petrophila* seems to be relatively low-water-using, with potted plants receiving water twice a week even in the hottest, driest time of the year in Tucson. As with most species, let the soil dry slightly before watering again. Because these grow in steep-walled canyons, they receive very little direct sun and in the hot, interior low elevation zone they are best grown in filtered sun most of the day—for instance, in the shade of a tree or under shade cloth. If neither option is viable, I would suggest spray-on sunscreen with an SPF of at least 70, or more seriously under a porch. Along the coastal zone, plants should be able to tolerate more sun, but would still probably benefit from some shade during the hottest part of the day during summer.

In nature, these rock-loving cliff-dwellers do not seem to need much actual soil—just a crack in the rock for seed to nestle down into, and enough soil for roots to set anchor. In cultivation, they seem to prefer a loose mix that drains extremely quickly and does not hold excess moisture. The addition of granite smashed into small chunks would look quite attractive as a top dressing for plants grown in decorative pots.

LANDSCAPE VALUE

Use *Agave petrophila* as a perfectly staged specimen plant in a decorative container and place it in a highly visible spot to show off the many blue ribbons it is sure to win when entered in a cactus and succulent show. A plant of any size, with its perfectly symmetrical rosette of narrow, needle-like leaves, makes a charming and impressive show piece when matched with an outstanding container.

This can possibly be used as a landscape plant in zones 10–11. Be sure to place it in a prominent spot in order to show off its striking form. Mix it with dainty, delicate flowering annuals such as *Eschscholtzia californica*, *Linaria maroccana*, *Linum grandiflorum*, and *Nemophila menziesii*.

Agave polianthiflora Gentry

POLIANTHES RED FLOWER AGAVE

White bud prints and marginal threads make *Agave polianthiflora* a decorative little plant.

The species name refers to the pinkish red to red, tubular flowers that bear a striking similarity to the flowers of the genus *Polianthes*.

FIELD NOTES

Agave polianthiflora can be found growing on rocky outcrops with pines and oaks in eastern Sonora and adjacent western Chihuahua, Mexico, between 4000 and 6500 feet (1200–2000 meters) elevation. In fact, there are a couple of relatively accessible spots where one can see this little gem growing in the wild. On Mexico Highway 16, as you drive from Hermosillo, Sonora east up into the Sierra Madre towards Ciudad Chihuahua, you pass the town of Yécora nestled in the oaks and pines. If you travel this road in the summer, go about thirty to forty miles east of Yécora and start looking for this little agave's telltale pinkish red flowers on stalks poking out from behind rocks and above the grasses. If you stay overnight in Yécora, be sure to get an early start as you want to photograph the flowers with early morning light and not as the sun is setting behind the mountains.

The Parque Nacional Cumbres de Majalca in northwestern Chihuahua is home to some very nice specimens of *Agave polianthiflora*. Here, plants can be seen inhabiting small pockets of soil in large boulders up above the roadway. Look for the short stalks with the long, pinkish red flowers, and then screech to a stop so you can scramble around on the large, rounded boulders to capture the plants with your camera.

DESCRIPTION

This one falls into the extra small category with the rosette reaching 3–8 inches tall by 5–12 inches across (8–20 by 12–30 cm). In habitat, the rosettes are usually single, sometimes producing a few offsets and forming small colonies to 12–18 inches (30–45 cm) across. Dark green leaves are narrow, linear lanceolate, kind of like a barbeque skewer, 4–8 inches long by ½ inch wide (10–20 by 1.3 cm), widest at the middle with a long taper to the tip. There are minute teeth near the base and white fibers in the upper half, while the grayish terminal spine is small and weak, about ¼ inch (0.6 cm) long and easily broken. With this leaf shape one could put feathers at the base and use it as a dart at the local pub.

The spicate flower stalk reaches 4–6½ feet (1.2–2 meters) tall with distinctive, 1½ inch (38 mm) long, pinkish red to red, tubular flowers, usually in pairs at each node, in the upper one third of the stalk. These are followed by the small, colorful seed capsules that look like small cherries before they ripen.

ABOVE The characteristic long, red, tubular flowers of *Agave polianthiflora* are hummingbird magnets.

OPPOSITE *Agave polianthiflora* nestled against a rock along Mexico Highway 16, east of Yécora in east-central Sonora

Young seed capsules on *Agave polianthiflora* look good enough to eat.

CULTURE

Although *Agave polianthiflora* has been grown successfully outdoors in Albuquerque, New Mexico, where the all-time low has been recorded at –11 degrees F (–24 C), it is considered a zone 7a–11 plant and should be reliably hardy to the 0–5 degrees F (–15 to –18 C) range without being damaged. If kept dry in winter, plants can be grown in the Pacific coast states, across the southern states, and up the Atlantic coast at least as far north as Raleigh, North Carolina. This species has been grown successfully in all southwestern U.S. zones.

These grow relatively quickly, reaching flowering size in less than ten years if given supplemental water during the growing season. The plants are frequently found growing on thin soil with sandy grit and small rocks on top of large, granitic boulders, indicating that the water needs are minimal in all zones. In the hot, interior, low elevation zone, it is best to grow this one in a bit of afternoon shade in the summer, while in the cool, coastal, mid- and high elevation zones plants can tolerate full sun. Under cultivation, plants tend to develop an open form and are subject to rot if given too much water.

Keeping the native soil in mind, cultivated plants should be in soil with coarse sand, small pebbles and very little organic matter. The coarse material combined with minimal water will help to prevent the roots from rotting.

LANDSCAPE VALUE

Agave polianthiflora makes a nice specimen in decorative pots, and works well tucked in among boulders with cactus, other succulents, and small flowering perennials. Because it reaches maturity quickly, it can be grown for the showy red, hummingbird-attracting flowers.

Agave polianthiflora, *A. parviflora* and *A. toumeyana* look very similar and can be difficult to tell apart. For advice on doing so, see "Comparing Look-Alikes."

Agave potatorum Zuccarini

BUTTERFLY AGAVE, PAPALOMETL

A striking specimen of *Agave potatorum* with its prominent mammillate leaf margins

The species name is derived from the Latin *potator* which means "of the drinkers," possibly referring to the fact that the locals make mescal from the plants.

FIELD NOTES

Agave potatorum is found in many widely scattered localities in the southern Mexican states of Puebla and Oaxaca, generally between 4000 and 7500 feet (1200–2300 meters) elevation, and is relatively common in many areas. This species either is a highly variable species, or is on the verge of becoming several, very closely related species, as indicated by the many names applied to plants that were collected and sent to European agavologists in the mid- to late 1800s. Even Gentry, an agave guru, admitted that it is a taxonomic mess. One of the most beautiful forms, with large mammillate margins, can be seen in the hills around the town of El Camerón in south-central Oaxaca.

A beautiful drive, along which one is likely to encounter a wide range of variability in the species, is on the Cerro Las Flores loop in southern Oaxaca. The loop road starts off of Mexico Highway 190 near the Presa Benito Juárez, and heads north, looping to the east around the Cerro Las Flores mountain before eventually heading southeast and hooking up with Mexico Highway 185. As I write this in 2010, the road is mostly a bumpy, dirt road barely wide enough to fit two vehicles. The Mexican government is building a new highway that will alter the route a bit, making the drive a little faster—that is, until the thin layer of pavement becomes full of potholes and the patches that are subsequently created by workers either higher or lower than the existing pavement, forcing normal drivers to go as slow as they would on the old dirt road! But there are a lot of really interesting plants on this loop and it is well worth spending a full day exploring, regardless of the condition of the road.

Agave potatorum is used in the making of Tobalá mescal throughout much of its range in central Oaxaca. This is one of the more expensive types of mescal, partly because the plant is not cultivated for this purpose and only wild plants are used.

DESCRIPTION

Although *Agave potatorum* is a variable species, it is generally recognizable and not easily confused with other agaves except *A. isthmensis*. Some of the variability might be derived from hybridization with other species, but with some practice, an agavephile is usually able to identify

A. potatorum. It is a non-offsetting type, with the rosette reaching about 1–1½ feet tall by 1½–3 feet across (30–45 by 45–90 cm), or maybe a little bit wider under cultivation. Gray-green to blue-gray or even nearly powdery white, 10–15 inch long by 3½–7 inch wide (25–40 by 9–18 cm) leaves are broadly obovate with the widest part of the leaf above the middle, gradually narrowing to the base. The leaf margins are crenate to mammillate ⅕–⅖ inch (5–10 mm) long, with grayish brown teeth perched upon noticeable teats that create impressive bud imprints on the surrounding leaves. Some of the best forms have a wiggly, nearly 2 inch (5 cm) long terminal spine with a broad groove on top.

At the end of its life, the plant will shoot out a 10–20 foot (3–6 meter) tall flower stalk, with fifteen to thirty short branches in the upper one half to one quarter of the shaft. The end of each side branch is loaded with several 2–3 inch (5–7.5 cm) long, light green to yellowish flowers frequently tinged red or purplish when in bud prior to opening.

A young specimen of *Agave potatorum* tucked in among some rocks

Agave potatorum has a tall, thin inflorescence and many side branches loaded with bright yellow flowers.

CULTURE

Agave potatorum is a bit frost sensitive, suffering damage when winter lows drop into the middle to high 20s F (−3 to −4 C) and outright death if subjected to low 20s F (−5.5 C) without some sort of cover blanketing the plant. The plants should be fine in zones 9b–11, or the low elevation southwestern U.S. zone. *Agave potatorum* can reliably be grown as a landscape plant in the mild winter zones of southern California and in other regions of the Pacific coast states and Florida that are frost free or experience mild, infrequent, short-duration frost. This one can also be grown in the hot, interior low elevation zone in the southwestern United States as long as plants are given some relief from the blazing, hot afternoon summer sun.

Butterfly agave has a moderate growth rate, taking several years to achieve flowering size—so you will have a beautiful specimen for a long time. In habitat, the plants seem to favor areas that receive a good deal of summer rainfall. Although they do not need much, if any, supplemental water in the cooler temperatures of late autumn until early spring, these plants relish extra water in the heat of summer in the hot, interior, low elevation and mid-elevation zones. In the cooler coastal, low elevation zone of southern California, plants can get by with minimal supplemental water in the summer and no extra water in the winter.

These grow best if given a bit of midday shade in the hot, interior, low elevation and mid-elevation zones. They can tolerate full sun in the milder climate of the coastal low elevation zone in southern California. In habitat, the plants frequently grow in soil with extra leaf litter or surrounded by small shrubs that help to keep the soil a little cooler. With that in mind, put these plants in a soil with good drainage and add a layer of compost or leaf litter on top of the soil to help it retain moisture and cool the temperature.

LANDSCAPE VALUE

Agave potatorum looks great as a specimen plant in a large, decorative container. As a landscape plant, use it in among large boulders, and mix with low-growing shrubs and perennials to help cool the soil.

TAXONOMIC NOTES

In 1993, Abisaí García-Mendoza and Felípe Palma Cruz described *Agave isthmensis*, distinguishing it from *Agave potatorum*. See "Comparing Look-Alikes."

Agave potatorum 'Snowfall'

This variegated form of *Agave potatorum* will reach a full size of about 2.5–3 feet (75–90 cm) across, and has striking creamy yellow coloring along the leaf margins. 'Snowfall' will tolerate full sun in coastal southern California and other mild climate regions, but will benefit from some shade in the hot, interior, low elevation and the mid-elevation southwestern U.S. zones. In hardiness it is the same as the species, needing some protection from winter temperatures in the mid- to high 20s F (−3 to −4 C).

RIGHT The wiggly terminal spines on leaves of *Agave potatorum*

FAR RIGHT *Agave potatorum* 'Snowfall'

Agave potrerana Trelease

POTRERO AGAVE

A stout specimen of *Agave potrerana* growing in rocky soil in Santa Clara Canyon, northern Chihuahua

One meaning of the Spanish word *potrero* is pasture ground, and *Agave potrerana* occurs in grasslands in northern Mexico.

FIELD NOTES

When driving south on Mexico Highway 45 north of Ciudad Chihuahua, find the dirt road that takes you to Santa Clara Canyon and head back about four miles to the rocky hills that hold a small population of *Agave potrerana*. Pull off the road, and make the short hike up the hill where a few of the plants grow. My friends Rob Nixon and Brian Kemble and I made this our summer vacation and were rewarded by finding the plants in glorious flower!

Plants of *Agave potrerana* are found in only a few localities in the Mexican states of Chihuahua and Coahuila from about 5000 to 8000 feet (1500–2500 meters) elevation.

DESCRIPTION

The plant is a solitary rosette that usually tops out at about 2½–3 feet tall by 4–6 feet across (0.75–0.9 by 1.2–1.8 meters) from leaf tip to leaf tip. The light to dark green, lance-shaped, 16–30 inch long by 2½ inch wide (40–75 by 6.5 cm) leaves usually have a slightly bluish cast and a continuous, woody margin edged with small yet annoying teeth that break off easily, getting stuck in fingers and forearms. The 1–1½ inch (2.5–3.8 cm) long, needle-like spine has a wide, shallow groove on top.

As your plant reaches the end of its life, an impressive, unbranched flower stalk densely packed with pink or red, 2 inch (5 cm) long flowers with bright yellow stamens will shoot forth, growing either straight up or arching over, in late spring or early summer, eventually reaching a length of anywhere from 13–23 feet (4–7 meters).

CULTURE

Agave potrerana is hardy to at least the high teens F (−7 to −8 C), and probably down to single digits F based on where the plants grow naturally. It is easily a zone 8b–11 plant, and should also be tried in zones 7b–8a. It can be grown in the ground in most areas of the Pacific coast states, across the southern states, into the southeast, and up the Atlantic coast as far north as North Carolina. They make great landscape plants in the low elevation southwestern U.S. zone, and at least in Tucson and Green Valley in the mid-elevation zone, and would probably take the

ABOVE A specimen of *Agave potrerana* in full bloom, found growing on a grass-covered slope in Santa Clara Canyon, northern Chihuahua

LEFT The showy red flowers of *Agave potrerana* in mid-June

winter lows in almost all of the high elevation zone cities except for Albuquerque and Santa Fe in New Mexico.

Plants have a moderate growth rate, taking several years to achieve flowering size, at which time you will be rewarded with one of the most spectacular sights ever. As they are found growing on dry, rocky slopes, these should be able to survive on very little supplemental water. My one potted plant is out of sight, out of mind, so to speak, and survives my sporadic summer watering which happens once every two or three weeks at best. This, along with the meager summer rainfall of about 4–5 inches (10–12.5 cm), amounts to about 10–12 inches (25–30 cm) of water from spring until the start of autumn.

They can tolerate full sun in the milder climate of the coastal, low elevation zone in southern California and the middle elevation zone, but seem to relish very light shade in the hot, interior, low elevation zone in the southwestern United States. In habitat, the plants' inclination to grow on slopes in rocky soil, tucked in among large boulders and mixed with seasonal grasses, indicates that they prefer a soil with good drainage and a bit of organic matter.

LANDSCAPE VALUE

Agave potrerana can be mixed in among large boulders, and with a sprinkling of low-growing shrubs and perennials to provide seasonal color and help cool the soil. Place it in a spot with high visibility to best display your plant when the time comes for it to shoot the incredibly colorful flower stalk. Some nice companion plants for the low and mid-elevation southwestern U.S. zones would include *Baileya multiradiata*, *Calliandra eriophylla*, *Chrysactinia mexicana*, *Glandularia gooddingii*, *Salvia greggii*, *Scutellaria suffrutescens*, *Tetraneuris acaulis*, and *Zinnia acerosa*.

TAXONOMIC NOTES

Howard Scott Gentry placed *Agave potrerana* in the Marginatae group but noted that it has no close relative.

Agave 'Royal Spine'

ROYAL SPINE AGAVE

The beautiful black margins and terminal spines of *Agave* 'Royal Spine' stand out next to the steely green leaves.

The cultivar name is a play on words derived from the two parent species, *Agave victoriae-regiane* (the royal part) and *A. macroacantha* (the spine part).

FIELD NOTES

Agave 'Royal Spine' is a hybrid of *A. victoriae-reginae* and *A. macroacantha*, and is making its way into the horticulture trade thanks to fellow agave enthusiast Allen Repashy, who purchased the original plant from a former propagator at TropicWorld Nursery in Escondido, California. The man told Allen that he had dusted pollen from *A. macroacantha* onto *A. victoriae-reginae*, making it the seed parent for this particular hybrid. Allen bought a total of seventy-five plants, all of which were nearly identical. The best one was selected and given to Randy Baldwin at San Marcos Growers, who came up with the name 'Royal Spine'. This name commemorates the regal lineage of *A. victoriae-reginae* and the long terminal spine of *A. macroacantha*. The plant has since been put into tissue culture and should be a major hit in the nursery trade.

DESCRIPTION

Agave 'Royal Spine' forms an attractive, uniform, dense rosette reaching about 1¼–1½ feet tall by 2–2½ feet across (38–45 by 60–76 cm) with deep steel-green leaves that are linear-lanceolate (imagine a bayonet used by Civil War soldiers), measuring about 10–12 inches long by 2 inches wide (25–30 by 5 cm). The leaf edges are devoid of teeth, a characteristic derived from the *A. victoriae-reginae* parent, instead having a continuous dark brown to black margin that leads into the dark brown to black, very stout terminal spine. As of this writing, the inflorescence is unknown.

CULTURE

Agave 'Royal Spine' is a solid zone 8b–11 plant, tolerating temperatures to at least the high teens F (−7 to −8 C), and should be an excellent landscape specimen in the drier regions of the Pacific coast and Gulf coast states. Plants are able to withstand winters in the cool, coastal and hot, interior low elevation zone and mid-elevation zone cities. Plants ought to be tested in the cities of Sierra Vista, Mesilla, and El Paso of the high elevation zone.

The growth rate is slow, so that you will have this one around for quite a while before it up and flowers, dies, and needs to be replaced. Young plants do have a tendency to rot if planted too low or kept too wet. Established plants are water misers like the parents, yet they are able to tolerate infrequent supplemental water in the summer.

Grow it in full sun to produce the most compact and regal form. Put it in a soil that has very good drainage with additional gypsum worked into the top 3–4 inches (7.5–10 cm) periodically, and keep the water to a minimum to avoid any abnormally stretched-out growth and rotting of the roots.

LANDSCAPE VALUE

Agave 'Royal Spine' makes a great container plant as long as the container is large enough. In time, the plant will form a nearly perfect, ball-like shape that makes for an eye-catching specimen. Put one each in several large pots, and make a statement with a nice grouping of these beauties. They also work great in the ground and blend well with colorful perennial wildflowers and small shrubs. Try mixing it with *Glandularia gooddingii*, *Penstemon* species, *Thymophylla pentachaeta*, or *Zinnia grandiflora* for a seasonally colorful display.

The dark steely green leaves combined with the dark brown or black terminal spine create a spectacular combination on a full-sized plant.

Agave salmiana Otto ex Salm-Dyck

MAGUEY DE PULQUE

Agave salmiana growing near the ruins of Mineral de Pozos in Guanajuato, Mexico

Agave salmiana is widely cultivated in central Mexico for its use in making the alcoholic drink pulque, as well as for cattle forage.

FIELD NOTES

Agave salmiana has been cultivated for centuries. It grows throughout much of central Mexico at elevations ranging from 5600 to 8800 feet (1700–2700 meters). One of the easiest ways to see some really cool specimens is to venture just southwest of the city of Tehuacán in Puebla, where they can be found growing out in the open desert along with tall yuccas and a variety of desert shrubs.

DESCRIPTION

Agave salmiana is a large to extra large species, and the popular var. *ferox* is readily identified by its rather sizable, urn-shaped rosette with bright green leaves that grow up and curve out and away from the center. The plant can grow to 3–5 feet tall by 4–8 feet across (1–1.2 by 1.5–2.5 meters), freely producing offsets around the base. Bright green to dark green leaves are broadly oblanceolate, narrower near the base and widest above the middle, and 24–36 inches long by 7–12 inches wide (60–90 by 18–30 cm) with a shortly acuminate taper to the 2–3 inch (50–75 mm) long, dark brown decurrent spine. The leaf margins are crenate with large, brown or dark gray teeth perched upon noticeable teats that leave a lasting impression on the surrounding leaves.

After many years of living the good life, the plant will eventually shoot forth its 20–25 foot (6–7.6 meters) tall, branched flower stalk that is heavily clothed in thick, somewhat fleshy, overlapping bracts and topped by fifteen to twenty side branches in the upper one third of the shaft. Each side branch is packed with many 3–4 inch (7.5–10 cm) long, bright yellow flowers, clustered at the ends.

CULTURE

Agave salmiana var. *ferox* is the most commonly cultivated form of *A. salmiana* for landscape use in the southwestern United States. A good, solid zone 7b–11 plant, it tolerates winter lows down to 5 degrees F (–15 C) with no damage. Plants can be grown in the ground throughout the Pacific coast states, across the southern and southeastern states, and up to North Carolina. They make large landscape specimens in the low and mid-elevation zones of the southwestern United States, and probably in all cities in the high elevation zone except for Albuquerque and Santa Fe.

The moderate growth rate is ideal as these plants can get quite large. Keeping the supplemental watering to a minimum in cooler climates will slow the growth a bit and help to keep the plants at a manageable size. However, plants in the hot, interior, low elevation zone need some supplemental water during the brunt of summer.

Plants will tolerate full sun in all areas where they are easily grown, and are not picky about the soil as long as excess water drains away and roots are not subject to soggy feet.

LANDSCAPE VALUE

Because of its large size, *Agave salmiana* var. *ferox* requires ample room in the landscape. Plants combine nicely with a variety of other succulents and desert-adapted large shrubs. Some great companion plants include *Buddleja marrubiifolia, Calliandra californica, Dalea frutescens, Larrea divaricata, Leucophyllum laevigatum, Salvia greggii,* and *Scutellaria suffrutescens.*

CULTIVAR

Agave salmiana var. *ferox* 'Butterfingers'

Agave salmiana var. *ferox* 'Butterfingers' is differentiated by its smaller size, reaching about 3 feet tall by 4 feet across (0.9–1.2 meters), and by the broad swaths of creamy yellow variegation along the margins of the dark green leaves. Plant Delights Nursery received a plant from the garden of Marsha McPhetters in California.

A light-green-leaved specimen of *Agave salmiana* growing on the Cerro La Laja in Querétaro, Mexico

Agave schidigera Lemaire

A dark green specimen of *Agave schidigera* in Tucson

Charles Lemaire got creative when describing this species. The Greek root *schid* means splinter and *gera* means old age. Combine the two and we have "splintering in old age," possibly in reference to the marginal threads peeling away from the edge as the leaf matures.

Agave schidigera is widespread throughout much of west-central Mexico from 1500 to 8500 feet (450–2600 meters) elevation, but frequently grows in remote mountains far from easy roadside access. The exceptions are the plants seen along Mexico Highway 40, famously called the Mazatlán-Durango Highway. There, plants can be seen clinging to steep roadcuts as you climb up into the oak and pine zone near the border of Sinaloa and Durango near Puerto El Espinazo del Diablo, or the Mountain Pass of the Devil's Spine, in reference to the crest of the Sierra Madre Occidental. I have not been on this highway since the late 1990s, and have heard that there is construction on a new freeway to replace the old two-lane road that snakes its way through the Sierra Madre. Hopefully both will be accessible, as there are a lot of really fun plants to be seen on the original road. One of those is *A. schidigera* which, when seen in silhouette against the sky, looks quite remarkable, especially with the tall spicate flower stalk thrust straight up into the air, holding deep wine purple flowers.

Drive along the road from San Luis de la Paz to Xichú in Guanajuato, and stop about twenty-four miles from Mexico Highway 57. Look out over the landscape and notice the distant peak. Hike up there to find *Agave schidigera* plants, some of which might even be colored up red in times of stress, intense sun or the fact that they are flowering. Be prepared for a bit of hike; even though it is not rugged, there is a fair amount of uphill to get to the plants.

For a real adventure, take a drive to the Sierra Chapultepec of Zacatecas, which is about twenty-five miles northwest of Fresnillo in Zacatecas. It is another long hike to the top of the distant peak, but you will be rewarded with excellent specimens of *Echeveria cante* and *Agave schidigera*. Be sure to carry plenty of water for the long and arduous hike up to the oaks and pines.

Typically *Agave schidigera* is considered a medium-sized species, usually staying about 1½–2½ feet tall by 2½–3 feet across (45–75 by 75–90 cm), though the rare specimen grown in some shade with a lot of water can reach 4 feet (120 cm) across. Medium to dark green leaves are shaped like a bayonet, typically widest at or below the middle, 12–16 inches long by ½–1½ inches wide (30–40 by 1.5–4 cm), lightly or heavily white-marked on both surfaces, and occasionally tinged red or purple. Toothless along the margin, leaves instead are lightly to heavily laden with coarse, white threads that can be used as dental floss in a pinch, and are terminated by a small yet sharp spine.

In the heat of summer, when the plant has led a long and fulfilling life and reached the right age, an unbranched flower stalk will shoot up from the center, generally hitting a maximum height of 12–15 feet (3.6–4.5 meters). This stalk is densely packed with 1½ inch (4 cm) long flowers that can be the deep red color of a fine Merlot wine, to purple-red or reddish yellow, crowded into the upper two thirds.

CULTURE

This is such a wide-ranging species in habitat that the cold-hardiness will vary depending on the original locality. Most forms should be fine in mild winter regions of the Pacific coast states, and the southern and southeastern states. Further up the Atlantic coast, only the hardiest forms will work outdoors. This makes a nice, symmetrical landscape plant in the mid-elevation, and cool, coastal and hot, interior low elevation zone and southwestern U.S. zones. From personal experience, I can tell you that *Agave schidigera* has been grown in Tucson (zone 8b, mid-elevation zone) since the mid-1980s and experienced 17–18 degrees F (−8 C) with no damage.

Plants have a moderately fast growth rate, depending on the culture, and can reach flowering size in ten to twenty years from seed. These are opportunistic when it comes to water, having a faster growth rate when given consistent supplemental water in the summer. Plants in full sun will thrive with a good, thorough root zone soaking once every seven to ten days in the hot zone, and once every ten to fourteen days in the mid-elevation and coastal zones.

The amount of sun they can tolerate will vary with elevation zone and watering practices. In the hot, interior, low elevation zone, plants should receive a bit of relief from the blazing sun in midsummer, while those in the mid-elevation zone need mostly full sun as they tend to stretch with too much shade. Plants growing in the coastal zone should receive full sun all the time.

The flowers of *Agave schidigera* in a Tucson landscape

Place them in a soil that has decent drainage and they are happy as can be. They seem to grow just fine in a rocky clay soil or a sandy soil.

LANDSCAPE VALUE

Agave schidigera looks great either singly or when massed in groups, planted near large boulders, mixed with cactus and other succulents, or tucked in with flowering perennials or small shrubs. Some of the usual culprits make excellent companion plants. Try using *Baileya multiradiata, Calliandra eriophylla, Chrysactinia mexicana, Dalea capitata, Eschscholtzia californica, Glandularia gooddingii, Penstemon superbus, Salvia greggii, Scutellaria suffrutescens, Tetraneuris acaulis,* and *Zinnia grandiflora.* With its white markings and marginal threads, this cool plant will decorate any garden or container.

CULTIVARS

Agave schidigera 'Black Widow'

'Black Widow' has not been around long enough for us to know much about its eventual size, but it appears to be a nice tight rosette that might stay on the small end of the range for the species. This is a result of a reversion to the green form during tissue culture of the variegated form 'Shira Ito No Ohi'. The culture for this cultivar is the same as for the species. It is hardy to at least the low 20s F (−5 to −6 C) if kept dry, and if daytime temperatures are sufficiently high to allow the plants to warm up. Water use is relatively low, with established plants needing a thorough soaking once every one to two weeks in the heat of summer and once every four to six weeks in winter.

Agave schidigera 'Durango Delight'

Plants of 'Durango Delight' develop more symmetrical rosettes than those in other populations do, and frequently have dark red-purple flowers. Seed was collected from plants growing along Mexico Highway 40 between Mazatlán and Durango in the late 1980s. The culture for this cultivar is the same as for the species. Plants are hardy to at least the mid-teens if kept dry, if duration of cold is short, and if daytime temperatures are sufficiently high, allowing the plants to warm up. Water use is relatively low, with established plants needing a thorough soaking once every one to two weeks in the heat of summer and once every four to six weeks in winter.

Agave schidigera 'Shira Ito No Ohi'

'Shira Ito No Ohi' is a variegated form of *Agave schidigera* that originated in Japan. The plants are perfectly symmetrical rosettes, with the narrow, knife-blade leaves having creamy yellow edges on either side of the dark green central stripe. Tony Avent has had this for several years, and his largest plant in a container is about 10 inches tall by 12 inches across (25 by 30 cm). Tony received a plant from Renny Wong and subsequently had them tissue cultured, making them more readily available to the masses.

'Shira Ito No Ohi' was not hardy for Plant Delights Nursery in zone 7b, while one plant in Tucson (zone 8b) was exposed to winter temperatures of 22–23 degrees F (–5 to –6 C) without damage. This one is probably best grown in a large, decorative container in order to showcase the distinctive variegation. Plants seem to prefer light shade throughout the desert southwestern United States. It is a low-water-using cultivar that grows best in a soil with very good drainage. The growth rate is quite slow, owing to the large proportion of variegation, especially when grown in a container, and it will take many years to achieve full size.

With its creamy yellow variegation, *Agave schidigera* 'Shira Ito No Ohi' looks great in a custom pot by Mike Cone.

Agave 'Sharkskin'

SHARKSKIN AGAVE

Agave 'Sharkskin' in habitat east of Saltillo in Coahuila, Mexico, showing its thick leaves and open rosette

The cultivar name refers to the rough leaf surface that reminds one of a shark's skin.

FIELD NOTES

Agave 'Sharkskin' is widely considered to be a naturally occurring hybrid between *A. nickelsiae* (= *A. ferdinandi-regis*, *A. victoriae-reginae* var. *laxior*) and *A. asperrima*. It was originally found near Saltillo, Coahuila, in northeastern Mexico. The plants there are quite impressive even when living the hard life in the hardcore, dry desert habitat. Plants occur on a south-facing ridge, and even though the population is relatively small, the few hybrids that occur there are quite stunning.

DESCRIPTION

'Sharkskin' is an attractive, few-leaved, open rosette, 2–3 feet tall by 2½–3½ feet wide (60–90 by 75–100 cm). Thick, rigid, dark olive green leaves are 18–24 inches long by 3½–5 inches wide (45–60 by 8–12 cm), widest from near the base to the middle, deeply channeled to folded near the tip, and lacking teeth along the edges, instead having a prominent, continuous, dark gray or black margin that extends into the vicious, ¾–1 inch (2–2.5 cm) long, dark grayish to black terminal spine. Plants will produce offsets, eventually forming small colonies, though this can take a multitude of years to occur. The tall, narrow flower stalk is intermediate between the two basic types, being narrow, more like the spicate type of *Agave victoriae-reginae* but with very short side branches.

CULTURE

'Sharkskin' is hardy to at least single digits F (−12 to −13 C), and is considered a solid zone 7b–11 plant. This handsome cultivar makes a stately landscape plant in the drier parts of the Pacific coast and Gulf coast states, and even up the Atlantic coast to North Carolina. The plant makes an attractive, very stout specimen in the low and mid-elevation southwestern U.S. zones.

The growth rate is quite slow, having inherited this characteristic from both of its pokey parents, and will take its sweet time in growing up and showing the sculptural masterpiece everybody raves about. Coming from a dry hill near Saltillo, the plants are adapted to about 12 inches (30 cm) of annual rainfall with the majority falling in the summer and early autumn. These plants will grow fine with minimal supplemental water in most parts of the desert southwestern United States. My plants

in Tucson are given supplemental water once every three weeks when the temperatures hit high 90s to low 100s F (35–39 C), and would need watering about twice that often in the really hot, interior, low elevation zone.

A true desert rat, 'Sharkskin' is best grown in full sun in all southwestern U.S. zones to achieve the densest form possible. The dry, rocky hill where I have seen similar hybrids is primarily limestone derived, indicating that the plants are tolerant of high pH and prefer really good drainage.

LANDSCAPE VALUE

'Sharkskin' makes a stately, dramatic form in the garden and can be used singly to attract the eye, or grouped for a bold, dramatic statement. Surround a large specimen with low, colorful, flowering perennials and small shrubs for a truly outstanding effect in your garden. Some nice companion plants include *Baileya multiradiata*, *Calliandra eriophylla*, *Chrysactinia mexicana*, *Penstemon* species, *Thymophylla pentachaeta*, and *Zinnia grandiflora*.

TAXONOMIC NOTES

The form being grown at San Marcos Growers is from the Huntington Botanical Garden, from material originally collected by Myron Kimnach and Gary Lyons on May 21st, 1971, in Coahuila. There are reports of the same or a similar hybrid having been collected by Charlie Glass and Bob Foster.

A plant being offered as *Agave* 'Sharkskin Shoes' originally came from the Ruth Bancroft Garden in Walnut Creek, California. Randy Baldwin at San Marcos Growers has grown both *A*. 'Sharkskin' and *A*. 'Sharkskin Shoes', indicating there is little difference between the mature plants. However Carl and Wade at Yucca Do believe that there is enough difference to maintain them as separate cultivars. Because there is conflicting opinion as to whether or not they are the same, *A*. 'Sharkskin Shoes' is left as a separate cultivar. The rosette is more densely leaved, and the leaves appear to be narrower and more blue-green.

Agave 'Sharkskin' growing with other succulents along with flowering shrubs and perennials in a Tucson, Arizona, landscape

Agave shawii Engelmann

SHAW AGAVE

A near-perfect specimen of *Agave shawii* north of Colonet along Mexico Highway 1 in Baja California Norte

George Engelmann honored Henry Shaw, founder of the Missouri Botanical Garden, by naming this species after him.

FIELD NOTES

Agave shawii is found in a couple of localities around San Diego, but is very common across the border in Baja California from near sea level to 1650 feet elevation (below 500 meters). At one time the plant was more widespread in San Diego County, but development along the coast and the harvest of plants for potential fiber use decimated the U.S. population. In *Cacti, Agaves, and Yuccas of California and Nevada*, published in 2008, Stephen Ingram noted that plants were introduced into Torrey Pines State Reserve and the Cabrillo National Monument and appeared to be reproducing.

A drive down Mexico Highway 1 along the coastal region in northern Baja California will reveal some otherworldly landscapes, with *Agave shawii* a prominent fixture in several spots. Look for hillsides full of spectacular rosettes starting about six miles north of the town of Colonet. Look for the rare plant that stands out in the field with leaves of light yellow green blushed with orange-red. As you move further south there are more populations of pure *A. shawii*, but as you turn inland at El Rosario and head away from the coast the plants morph into *A. shawii* ssp. *goldmaniana*. These two are not easily distinguished, but Gentry indicated that the flower stalk of ssp. *goldmaniana* is longer than broad, with the bracts smaller and not closely clustered, while the leaves are long acuminate. Compare to the flower stalk of ssp. *shawii*, which is as wide as it is tall, with large, succulent bracts closely clustered together, and short acuminate leaves.

DESCRIPTION

Agave shawii forms small to medium rosettes, ranging from 1–2 feet tall and 1–3 feet across (30–60 by 30–90 cm). In time, the plants can develop trunks that snake along the ground, eventually forming huge colonies up to 6–9 feet (1.8–2.75 meters) across, with branches arising from the leaf axils. Light to dark green, broad, sword-shaped leaves are 8–20 inches long by 3–8 inches wide (20–50 by 8–20 cm). Reddish brown or dark chestnut brown to grayish white marginal teeth are quite variable in size and shape, from short and straight to longer, curving and quite gnarly, leaving wicked bud imprints in the surrounding leaves. The stout, reddish brown to grayish white terminal spine is about 1–1½ inch

(25–38 mm) long, broad at the base, openly grooved above, and decurrent to halfway down the leaf or as a continuous margin for the whole length.

In the spring, a mature specimen of *Agave shawii* will send up its stout, 6½–13 foot (2–4 meter) tall, branched flower stalk that is shrouded in thick, purplish bracts and topped by ten to fourteen colorful side branches packed with reddish to purplish flower buds that eventually open to reveal bright golden yellow, 3–4 inch (7.5–10 cm) long flowers.

CULTURE

Plants have proven hardy to at least the low 20s F (−5 to −6 C), and should be hardy in zones 9a–11. They should make great landscape specimens throughout much of the Pacific coast states. They can be grown without damage in the cool, coastal and hot, interior low elevation zone, in most parts of Tucson in the mid-elevation zone, and in protected microclimates in much of the rest of the mid-elevation zone.

This is a very slow growing species, and will take many years to reach a mature size, so start with larger plants when planting in the landscape. Once established, the plants are low-water-using but will respond to supplemental summer water in the mid-elevation and hot, interior, low

elevation zones. Because it is adapted to winter rainfall and summer drought, take care not to give it too much summer water; just apply frequently enough to get the plants through the summer heat. Avoid letting water remain on leaves overnight as this can lead to rot.

Plants grow well in full sun in the coastal, low elevation zone and in the mid-elevation zone during the cooler months of autumn through spring, but relish a bit of afternoon shade in the summer, especially in the very hot, interior, low elevation zone. Plants do not require any special soil type, but excellent drainage is imperative to reduce the risk of anthracnose, a disease caused by the fungus *Colletotrichum*. The typical symptom for this fungus is the formation of concentric rings of black or reddish brown spots on the leaves.

LANDSCAPE VALUE

Agave shawii grows naturally with chaparral vegetation, and mixes nicely with low-water-using shrubs such as *Calliandra californica*, *Dalea bicolor*, *Leucophyllum* species, *Rhus integrifolia*, *Rosmarinus officinalis*, *Ruellia peninsularis*, *Salvia clevelandii*, *Simmondsia chinensis*, *Sophora secundiflora*, and *Vauquelinia californica*.

A specimen of *Agave shawii* growing within sight of the Pacific Ocean near Eréndira in Baja California Norte

Agave shrevei Gentry

SHREVE AGAVE

The large rosette of *Agave shrevei* ssp. *magna* is easily recognizable.

Forrest Shreve, an early twentieth century ecologist in the southwestern United States, was honored by Howard Scott Gentry in the naming of this notable species.

FIELD NOTES

With three subspecies, *Agave shrevei* can be found in several places between 3000 and 6000 feet (900–1800 meters) elevation in the Sierra Madre Occidental in the Mexican states of Sonora and Chihuahua. Some fine specimens of ssp. *shrevei* can be seen on the hills around the Yécora area in east-central Sonora as you drive along Mexico Highway 16 from Hermosillo to the Cascada de Baseseachi in Chihuahua. Look for plants with exceptionally nice teeth and terminal spines as these make the best bud imprints.

Plants of ssp. *magna* can be seen as you continue along Mexico Highway 16 past the Cascada de Baseseachi and towards Ciudad Chihuahua; this subspecies tends to be larger with wide-spreading leaves and a more open rosette than ssp. *shrevei*. Subspecies *matapensis* plants can be found in the mountains near the town of Matape in east-central Sonora, and form some of the nicest plants, with beautiful, rounded rosettes.

In some parts of Sonora and Chihuahua, *Agave shrevei* grows intermingled with *A. wocomahi* from which it can be a little difficult to separate when not in flower. However, it is readily separable with flowers.

DESCRIPTION

Agave shrevei is a small to medium-sized species with individual rosettes reaching 1¼–2 feet tall and 1½–3 feet across (40–60 by 45–90 cm). Ovate to lanceolate, light gray to glaucous blue leaves are 8–24 inches long by 3–4 (rarely 7) inches wide (20–60 by 8–10 cm [rarely 18 cm]) and have a long taper to the tip. Dark brown, curved marginal teeth are small to large, terminating the mammillate bumps along the edges. The stout, brown, needle-like terminal spine is about 1–2 inches (2.5–5 cm) long.

Come summer, when the plant is the right age or size, your prized specimen will send forth an 8–16 foot (2.5–5 m) tall, branched flower stalk with several side branches, each branch holding small clusters of 2½ inch (6.5 cm) long, light green to pale yellow flowers that will be abuzz with bee and hummingbird activity during the day.

CULTURE

All three subspecies are hardy in zones 9a–11, and are especially good landscape plants in the cool, coastal and hot, interior low elevation southwestern U.S. zone, while ssp. *magna* and *matapensis* are fine for zones 8b–11, and are hardy in the mid-elevation southwestern U.S. zone. All subspecies can be used as landscape plants in much of the Pacific coast states except the cold and very wet parts. They should be fine along the Gulf coast and most of Florida, but marginal inland. This is a slow growing species, and will take many years to reach a good size, so start with larger plants when planting in the landscape.

Once established, these are low-water-using, but will respond to supplemental summer water in the mid-elevation and hot, interior, low elevation zones. Plants grow well in full sun in the coastal, low elevation zone and middle elevation zone, but relish a bit of afternoon shade in the very hot, interior, low elevation zone. These are not picky about the soil type as long as there is adequate drainage.

ABOVE The greenish flowers of *Agave shrevei*

OPPOSITE The light blue-gray leaves of *Agave shrevei* stand out against the rocks.

LANDSCAPE VALUE

Agave shrevei makes a great specimen plant, and those with really gnarly bud prints should be used where they can be seen on a regular basis. Mix with cactus and other succulents, and with perennial wildflowers and small shrubs that provide seasonal color. Some perfectly compatible flowering plants for the desert regions would include *Anisacanthus quadrifidus*, *Calliandra eriophylla*, *Chrysactinia mexicana*, *Ericameria laricifolia*, *Penstemon* species, and *Salvia greggii*.

Agave striata Zuccarini

ESPADIN, NEEDLE LEAF AGAVE

Perfectly rounded spheres of *Agave striata* growing near Miquihuana in southern Tamaulipas

The species name is derived from the Latin *stria*, meaning furrow or steak—which accurately describes the thin, longitudinal furrows in the leaves.

FIELD NOTES

Agave striata has a widespread distribution in eastern and central Mexico, occupying elevations between 2200 and 7000 feet (670–2100 meters). Leaf color is extremely variable and plants can be found with light to medium-dark green, blue-green, or silvery blue leaves, and even bicolored leaves that are mostly purplish red with green near the base.

Driving just about anywhere in eastern Mexico will almost certainly result in coming across this species; try heading down Mexico Highway 45 in Zacatecas and look on low-lying hills with limestone soil. Some spectacularly large clumps 8–10 feet (2.4–3 meters) across can be seen standing guard over broad valleys.

Some of the coolest forms have to be the really silvery blue-leaved plants mixed in with green-leaved plants just east of Doctor Arroyo in Nuevo León.

On Mexico Highway 85 about twelve miles northwest of Pachuca, keep an eye out for the bizarrely branching form of *Fouquieria splendens* growing on pure limestone outcrops, and you will probably spot some specimens of *Agave striata* with tricolored leaves that are green at the base, changing to pinkish red and finally a deeper reddish purple at the tip. If you wander around looking at these beauties, you might want to wear a full covering of leather motorcycle clothes to prevent ripping open tender flesh in the event that you stumble on the sharp-edged rock.

On the road to Guadalcázar in San Luis Potosí, I saw a relatively dwarf form growing on chalky limestone soil. The plants there top out at about 1 foot tall by 1 foot across (30 by 30 cm) and form small clumps to only 2½–3 feet (76–90 cm) across.

DESCRIPTION

With wide diversity within the species, one could not blame *Agave striata* for being somewhat schizophrenic. Individually, each form is distinctive, but collectively they are readily identified as one conglomeration. It is an offsetting type, and although there are exceptions, the individual rosettes generally reach a maximum size of about 1½ feet tall and 2 feet across (45 by 60 cm). There are dwarf forms that are quite shy

ABOVE *Agave striata* with purplish red and green leaves growing near Pachuca in Hidalgo

RIGHT Reddish purple stamens pop out against the greenish petals of *Agave striata*, attracting bees to the flowers.

about bulking up and stay at about 1 foot by 1¼ feet (30 by 38 cm). Even though some of the largest rosettes will measure 3½ feet across (1 meter) from leaf tip to leaf tip, the effective garden size feels smaller because of the openness at the leaf tips. Small plants grow out of the leaf axils of this clumper, forming small to large, very dense masses anywhere from 2 feet to nearly 8 feet (0.6–2.4 meters) across!

To illustrate the variation, one need only look at the leaf color which can range from light green to medium green and is sometimes flushed with red or purplish red near the base; some plants have leaves that are nearly completely red or purplish red, while others even have silvery leaves. Regardless of color, most of these leaves are linear in shape, with longitudinal striations running along the length, 9–20 inches long by ⅕–⅖ inch across (25–50 cm by 0.5–1 cm), widest at or below the middle. They are thick, four-angled in cross section and quite stiff and rigid, with minute, evenly spaced teeth along the margin; the terminal spine is ⅖–2 inches (1–5 cm) long and quite lethal to the unsuspecting handler.

The narrow, unbranched inflorescence reaches 5–8 feet (1.5–2.5 m) tall and is covered with greenish yellow or, more commonly, reddish to purplish, showy flowers measuring 1–1½ inches (25–38 mm) long.

CULTURE

Hailing from the cold Chihuahuan Desert Region, *Agave striata* is generally undamaged when temperatures dip to 0 degrees F (–18 C) and can be grown throughout the Pacific coast states, across the southern states, into the southeast, and up the Atlantic coast at least to North Carolina. They make nice landscape plants in all southwestern U.S. zones as well as in zones 7a–11. Although individual rosettes have a moderate growth rate, achieving a decent size five or six years after planting in the ground, many years are needed for large clusters to form. Even though they are drought tolerant, plants will benefit from and respond to some supplemental summer water. Thoroughly soak the root zone, allowing the soil to dry before soaking again.

Grow these pincushions in full sun no matter what zone you are in. In habitat, these plants typically grow on thin soil over limestone or in pockets of sandy soil in limestone slabs, but they will tolerate almost any soil type in the landscape.

LANDSCAPE VALUE

Plants can be used to eventually cover a large expanse of ground if given ample room to develop. Mix with flowering perennials or low drought-tolerant shrubs. Use in a wild, desert or xeric garden with other Chihuahuan Desert plants like big yuccas and small shrubs such as *Chrysactinia mexicana*, *Salvia greggii*, or *Scutellaria suffrutescens*. Some really interesting combinations can be made with flowering perennials like *Baileya multiradiata*, *Conoclinium dissectum*, *Penstemon* species, and *Tetraneuris acaulis*.

Look for the plants with nicely colored leaves and use them for the form, color and texture that make them stand out in a xeric landscape.

A green-leaved form of *Agave striata* on the road to Guadalcázar in San Luis Potosí.

Agave stricta Salm-Dyck

SEA URCHIN AGAVE

The rounded spheres of *Agave stricta* look like misplaced sea urchins.

The tight balls of leaves were the inspiration for the species name *stricta*, based on the Latin *strict* which means tight or drawn together.

FIELD NOTES

The most accessible spot for viewing *Agave stricta* is near Tehuacán in Puebla, Mexico, where the plants can be found growing between 5500 and 6000 feet (1675–1800 meters) elevation. This once-pristine desert area is now frequently used as a trash dump; however, the plants are always spectacular and it is well worth seeking out the best angle for pictures while avoiding the trash strewn around.

The individual rosettes have over a hundred leaves and make dense, perfectly rounded spheres and large clusters sprawling across the desert floor. Lower leaves on some of the clusters will turn a deep purplish red or striking orange-brown under the stress of summer while the newer leaves remain bright green. This combination of color adds a bit of zing to the surrounding desert vegetation.

DESCRIPTION

With its hundreds of pointy, needle-like leaves, these dense, rounded spheres look like giant sea urchins invading the land. A safe size for the individual spheres is around 1½–2½ feet by 1½–2½ feet (45–75 by 45–75 cm), with ancient, multi-headed clumps reaching 8–10 feet (2.4–3 meters) across. Individual leaves are bright green to yellowish green, sometimes flushed with red or purple, narrowly linear, shaped a bit like curved sewing needles, and measure anywhere from 10–20 inches long and less than ½ inch wide (25–50 by 0.8–1 cm). The leaf margins are minutely serrated, much like a hacksaw blade—and they can inflict similar damage to the careless handler. The terminal spine is not long, just less than 1 inch (1–2 cm), yet it is needle-sharp and breaks off easily, so care should be taken when handling the plant.

The unbranched, 5–8 foot (1.5–2.5 meter) tall inflorescence usually begins to emerge in summer and is generally filled with dark red-purple to purplish red, 1 inch (2.5 cm) long flowers that fill the upper half of the stalk come late summer or early autumn.

CULTURE

Information on the hardiness of *Agave stricta* is conflicting. Mary Irish stated that plants were killed at 23 degrees F (–5 C) in Essex, England, yet other plants survived 17 degrees F (–8 C) in northern California and

A large colony of *Agave stricta* sprawls across the desert southwest of Tehuacán in Puebla.

A rosette of *Agave stricta*, showing the uniform shape and hint of purplish red at the ends of the leaves

10 degrees F (–12 C) in El Paso, Texas, with no damage. She speculated that this was due to either clonal variation or sensitivity to the wet climate of England. However, northern California can also be quite wet during winter. I suspect that the discrepancy is due to misidentification of the plants, and that those that survived the lower temperatures were actually the closely related *A. striata*, a hardy Chihuahuan Desert species that looks similar to and can be difficult to distinguish from *A. stricta*. To be on the safe side, consider them to be zone 10a–11 plants that are frost sensitive and need protection when winter lows start to dip

below freezing. They can be used as landscape plants only in frost-free areas of California and Florida. *Agave stricta* can be an excellent potted specimen anywhere, as long as it is protected from winter frost.

Plants have a moderate growth rate, and in most parts of the southwestern United States they are best grown in containers that can be moved under protection when frost hits. *Agave stricta* is a low to moderate water user, getting by on being watered once or twice a month during winter but needing supplemental water once a week in the heat of summer. Plants seem to relish a bit of shade during the dog days of summer, especially in the hot, interior, low elevation and mid-elevation zones in Arizona, when summer highs top 100 degrees F (38 C).

As with most other species, place *Agave stricta* in a soil with fast drainage and a neutral to slightly alkaline pH.

LANDSCAPE VALUE

With its highly sculptural form and tight, ball-like rosettes consisting of numerous, needle-like leaves, *Agave stricta* makes a great specimen plant whether in a large, decorative container or in the ground. In areas where space and frost are not issues, plants can be grown with a variety of low-water-using perennials and small shrubs. In the cool, coastal low elevation zone, try mixing in some *Calylophus hartwegii*, *Conoclinium dissectum*, *Eriogonum fasciculatum*, *Polemonium caeruleum*, *Salvia dorrii*, *Salvia leucantha*, *Santolina rosmarinifolia*, *Thalictrum aquilegifolium*, *Trichostema lanatum*, or *Zinnia grandiflora*.

Agave titanota Gentry

ALABASTER WHITE AGAVE

Bluish white leaf color is the classic look for *Agave titanota*.

Howard Scott Gentry used the chalky white leaves as the basis for this species name; chalky is one meaning of the word *titan*, from Greek mythology.

FIELD NOTES

Looking for the classic whitish blue-leaved plants of *Agave titanota* at the original locality involves making your way to the town of San Antonio Nanahuatipam in northern Oaxaca, Mexico, and then hiring a local guide to lead you across the desert and through riverbeds to the hiking trail. There you must park your four-wheel-drive vehicle and make the nearly hour-long hike to the hill of sharp, fleshing-ripping limestone where you can scramble around looking at these beauties that occur from about 3200 to 4000 feet (975–1200 meters) elevation.

DESCRIPTION

Agave titanota is a solitary type, reaching about 1½–2 feet tall and 2–3½ feet across (45–60 by 60–100 cm). Although Gentry described the leaves as "alabaster white", I found that leaves at the type locality varied from light glaucous blue to bluish white. The leaf shape is linear-ovate to lance-ovate, with the broadest part near the middle. They measure 12–20 inches long and about 4–5 inches wide (30–50 by 10–12 cm), tapering to the stout terminal spine. The broadly conical, deeply grooved spine is dark brown to nearly black on new leaves, turning to ash gray on older leaves. The continuous, woody margin holds small to large teeth that create intriguing bud prints.

In habitat, the slender, 10–12 foot (3–3.6 meter) tall, unbranched flower stalk appears in autumn. The upper half is covered with 2 inch (50 cm) long, yellow flowers frequently tinged with a flush of purple.

CULTURE

This Oaxacan native is hardy to the high 20s f (−2 to −3 c) and is considered a zone 9b–11 plant, though it might be able to withstand lower temperatures if kept dry during the winter. *Agave titanota* can be grown as a landscape plant in frost-free regions of California and Florida, and possibly the hot, interior low elevation southwestern U.S. zone.

Experience has shown that *Agave titanota* is a moderately slow grower, taking several years to achieve mature, flowering size, and can last for many years. Average annual rainfall in the Rancho Tambor area is about

RIGHT A cluster of several young *Agave titanota* plants growing on the limestone soil at Rancho Tambor in northern Oaxaca

OPPOSITE Green-leaved plants, which resemble those being called *Agave* 'FO76' and *Agave* 'Sierra Mixteca', found growing in northern Oaxaca

15 inches (38 cm) with the majority falling from May through September, so *A. titanota* plants will need some supplemental water when the weather really heats up. Plants can be grown in full sun or very light shade, though they will need to be watered a bit more frequently in the hot, interior low elevation zone.

Plants grow naturally on cliffs and ledges composed of sharp ridged limestone, but they will grow in dry, rocky desert soil. Plant them directly in the ground without any amendments unless you have a heavy clay soil, in which case you might want to put them in raised planters.

They seem to be a favorite target of wildlife, as evidenced by leaves getting nibbled by woodrats, packrats and kangaroo rats.

LANDSCAPE VALUE

Agave titanota can be used as a landscape plant in the low elevation zone, and would look great planted alongside xeric wildflowers and small shrubs. Try using *Baileya multiradiata, Chrysactinia mexicana, Conoclinium dissectum, Glandularia gooddingii, Lupinus sparsiflorus, Penstemon* species, *Salvia greggii, Tetraneuris acaulis, Thymophylla pentachaeta,* or *Viguiera stenoloba.* In the cooler, coastal zone, try using *Coreopsis grandiflora, Santolina rosmarinifolia,* and *Trichostema lanatum.*

TAXONOMIC NOTES

When Gentry described *Agave titanota* in 1982, he based his description on the plants found at Rancho Tambor which consistently have bluish white to glaucous blue leaves. As horticulturists have explored more areas in northern Oaxaca, more populations of plants that resemble *A. titanota* have been found. Some of these plants have bluish leaves while others have light green to dark green leaves. In the 1980s Felipe Otero collected seed in the Sierra Mixteca from plants that look similar to those with green leaves. Those green-leaved plants have been sold under the names *A.* 'FO76' and *A.* 'Sierra Mixteca'. Plants with green leaves have been found growing alongside those with blue leaves in Oaxaca, leading some agave fanatics to speculate that *A. titanota* might be more variable than Gentry originally thought. With their green leaves, the plants known as *A.* 'FO76' and *A.* 'Sierra Mixteca' certainly have a different look horticulturally, and whether or not they are lumped together botanically, the names ought to be maintained as cultivar names to distinguish them from their bluish-white-leaved brethren.

Agave titanota belongs to the group Marginatae. David Bogler, a taxonomist best known for his work on *Dasylirion*, studied the DNA of this group but was unable to find a definitive molecular marker that could be used for species recognition. Howard Scott Gentry indicated that there are "some poorly defined specific boundaries in large variable intergrading complexes, such as that of *Agave ghiesbreghtii-Agave kerchovei* and *Agave obscura-Agave horrida*." He went on to suggest that these complexes need more study, with attention paid to their leaf anatomy, chemistry, cytology, and other characteristics. Now it seems that *A. titanota* should be included in a comprehensive taxonomic study of these species complexes.

Agave toumeyana Trelease

TOUMEY AGAVE

Agave toumeyana var. *bella* along the Barnhardt Trail in the Mazatzal Mountains in central Arizona

Agave toumeyana will hybridize with *A. chrysantha* to form the attractive *A.* ×*arizonica*.

FIELD NOTES

Quite a few different trails begin in the Barnhardt Trail parking area in the Mazatzal Mountains south of Payson off of Arizona State Route 87. Locate the correct one, and take a leisurely hike west up into the mountains. While on the trail, look to the rocky outcrops and you are likely to see some very nice clumps of *A. toumeyana* var. *bella* sunning themselves among the lichen-covered boulders. These cute, perfectly symmetrical rosettes develop offsets and form clusters up to 2 feet (60 cm) in diameter. If you visit in the heat of summer, chances are good that you will find plants in bloom.

Agave toumeyana is found only in central Arizona, from 2000 to 5000 feet (600–1500 meters) elevation, growing on limestone and volcanic rock with high-desert vegetation, into chaparral, and even creeping into the lower elevation pine tree habitats. *Agave toumeyana* var. *bella* is found between 2625 and 5575 feet (800–1700 meters) elevation in the Sierra Ancha, New River Mountains, Mazatzal Mountains, Bradshaw Mountains, and the Wet Beaver Creek drainage in central Arizona.

DESCRIPTION

Agave toumeyana is an offsetting species, and while individual rosettes are only 6–16 inches tall and about 8–24 inches across (15–40 by 20–60 cm), they can form large, dense colonies. Some of these clusters can become quite old and even form fairy rings as the central rosettes die out over time. Light green to dark green, 6–18 inch long by ³/₅–⁴/₅ inch wide (15–46 by 1.5–2 cm), narrow leaves are straight or slightly curved and shaped somewhat like the sabers used extensively in the Napoleonic Wars in the early 1800s. The leaves have prominent white bud printing on both surfaces, and lack marginal teeth, instead having thin, white fibers along the edges, while the conical terminal spine is less than 1 inch (2.5 cm) long.

The slender, unbranched, 5–10 foot (1.5–3 meter) tall flower stalk appears in late spring to early summer, and is covered with 1 inch (2.5 cm) long, greenish yellow flowers in the upper one third of the shaft.

Variety *bella* differs in that the rosette is smaller and more compact, reaching about 4–8 inches tall and about 6–12 inches across (10–20 by 15–30 cm) with dense white bud printing on the leaves. Some growers

ABOVE A small cluster of *Agave toumeyana* var. *bella* growing among lichen-covered rocks in the Mazatzal Mountains in central Arizona

LEFT The dense rosette of decorative leaves on *Agave toumeyana* var. *bella*

are busy selecting forms that are the smallest and most densely covered with white bud printing on the leaves.

CULTURE

This central Arizona native is hardy to at least 10 degrees F (–12 C), is considered a zone 8a–11 plant, and can be planted in the ground throughout much of the Pacific coast states and along the Gulf coast if kept dry during the winter. However, variety *bella* is hardier and can be grown outdoors in places as cold as Santa Fe, New Mexico, and Raleigh, North Carolina, as well as in all southwestern U.S. elevation zones.

Agave toumeyana, which can last for many years, is a slow grower and will take several years to achieve mature, flowering size, eventually developing large clusters. It is found in areas that receive anywhere from 15 to 25 inches (38–64 cm) of annual rainfall that is split nearly evenly between winter and summer. Plants can be grown in full sun throughout the southwestern United States, although they will need to be watered a bit more frequently in the hot, interior low elevation zone than they will in the other zones.

These are found growing naturally on open, rocky ledges composed of limestone or volcanic rock, and will grow in dry, rocky desert soil. Plant them directly in the ground without any amendments unless you have a heavy clay soil, in which case it is a good idea to add some sand or rock. Plants definitely benefit from being in raised planters in high rainfall areas.

LANDSCAPE VALUE

Being an extra small to small species, *Agave toumeyana* is best used in a small landscape where the plants will not be lost among large plants, or in an area that is highly visible from a patio or entry. Try mixing with annuals or small perennials, for splashes of periodic color. Some great companion plants in the hot, interior, low elevation zone and the mid-elevation zone would include *Baileya multiradiata*, *Calylophus hartwegii*, *Conoclinium dissectum*, *Lupinus sparsiflorus*, *Penstemon* species, *Tetraneuris acaulis*, *Thymophylla pentachaeta*, and *Zinnia grandiflora*. In the cooler, coastal zone, try using *Coreopsis grandiflora*, *Santolina rosmarinifolia*, and *Trichostema lanatum*.

Agave utahensis Engelmann

UTAH AGAVE

The red soil in Red Rock Canyon Natural Conservation Area is a
perfect backdrop for *Agave utahensis* var. *nevadensis*.

Although named for the state of Utah, this agave is also found in the adjacent states of Nevada, Arizona, and California.

FIELD NOTES

Agave utahensis has the most northerly distribution, being found in northern Arizona, southeastern California, southern Nevada, and southern Utah from 2000 to 8250 feet (600–2500 meters) elevation. There are two subspecies (ssp. *kaibabensis* and ssp. *utahensis*) and three varieties, with the two most sought-after varieties being var. *eborispina* and var. *nevadensis*. Both of these varieties are found in southern Nevada and adjacent southern California.

At Red Rock Canyon National Conservation Area just west of Las Vegas in southern Nevada, I found *Agave utahensis* var. *nevadensis* growing off the beaten path, tucked in among large boulders. To find these plants, you almost have to know where they grow, or visit in the summer when the flower stalks are visible above the boulders. Many of the plants fit the classic description for var. *nevadensis*—smaller rosettes, glaucous bluish gray leaves, and shorter, brownish white terminal spine—while others seem to want to become var. *eborispina*, with greener leaves, stouter teeth, and a longer terminal spine. I also visited another population of var. *nevadensis* at the crest of the pass in the Spring Mountains along Nevada State Route 160 between Las Vegas and the UFO hotspot of Pahrump. This spot is only thirteen miles by jet pack from the Red Rock Canyon plants, and not surprisingly, the plants there fit the description for var. *nevadensis*.

Agave utahensis var. *eborispina* can be seen in several spots in the mountains around Las Vegas; I have been up both Kyle Canyon and Lee Canyon in the Charleston Mountains off of Highway 95 northwest of the city. It takes a bit of hiking around to find them, but once you do, you will be rewarded with some awesome-looking plants. Some of the nicest plants of var. *eborispina* I have seen are in Peek-A-Boo Canyon, which is north of Las Vegas and about twenty-nine miles as the crow flies from Red Rock Canyon National Conservation Area. Make sure you have emptied your bladder before you travel the seventeen miles of bumpy dirt road to Peek-A-Boo Canyon. The majority of plants there look like classic var. *eborispina*, with greener leaves, larger, white teeth, and a slightly longer, terminal spine colored a mix of white and rusty, chocolate brown and decurrent down to the first two or three pairs of teeth. Some of the terminal spines on these plants are quite wiggly, and

ABOVE *Agave utahensis* var. *eborispina* on sharp limestone in the Nopah Range in southeastern California

LEFT *Agave utahensis* var. *nevadensis* in the pebbly limestone of the Spring Mountains in southern Nevada

look as though they came from another planet. Some of the larger specimens of var. *eborispina* are found in the Nopah Range of southeastern California. Because the plants here grow on steep slopes of sharp limestone, you might want to wear full body armor or thick leather clothing when scrambling around in search of the best plants to photograph.

You may be wondering why the big deal about whether or not the plants look more like var. *nevadensis* or var. *eborispina*; however, once you see the long, often squiggly terminal spine of the latter, you will be stuck on that one forever!

DESCRIPTION

Regardless of the subspecies or variety, *Agave utahensis* is an attractive plant. Rosettes of ssp. *utahensis*, including both var. *eborispina* and var. *nevadensis*, will reach about 6–12 inches tall by 6–18 inches across (15–30 by 15–45 cm), while rosettes of ssp. *kaibabensis* are larger, reaching 8–24 inches tall by 16–39 inches across (20–60 by 40–100 cm). *Agave utahensis* ssp. *kaibabensis* is solitary, but var. *eborispina* and var. *nevadensis* will produce identical little clones around the base of the mama plant, and form clusters to 18–24 inches (45–60 cm) across. This can take quite a while, however, so plan on living in one spot for several years to get the full effect of this wonderful, wickedly spined plant. The distinctiveness of the two looks created by the extremes of the varieties cannot be emphasized enough, and collectors ought to look for the most bizarre and intriguing forms.

Variety *nevadensis* is grown primarily for its perfectly symmetrical rosette of intense blue-green leaves, with the small teeth and relatively short (when compared to variety *eborispina*) terminal spine that are almost afterthoughts rather than significant components of the overall look. On the other hand, the large, coarse teeth resembling those used by sharks to rip into flesh, and the long, often quite wiggly and squiggly terminal spines are the main features that give var. *eborispina* its appeal.

The leaf color varies from the intense blue-green of var. *nevadensis* to the darker green of var. *eborispina*. The teeth also vary dramatically, the small, almost insignificant teeth of var. *nevadensis* to the large, crosscut, ripping saw-like teeth of var. *eborispina*. Throw in the long, squiggly terminal spine and *Agave utahensis* var. *eborispina* is one of the most attractive miniature species.

The inflorescence varies from spicate to racemose to narrowly paniculate, reaching a height of 6–13 feet (2–4 meters), and is loaded

A long, straight-spined plant of *Agave utahensis* var. *eborispina*

with 1 inch (2.5 cm) long, yellowish flowers between late winter and summer.

CULTURE

Agave utahensis is one of the hardiest agaves being grown. However, it is winter wet rather than cold that limits where it can be planted in the ground. Plants are reliably hardy in zones 7a–11, though David Salman of Santa Fe Greenhouses grows this one outdoors and indicates that it is hardy in zone 5a as long as it is kept dry. Plants can be grown in all elevation zones throughout the southwestern United States as long as they are kept very dry in winter weather. Otherwise, the plants should be grown as prized potted specimens and kept under cover.

The growth rate is quite slow and the plants will be around for many years, especially when the offsetting component is taken into account. Occurring in areas that receive about 4–5 inches (10–13 cm) of annual

A young, bluish green plant of *Agave utahensis* var. *eborispina*

rainfall, they are quite drought tolerant. In fact, too much water, rather than too little, can cause their demise.

Plants in the ground should be grown in full sun from morning until early afternoon, at which time they should get a reprieve from the sun. Those in pots can tolerate at least a bit of afternoon shade in the hot, interior, low elevation zone and in other areas that routinely experience summer highs over 100 degrees F (38 C).

For plants being grown in containers, use a soil with absolutely perfect drainage, and monitor the frequency of watering to minimize excess water around the roots. Plants in the ground are fine in most desert soils as long as drainage is good and watering is kept to a minimum.

Did I mention that it is critical to keep the soil from remaining wet for a prolonged period, in order to minimize the potential for rotting the roots?

With its attractive looks, *Agave utahensis* is probably best grown in a decorative container and placed where it will be highly visible. Plants can be used in the ground, but seem to get lost if the area is too large.

The long, wiggly terminal spine of var. *eborispina* makes for a truly unusual effect on a full-grown rosette, looking like a spiky hairdo on a cartoon character.

TAXONOMIC NOTES

Howard Scott Gentry separated *Agave utahensis* into ssp. *kaibabensis* (from the Kaibab Plateau in northern Arizona), var. *nevadensis*, and var. *eborispina,* based on the length and color of the terminal spine—variety *nevadensis* having a brown to whitish terminal spine measuring 1½–3 inches (4–8 cm) long, and var. *eborispina* having an ivory white one measuring 4 inches nearly 8 inches (10–20 cm) long! In *Flora of North America*, Reveal and Hodgson clarified the classification, recognizing two subspecies: ssp. *kaibabensis* and ssp. *utahensis*. They subdivided the latter into var. *utahensis*, var. *nevadensis*, and var. *eborispina*. When shopping for these plants, be sure to pick the one you like the most, regardless of the subspecies to which it belongs.

Agave victoriae-reginae T. Moore

QUEEN VICTORIA AGAVE

The most compact plants of *Agave victoriae-reginae* are highly decorative.

English gardener/botanist Thomas Moore paid his respects to the alluring Queen Victoria by naming this regal species in her honor.

FIELD NOTES

Agave victoriae-reginae is a Chihuahuan Desert species found in few yet widely separated localities. It occurs in at least six spots, all between 4000 and 5000 feet (1200–1500 meters) elevation. This limited distribution apparently led to its inclusion on the CITES (Convention on International Trade in Endangered Species) list, which places restrictions on the collection and trade of the plants. The most famous locality is in Huasteca Canyon outside of Monterrey, Mexico, where plants occur by the tens of thousands, with some attractive specimens to be seen. To get to the best plants in Huasteca, one must negotiate the streets of Monterrey, and then travel beyond the pavement along a dirt road that has not seen the blade of a road grader in many years. Easier to drive to is an area called Cañon Ventanillas along Mexico Highway 30 in Coahuila. Some plants are seen growing on the vertical, limestone walls on the east side of the road, but others can be found below those walls and more easily photographed.

DESCRIPTION

Although this species exhibits quite a bit of variability as witnessed by the eight "rather well marked forms" listed by Breitung in 1960, it is still easily recognizable by the dense, generally single rosette of light green to dark green leaves, each lovingly hand-painted by the agave gods with decorative white bud prints. In cultivation, plants are either solitary or will produce few to many offsets, especially when young. Depending on the form, the rosette will grow to 9–15 inches tall by 10–24 inches across (23–38 by 25–60 cm). Thick, rounded to keeled leaves are 4–8 inches long by 1½–2 inches wide (10–20 by 4–5 cm) and toothless along the margin, instead having a continuous white border. On some plants, the dark brown to black terminal spine is small and nearly invisible, escaping notice until it stabs the careless handler, while in others it is quite long, shouting out a fair warning before impaling tender flesh. In summer, a 10–16 foot (3–5 meter) tall, spicate inflorescence, packed with 1 inch (2.5 cm) long, yellowish green, reddish, or purplish flowers, reaches toward the sky. Striking as they may be, none of these forms even remotely compares to the lovely Queen Victoria herself, who reigned from 1837 to 1901.

CULTURE

Plants are known to have withstood winter lows down into single digits F (−12 to −13 C) in Rhode Island and North Carolina without damage, and can probably be considered zone 7b–11 plants. They can be grown in all southwestern U.S. zones without fear of damage.

This is one of the slowest growing species, taking up to twenty or twenty-five years to reach flowering size, but then you are rewarded with a tall stalk of reddish or purplish, rarely yellowish flowers. Once established, plants are quite drought tolerant, but those growing in the hot, low elevation zone will look better if the root zone is given a thorough soaking once every ten to fourteen days. Plants in the mid-elevation zone will relish a thorough soaking once every fourteen to twenty-one days when temperatures creep up above 90 degrees F (32 C) during the day.

Established plants of *Agave victoriae-reginae* can tolerate full sun in all zones except the hot, interior, low desert and the hotter parts of the mid-elevation zone where they will appreciate a bit of afternoon shade in the summer. Young plants especially will benefit from summer shade in the mid- and low elevation zones. Plants are accustomed to growing on steep walls of limestone or very dry, gritty soils, so they should be put in an area that has impeccable drainage.

LANDSCAPE VALUE

The small size of *Agave victoriae-reginae* lends itself to use in either small spaces or mass plantings in larger areas. Tuck several of these in with seasonally flowering perennials to give colorful interest at various times of the year. Plant several in a raised planter, mix with cactus and other succulents, or use in large decorative pots. Try to collect as many forms as possible by searching through blocks of seed-grown plants.

For a truly interesting effect, mass together as many different forms, in various sizes, as you can find.

TAXONOMIC NOTES

Of the eight forms listed by Breitung, only the one he called forma *nickelsii* (now considered a distinct species: *Agave nickelsiae*) is found growing as a separate population in the wild. All of the others can be found mixed together in the Huasteca Canyon locality. Although a couple of forms have persisted in horticulture, most seem to have been selected as

One often finds *Agave victoriae-reginae* growing on the edges of steep rock outcrops in northern Mexico.

ABOVE A dense rosette of *Agave victoriae-reginae* growing on rock near Cañon Ventanillas

RIGHT The terminal spine on *Agave victoriae-reginae* is usually quite small, but still very sharp.

oddball types from a batch of seedlings, and have fallen from cultivation and subsequent horticultural literature.

Several variegated clones of *Agave victoriae-reginae* have made their way into the horticulture trade. The most popular ones have either yellow or white margins which contrast with the deep green central portion of the leaves. The intensity of variegation varies from one clone to another, and seems to also be affected by the age of the plants, and quite possibly the growing conditions as well. The culture for these variegated forms is the same as for the non-variegated plants. The following variegated cultivars are among the more popular ones, and are sometimes available at specialty nurseries. With time, each forms perfectly symmetrical rosettes to about 10–12 inches tall and 12–18 inches across (25–30 by 30–45 cm).

Agave victoriae-reginae 'Kazo Bana'

'Kazo Bano' differs from the species in having broad butterscotch-gold margins on the leaves. This is sometimes sold as 'Golden Princess', but 'Kazo Bana' is the valid name for this cultivar which was named by Yoshimichi Hirose, a noted variegated plant enthusiast from Japan.

Agave victoriae-reginae 'Snowburst'

'Snowburst' differs from the species in having broad stripes of creamy white along the margins of the dark green leaves, and noticeable terminal spines.

Agave victoriae-reginae 'White Rhino'

'White Rhino' differs from the species in having broad stripes of white along the leaf margins as well as very short terminal spines.

Agave vilmoriniana Berger

OCTOPUS AGAVE

The truly unique look of *Agave vilmoriniana* gave rise to the common name of octopus agave.

This unique plant was named by Alwyn Berger in honor of M. Maurice de Vilmorin (1849–1918), who was instrumental in developing the National Arboretum of Les Barres just south of Paris.

FIELD NOTES

Driving along the twisting, turning roads through the foothills and steep-walled canyons of eastern Sonora, you can spot this amazing cliff dweller clinging to vertical rock faces between 2000 and 5500 feet (600–1675 meters) elevation, and from a distance you might think that aliens have landed and are advancing over the most rugged terrain by virtue of sticky pads on their deeply guttered appendages. Upon closer inspection, you notice these aliens are actually plants, and possibly you might ponder how and why they end up in some of the situations in which they find themselves. Occasionally plants are seen on the open, gentler slopes, but the ones with the droopiest, most twisted leaves and the most interesting forms are those on the steep, virtually inaccessible rock faces. Take Mexico Highway 16 east out of Hermosillo, through the foothills of the Sierra Madre Occidental towards the town of Yécora. As you snake your way along the narrow, two-lane road, dodging potholes and oncoming cars and trucks, you come to realize that somehow the term *highway* just does not seem appropriate. While avoiding the potholes and oncoming traffic, remember to occasionally look for these beautiful plants growing precariously on the steep canyon walls and vertical road-cuts, and envision creating a large canyon in your yard peppered with these marvelous plants and their long, drooping leaves.

DESCRIPTION

Octopus agave is a moderately large, solitary rosette, usually reaching 3–4 feet tall and 4–6 feet across (0.9–1.2 by 1.2–1.8 meters), and is noted for its deeply guttered, arching, frequently twisting, light green to medium green leaves that make this plant instantly recognizable. These 3–4 foot (0.9–1.2 meter) long leaves have small, weak marginal teeth and a short, somewhat tame terminal spine reaching less than 1 inch (2.5 cm) long.

When springtime rolls around, the 10–16 foot tall (3–4.8 meter), spicate inflorescence covered with 1½ inch (3.8 cm) long, golden yellow flowers makes quite an impressive display. This is one of the few species that produces thousands of small plantlets on the flower stalk once flowering has finished, rendering a once-hard-to-acquire plant virtually worthless to the specialty grower.

A roadcut full of *Agave vilmoriniana* plants on the drive from Hermosillo to Yécora in Sonora, Mexico

CULTURE

The more northern forms of can withstand winter lows into the low 20s F (−5 to −6 C) with little or no damage to the leaves. A zone 9a–11 species, *Agave vilmoriniana* can be used in the landscape in the mild winter regions of the Pacific and Gulf coast states. In the southwestern United States, it can safely be grown in the cool, coastal and hot, interior low elevation zone, and in most places in the mid-elevation zone.

Super-fast-growing when given supplemental water, these plants have been known to flower as soon as four to five years after planting. They are low-water-using enough that they only need to be watered once a month even in the hot, interior, low elevation zone. In southwestern U.S. landscapes they tend to be watered too frequently and grow too quickly, shortening the lifespan. Once plants are established, grow with minimal water and let them develop some character.

Although in nature plants grow on cliffs where they receive shade for part of the day, these can tolerate full sun in all regions in which they are winter hardy. This one is not picky and will grow in just about any soil type from heavy clay to sandy, as long as the watering is adjusted accordingly.

LANDSCAPE VALUE

Place *Agave vilmoriniana* on steep, shady embankments to simulate its natural habitat and recreate the floppy form that is so unusual. If space allows, plant several octopus agaves by themselves for a truly interesting landscape, or mix in several medium-sized shrubs with showy flowers to create a visual feast of color and texture. Some great companion shrubs with showy flowers include *Anisacanthus quadrifidus, Calliandra californica, Dalea frutescens, Justicia californica, Leucophyllum candidum, Ruellia peninsularis*, and *Tecoma stans*.

The twisting, arching, deeply channeled leaves set this unconventional plant apart from all other species.

CULTIVAR

Agave vilmoriniana 'Stained Glass'

'Stained Glass' grows as large as the species, reaching 4 feet tall and 5–6 feet across (1.2 by 1.5–1.8 meters). The narrow, medium green, deeply guttered leaves differ by having distinct creamy yellow variegation along the leaf margins. The flowers appear to be the same as those of the species.

The original plant was given by Charlie Glass to the brothers Don and Dave Harris, both Santa Barbara plantsmen. The Harris brothers asked that it be given a name to honor Charlie Glass, and San Marcos Growers decided upon 'Stained Glass' to describe the creamy yellow leaf edges and to honor Mr. Glass.

The culture is the same as for the species: hardiness to the low 20s F (−5 to −6 C), fast growth, full sun to light shade, moderately drought tolerant, not fussy about soil.

Agave vilmoriniana is spectacular when in full flower as in this Phoenix, Arizona, garden

Agave wocomahi Gentry

WOCOMAHI

A large specimen of *Agave wocomahi* growing near Yécora in Sonora is a magnificent sight.

Howard Scott Gentry used the local Warihio Indian name of wocomahi for this species, which is sweet, good for eating and useful in the making of the alcoholic drink mescal.

FIELD NOTES

When traveling through the mountains of east central Sonora and adjacent Chihuahua between 4500 and 8100 feet (1370–2470 meters) elevation, be on the lookout for these large plants with big, gnarly teeth. Some awesome specimens can be seen while tooling along Mexico Highway 16 in the vicinity of Yécora, Sonora. I have seen some very fine specimens on the way to Basaseachi Falls in Chihuahua, which at 807 feet (246 meters) is the second highest waterfall in all of Mexico. One year, during a trip in January, my friend Dave Palzkill and I found plants covered in snow! While looking at the plants, make a point of finding the ones with the most incredible teeth and wicked spines perched on rock outcrops and ledges.

DESCRIPTION

Agave wocomahi is a solitary, medium to medium-large species, ranging in size from 3 to 5 feet tall by 4–6 feet across (0.9–1.5 by 1.2–1.8 meters) before flowering. Some of the most intriguing forms have dark green to glaucous green, lanceolate-ovate leaves, measuring up to 2–3 feet long by 6–8 inches across (0.6–0.9 by 15–20 cm) at the widest point which is generally above the middle. The large, wicked teeth are perched atop prominently mammillate margins, and make very impressive bud prints on the surrounding leaves. The vicious, stout terminal spine is straight or wiggly, dark brown to nearly black, with an open groove above, and measures 1–2 inches long (25–50 mm).

A 10–16 foot (3–5 meter) tall, narrowly branched flower stalk appears in summer or fall. The stalk has eight to fifteen side branches, each loaded with 2½–3 inch (65–75 mm) long, yellow flowers clustered at the tips.

CULTURE

Agave wocomahi has been exposed to winter lows in the high teens in Tucson without damage, and should be a great landscape plant in the drier regions of the Pacific and Gulf coast states. Easily hardy in zones 8a–11, the cool, coastal and hot, interior low elevation and mid-elevation southwestern U.S. zones, and warmer microclimates in the high elevation zone.

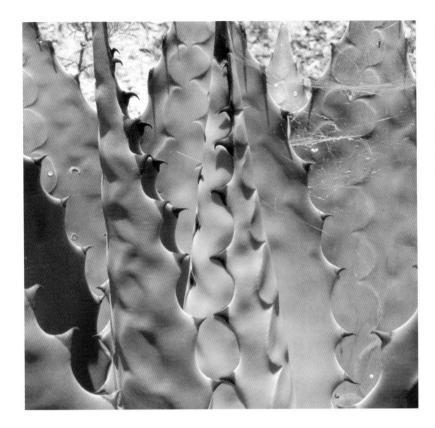

Plants have a moderate to moderately fast growth rate, achieving mature size in ten to fifteen years. *Agave wocomahi* is relatively drought tolerant, but will also grow faster with supplemental water during the growing season. In the hot, interior low elevation zone, the root zone should be thoroughly soaked once every two to three weeks when the daytime temperatures are consistently above 85–90 degrees F (29–32 C), and then stepped up to once every one to two weeks when the full brunt of summer hits. In the cooler coastal and mid-elevation zones, plants will be fine with a thorough soaking of the root zone once every two to three weeks from spring until autumn.

Plants will benefit from some midday or afternoon shade in the hot, interior, low elevation zone of the desert southwestern United States. They will tolerate full sun or some midday shade in the mid-elevation zone, while in the cooler coastal zone and high elevation zone plants will thrive in full sun.

Plants will grow fine in most soil types, from heavier clay to a faster-draining sandy type, as long as the watering is adjusted accordingly.

ABOVE The bright yellow flowers of *Agave wocomahi*

RIGHT *Agave wocomahi* makes a remarkable landscape plant, as seen in a Tucson garden.

LANDSCAPE VALUE

Use *Agave wocomahi* as a large specimen plant in a xerophytic or dry garden, in a cactus and succulent garden, or mixed with low-water-using flowering shrubs and perennials. In the hot, low elevation zone, plant in the filtered shade of a native or near-native tree such as *Acacia berlandieri*, *Eysenhardtia orthocarpa*, *Lysiloma watsonii* ssp. *thornberi*, or *Parkinsonia microphylla*. Take advantage of the forms of *Agave wocomahi* that have large, extremely wicked, gnarly teeth that make really interesting bud imprints on the leaves.

Agave xylonacantha Salm-Dyck

WOODY SPINE AGAVE

Agave xylonacantha growing on a limestone slab west of Zimapán in Hidalgo, Mexico

Agave xylonacantha
growing on a limestone
slab west of Zimapán in
Hidalgo

The species name *xylonacantha* is derived from the Greek *xylo*, meaning wood, and *acanth*, meaning spine or thorn, referring to the prominent spine and often bizarre woody teeth.

FIELD NOTES

Watch for this unusual, narrow-leaved species growing out of cracks and crevices in the limestone as you drive through the arid barrancas in central Hidalgo, Mexico, between 4200 and 6200 feet (1280–1900 meters) elevation. Look for the specimens with the waviest leaves and the bizarre bi-, tri-, and sometimes quad-cuspid teeth along the leaf edges. It seems that no matter how many photographs one looks at, they will pale in comparison to actually seeing this plant in habitat. Be cautious as you take pictures while in the cactus hotspots known as the Barranca de Tolentango and the Barranca de Metztitlan, as the locals might stop and tell you it is forbidden to take photos. This can be disturbing as it might dampen your enthusiasm for the grandeur of the scenery.

Northwest of the town of Zimapán in Hidalgo, I saw the most spectacular *Yucca querétaroensis* standing guard over some of the most breathtaking scenery in Mexico. If you bump your way along the washboarded dirt road, look for the several large stands of very nice *Agave xylonacantha* plants growing on the solid limestone rock in full, open exposure. Be sure to get pictures of the agaves growing on the rooftop of one of the buildings as you take this teeth-rattling road.

From the town of Zimapán, take the road to Querétaro over the Rio Moctozuma made possible by the dam that resulted in the flooding of *Echinocactus grusonii* (golden barrel) habitat. Along this road, you will see some impressive stands of *Agave xylonacantha* growing on huge slabs of solid limestone. Look for the plants with the most outrageous marginal teeth imaginable and those tucked into small pockets of soil.

DESCRIPTION

Rosettes of *Agave xylonacantha* are few-leaved, with an open form that helps to show off their outlandish teeth. Mature plants are solitary or occasionally offsetting, can reach to 1½–2½ feet tall by 3–4 feet across (50–75 by 120 cm), and develop an attractive, gnarly form. Light green, grayish green or yellowish green leaves are long and narrow, described as sword-shaped or lance-shaped, measuring 14–30 inches long by 2–4 inches wide (35–75 by 5–10 cm), widest near the middle with a long acuminate taper to the terminal spine. Woody leaf margin is continuous

between and over the prominent teats which are topped by the broad, woody teeth, some with two or more points. The light gray to nearly white, awl-shaped terminal spine is 1–2 inches long, flat to slightly grooved on the upper surface, and in a pinch can be used as a needle to mend ripped pants. Spend some time seeking out the plants that have leaves full of the sexiest, most sinuous curves imaginable.

The unbranched flower stalk climbs skyward in spring and summer, reaches 10–20 feet (3–6 meters) tall and is densely packed with 1½–2 inch (38–50 mm) long, greenish or pale yellow flowers with long reddish or purplish filaments in the upper one half to two thirds of the shaft.

CULTURE

Information about cold hardiness for *Agave xylonacantha* is still sketchy, but Irish indicated that plants subjected to winter lows of 23 degrees F (−5 C) in Essex, England, had no damage, but were killed at 17 degrees F (−8 C) in northern California. Plants in Tucson have survived several winters with overnight temperatures routinely reaching the low 20s F (−5 to −6 C), and plants in Raleigh, North Carolina, have survived temperatures even lower, though the species as a whole is marginal there. My own plant in Tucson finally flowered in 2007 and produced a couple of offsets that were undamaged when temperatures hit 22 degrees F (−5.5 C). The plants could be considered hardy in zones 8a–11, and could probably be used in the landscape in the drier parts of the Pacific and Gulf coast states and up the mild winter parts of the Atlantic coast states. They make a nice addition to the landscape in the cool, coastal and hot, interior low elevation and mid-elevation southwestern U.S. zones.

The growth rate varies with the amount of water applied during the growing season. Even though plants occur naturally on solid slabs of limestone in very arid regions, they will tolerate receiving supplemental water in the summer. However, be aware that they will then grow more rapidly, and in turn bloom and die more quickly.

Give this one plenty of sun without fear of sun burning the leaves. Even plants that are watered sparingly through the summer will survive with a slight lightening of the leaves. *Agave xylonacantha* is found naturally on limestone slabs with very little actual soil, and does not appear to have problems growing in non-limestone soil.

LANDSCAPE VALUE

Use *Agave xylonacantha* with other drought-tolerant plants in a xeric landscape. Try mixing with colorful perennials and small shrubs to provide year-round interest. Some perfect complementary plants include *Baileya multiradiata*, *Chrysactinia mexicana*, *Dalea frutescens*, *Ericameria laricifolia*, *Salvia greggii*, and *Tetraneuris acaulis*. Get up close and personal with the gnarly teeth by planting in large, decorative pots and placing them around the patio.

CULTIVAR

Agave xylonacantha 'Frostbite'

This cultivar was first offered commercially by Plant Delights Nursery in their spring 2010 catalog. The description indicates that it is a non-offsetting plant that forms a symmetrical rosette to 2½ feet across (0.76 meters). The 18 inch long by 1 inch wide (46 by 2.5 cm) leaves are medium green bordered by a wide creamy yellow edge that turns white as the leaves age.

The hardiness of 'Frostbite' is similar to that of the species, with plants being hardy in zones 8b–11. The growth rate is slower than that of the species, and plants require a bit more water and more shade, especially where daytime temperatures stay over 100 degrees F (38 C) for most of the summer.

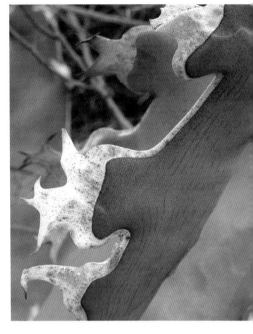

The bizarre teeth frequently found on *Agave xylonacantha*

Agave zebra Gentry

ZEBRA AGAVE

The crossbanded leaves on an *Agave zebra* plant growing with *Jatropha* species in the Sierra El Viejo

The heavy crossbanding on the leaves resemble stripes on a zebra, inspiring Gentry to give it this unique species name.

FIELD NOTES

Agave zebra is known to occur in only two mountain ranges in the northwestern Mexican state of Sonora from 1500 to 3000 feet (450–900 meters) elevation. One, the Sierra El Viejo, is fenced off with access restricted to bighorn sheep hunters and occasionally to botanists by prior arrangement. If one is able to secure permission, the white knuckle drive back to the plants is on another long, bumpy, unmaintained dirt road full of washboard ripples that seems to be the rule for reaching agave habitat throughout much of Mexico. If you have never driven on a road with these, just imagine driving over thousands of 4 inch (10 cm) high speed bumps placed 1 foot (30 cm) apart. The idea is, go fast enough and spend more time in the air, and you will hardly feel the constant jarring. Both *Agave zebra* and *A. pelona* occur in these mountains, with *A. zebra* occupying the sandy bajadas or the lower end of the sharp limestone mountains, while *A. pelona* is found higher up on the limestone. Occasionally the two will be seen growing together, but because the flower seasons do not overlap, hybrids are not known to occur. These two are quite distinct from each other, and both are isolated from any of their presumably closest related species.

DESCRIPTION

In habitat, *Agave zebra* is a solitary, medium-sized species that can grow to 1½–2½ feet tall by 3–4 feet across (0.5–0.75 by 0.9–1.2 meters), rarely reaching 5 feet (1.5 meters) across. Although solitary in habitat, plants in cultivation will sometimes produce offsets. The 20–30 inch long by 4–6 inch wide (50–80 by 12–17 cm), thick and rigid, beautiful powdery blue-gray, ovate-lanceolate leaves are deeply guttered, broadest near the middle, tapering to the acuminate tip. They are rough to the touch, feeling a bit like coarse sandpaper, and distinctively crossbanded on both sides of the leaves, giving rise to the species name of *zebra*. The sharp, stout terminal spine can get up to 3 inches (7.5 cm) long and inflict heavy damage to the legs of unwary passersby.

Some of the most remarkable specimens have the bluest, most deeply guttered leaves with broad, dark gray-green crossbands, and huge, brilliant reddish brown teeth on big teats along the leaf edges, all terminated by a long, wiggly spine.

When a plant reaches flowering age and decides it's time to go, the 20–26 foot tall (6–8 meter), branched panicle will begin to emerge in late spring, continue growing until early summer, and then bust out with 2 inch (5 cm) long, bright lemon yellow flowers clustered at the ends of the seven to fourteen short side branches radiating out from near the top of the main shaft.

Agave zebra has a tall, thin inflorescence with short side branches.

CULTURE

Plants have proven hardy to short durations of at least 15 degrees F (–9 C) if kept dry during the winter, and can be considered suitable for zones 8b–11. They should make attractive landscape plants in the mild-winter, dry regions of the Pacific coast and Gulf coast states. They are also readily grown as landscape plants in the hot, interior low elevation and mid-elevation southwestern U.S. zones.

They have a moderate growth rate, taking several years to achieve flowering age. Keep established plants on the dry side since too much water can lead to roots rotting and the kiss of death. Established plants growing in landscapes in the hot, low elevation zone and mid-elevation zone will grow fine with a thorough soaking of the root zone once or twice a month in the summer until the monsoons hit. They should not receive any supplemental water from autumn until spring.

Plants develop the best form and most intense color when grown in full sun even in the hot, interior, low elevation zone. Plants seem to be particularly susceptible to anthracnose, the leaf-spotting lesions caused by species of the fungus *Colletotrichum*. To minimize the occurrence of these lesions, place plants in full sun with good air circulation and make sure to plant them a little high, keeping the lower leaves just a bit above the ground even if that means propping up the plant with coarse gravel or rock, and avoid overhead watering.

Plants prefer to be planted on a slope in a fast-draining soil to keep excess moisture away from the roots. Try adding some limestone or gypsum to the soil to keep the plants healthy with a good balance of nutrients.

LANDSCAPE VALUE

Agave zebra is best used in a dry garden and mixed with other drought-tolerant plants, including flowering perennials and small shrubs. Some great flowering plants that mix well include *Baileya multiradiata, Chrysactinia mexicana, Dalea frutescens, Ericameria laricifolia, Glandularia*

ABOVE A heavily cross-banded *Agave zebra* specimen in the Sierra El Viejo

RIGHT An *Agave zebra* plant, with deeply folded leaves and large red teeth, in the Sierra El Viejo

gooddingii, *Penstemon* species, *Salvia greggii*, *Tetraneuris acaulis*, and *Viguiera deltoidea*. It does great in full sun in a cactus and succulent garden, and blends well with ephemerals that disappear when the weather gets hot. Some really nice companion succulents would include: other *Agave* species, *Dasylirion* species, *Echinocactus grusonii*, *Echinocereus* species, *Ferocactus* species, *Trichocereus* species, and *Yucca* species. It makes a great container plant, and does well if the container is shallow and the soil has fast drainage.

Use *Agave zebra* up close for the striking crossbanded, deeply guttered, powdery blue-gray leaves.

Comparing Look-Alikes

The puzzle of how to properly identify agaves has frustrated even the most devout agavephiles for many years. Despite being roughly 7.8 to 10.1 million years old, the genus is considered to be relatively young, with a high rate of speciation, resulting in several species looking similar vegetatively but having distinct floral differences. Also, some species have a wide range of forms, rendering it difficult to make general statements about their characteristics. Juvenile plants of closely related *Agave* species can look strikingly similar to one another, to the point where it is particularly hard to tell them apart. Finally, because there is variation within some of the species and the distinctions are nuanced rather than patently obvious, you will probably see a lot of terms such as *typically, generally, slightly, tends to be, a bit smaller,* or *a bit longer,* as well as any others that I can come up with in order to keep things interesting.

Differentiating between similar-looking species is not an exact science; in fact, quite a bit of voodoo and witchcraft is involved. However, I believe that, with enough pictures, practice, and sometimes the flip of

Agave parviflora ssp. *densiflora*

a coin, a person will have a 50-50 chance of being able to put at least a tentative identification on the plant in question. So if you wish to identify agaves without flowers, do not despair: you will either be right or wrong, and if you say the name loud enough and with enough conviction, you will believe yourself to be correct. So, armed with that bit of sage advice, let us take a look at some of the pesky look-alikes, starting with the groups that have smaller plants and working toward the groups with larger ones.

Agave parviflora, Agave polianthiflora, and *Agave toumeyana*

These small, closely related species can be difficult to tell apart vegetatively, as all have bud printing on the leaves and thin, white curly fibers along the leaf edges. But we will give it a go: let us take a look at the descriptions individually, and then figure out how to separate the three.

Agave parviflora

- Rosettes are 5–12 inches (13–30 cm) across.
- Plants are usually solitary, rarely producing offsets.
- Leaves are 2.5–6 (6–15 cm) inches long and abruptly acuminate at the tip.
- White fibers curve back to form an upside-down U, and are the thickest among the three species.
- Flowers are pale yellow, and less than 1 (2.5 cm) inch long.

Agave polianthiflora

- Rosettes can be the same size as those of *Agave parviflora*: 5–12 inches (13–30 cm) across.
- Plants are either solitary or produce offsets.
- Leaves are 4–8 inches (10–20 cm) long and acuminate at the tip.
- Thin, white fibers either look quite unruly, point towards the tip, or curl back away from the tip. Fibers are of medium thickness.
- Flowers are pink or pinkish red and 1.5 inch (4 cm) long.

Agave toumeyana

- At 10–15 inches (25–40 cm) across, rosettes are slightly larger than those of *Agave parviflora* and *A. polianthiflora*. Alternatively, if they are smaller as in var. *bella*, they are much denser than those of the other species.
- Plants offset profusely and form large colonies.
- Leaves are 8–12 inches (20–30 cm) long and acuminate at the tip.
- Thin, white curly fibers along the edge are the thinnest of among the three species.
- Flowers are greenish yellow and 1 inch (2.5 cm) long.

COMPARISONS

The plants are easily distinguished when in flower, as *Agave polianthiflora* has distinctive red to pinkish red flowers while the others have pale yellow or greenish yellow flowers. Of the other two, *A. parviflora* flowers are less than 0.75 inch (2 cm) long, easily distinguishing the plants from *A. toumeyana* which has flowers about 1 inch (2.5 cm) long.

The plants are a bit more difficult to differentiate when not in flower, but with diligence and a box of chocolates on which to munch while pondering the differences, it can be done with about as much accuracy as hitting a half-court basketball shot. The key, of course, is in the rosette and the leaves.

First, we can usually identify *Agave toumeyana* by the size of its rosette. At 10–15 inches (25–40 cm) across, it is slightly larger than those of both *A. parviflora* and *A. polianthiflora*, which each measure 5–12 inches (13–30 cm) across. Second, the leaves on *A. toumeyana* are longer, and narrower relative to their length, than the leaves of the other two. Third, the marginal fibers on the leaf edges of *A. toumeyana* tend to be more slender than those on both *A. parviflora* and *A. polianthiflora*.

To distinguish *Agave parviflora* from *A. polianthiflora* is quite a bit more difficult. First, the leaf tip on *A. parviflora* is at a more obtuse angle than the leaf tip of *A. polianthiflora*. Next, the leaves on *A. parviflora* tend to be broadest at or above the middle of the blade, while those on *A. polianthiflora* tend to be widest below the middle. Finally, the leaf fibers of *A. parviflora* tend to be shaped like an upside-down U while those of *A. polianthiflora* tend to be either straight or slightly curved back.

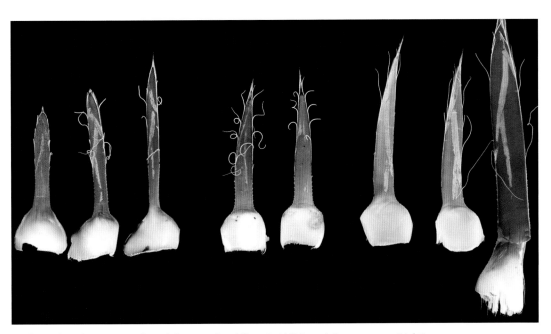

Leaf samples of *Agave parviflora* (left), *A. polianthiflora* (middle), and *A. toumeyana* (right)

Agave guadalajarana, Agave isthmensis, and Agave potatorum

Although *Agave guadalajarana* is not covered in this book, it is occasionally seen for sale in the southwestern United States, and so is compared to both *A. isthmensis* and *A. potatorum* due to its resemblance to them. *Agave guadalajarana* is sometimes confused with *A. potatorum* because they are about the same size and the leaves are somewhat similar. *Agave isthmensis*, on the other hand, looks like a dwarf form of *A. potatorum*, and actually has been sold as *A. potatorum* var. *verschaffeltii*. If you think you have one of these three, the best approach is to first determine whether or not you have *A. isthmensis*, because of its smaller size. The next step is to focus on the differences between *A. guadalajarana* and *A. potatorum*. Let us take a closer look at the descriptions of these three intriguing species and explore how to distinguish each from the other two.

Agave isthmensis

- Rosettes are small, measuring 4–5 inches tall by 6–8 inches across (10–13 by 15–20 cm) in one form and 8–12 inches tall by 10–15 inches across (20–30 by 26–40 cm) in the other.
- Plants produce few or many offsets.
- Leaves are powdery blue or gray-blue, obovate to spoon-shaped, and under 6 inches (15 cm) long and 3 inches (8 cm) wide.

Agave guadalajarana

- Rosettes are larger than those of the other two when mature, measuring 12–24 inches tall and 24–40 inches across (30–60 by 60–100 cm).
- Rosette form is generally more upright and denser than on *A. potatorum*.
- Plants are usually solitary.
- Leaves are powdery blue-gray to light gray-green and measure 12–18 inches long by 3–4.75 inches wide (30–45 by 7.5–12 cm).

Agave potatorum

- Rosettes are larger than those of *A. isthmensis* and slightly smaller than those of *A. guadalajarana*, measuring 12–18 inches tall by 18–36 inches across (30–45 by 45–90 cm).
- Rosette form is generally more open, frequently with leaves lying flatter.
- Plants are generally solitary.
- Leaves are gray-green to blue-gray or even nearly white, 10–15 inches long by 3.5–7 inches wide (26–40 by 9–18 cm).

COMPARISONS

The first step is to determine whether the specimen in question is *Agave isthmensis*, with its smaller rosettes reaching a maximum size of 6–15 inches (15–40 cm) across. Compare that to the rosettes of *A. potatorum*, which are roughly twice the diameter, reaching 18–36 inches (45–90 cm) across, and *A. guadalajarana* at 24–42 inches (30–60 cm) across. Even as a young plant, *A. isthmensis* is proportionally smaller than either *A. guadalajarana* or *A. potatorum*, along with being denser with more leaves for its size.

Distinguishing *Agave guadalajarana* from *A. potatorum* is a little more difficult. As younger plants growing in pots, *A. guadalajarana* tends to have more leaves with those near mid-rosette being held more upright. Contrastingly, *Agave potatorum* tends to have fewer leaves, with those near mid-rosette more splayed out, giving it a more open appearance. Some leaves on *A. guadalajarana* have smaller teeth in the valleys between the larger teeth perched on the prominent teats, whereas the leaves of *A. potatorum* almost never have smaller teeth in between the larger ones. As you grow these species, you will begin to notice subtle differences that will enable you to separate the two.

Young plants of *Agave guadalajarana* (left), *A. potatorum* (middle), and *A. isthmensis* (right)

Agave petrophila, Agave striata, and Agave stricta

These three are members of the group Striatae, with *Agave petrophila* having been recently described. *Agave stricta* is sometimes considered to be a subspecies of *A. striata*, but the two are maintained here as distinct species based on floral characteristics. The tube and tepals on *A. stricta* flowers are of equal length, but on *A. striata* flowers the tube is two to three times the length of the tepals. First, we shall look at the descriptions.

Agave petrophila

- Rosettes are 18–24 inches tall by 18–30 inches (45–60 by 45–75 cm) across.
- Plants produce few offsets in habitat, but more in cultivation.
- Leaves are light glaucous green, and linear lanceolate, meaning that they are slightly wider at the base and gradually tapering to the tip.
- The dark reddish brown terminal spine is small at only about 0.25 inch (0.6 cm) long.

Agave striata

- Rosettes are 12–36 inches tall and 18–40 inches across (30–90 by 45–100 cm).
- Plants produce abundant offsets in habitat and in cultivation.
- Leaves are variously colored, and linear in shape, meaning that they are about the same width from the base to near the tip before tapering quickly to the tip.
- The terminal spine is 0.4–2 inches (1–5 cm) long.

Agave stricta

- Rosettes are 18–30 inches tall by 24–40 inches across (45–75 by 60–100 cm).
- Plants produce abundant offsets in habitat and in cultivation.
- Leaves are bright green to dull green, and sometimes reddish purple near the base. They are narrowly linear, meaning that they are about the same width from the base to near the tip, and then taper quickly to the tip.
- The terminal spine is just under 1 inch (2.5 cm) long.

COMPARISONS

Although a close look at these species' flowers will reveal differences, we do not always have the luxury of having flowers on hand. Vegetatively, these look-alikes are easily confused unless the subtle details are examined closely, and even then there is some confusion between *Agave petrophila* and *A. stricta*. Because those two are so similar and very difficult to distinguish, it is probably easiest to begin by using a combination of characteristics to separate *A. striata* from the other two.

Agave striata is the easiest of the three species to recognize. Although they are all roughly the same size when fully grown, the three are easily identified when mature. It is when the plants are smaller that some confusion can

Young plants of *Agave stricta* (left) are easily distinguished from *A. striata* (right).

Compare young plants of *Agave striata* (left) with plants of *A. stricta* (middle) and
A. petrophila with frost-damaged leaves (right).

occur, especially between *A. petrophila* and *A. stricta*.

At 0.4–2 inches (1–5 cm) long, the terminal spine on *Agave striata* is generally longer than the spines on either *A. petrophila* or *A. stricta*. Young plants of *A. striata* have fewer leaves (generally thirty to thirty-five for plants filling out 3–4 inch [7.5–10 cm] pots), which at 5–10 inches (12.5–25 cm) are much longer than either *A. petrophila*, which generally has sixty or more leaves that are 1–3 inches (2.5–7.5 cm) long for plants filling out 3 inch (7.5 cm) pots), or *Agave stricta* which typically has seventy or more leaves that are 2–4 inches (5–10 cm) long for plants filling out 3 inch (7.5 cm) pots.

Agave petrophila versus Agave stricta

The final challenge is to separate *Agave petrophila* from *A. stricta*. Distinguishing between these two at any stage of growth is like pulling spines out of a dog's paw. It can be done fifty percent of the time, but it requires patience, persistence, a lot of practice, a little luck, and even a chocolate candy treat when you are finished. You really have to pay attention to detail.

Comparing young plants of the same age reveals that *Agave petrophila* tends to be a little smaller with fewer, broader, glaucous blue-green leaves. On the other hand, *A. stricta* leaves are bright to dull green or yellowish green and are sometimes colored reddish purple near the base. The leaves on young plants of *A. petrophila* tend to be just a little wider (0.25–0.3 inch [0.6–0.75 cm] across) at the widest point, compared to those of *A. stricta* which measure 0.18–0.25 inch (0.45–0.6 cm) at the widest point. The terminal spine on *A. petrophila* is generally a little shorter (less than or equal to 0.25 inch [0.6 cm]) while that of *A. stricta* is a bit longer at 0.5–0.9 inch (1.2–2.2 cm). If all else fails, set a glass of ice water next to the plant, and if it visibly shivers and asks for a winter jacket, you most certainly have *A. petrophila*!

Agave filifera, Agave geminiflora, Agave multifilifera, and Agave schidigera

We can divide these four closely related species into two pairs: *Agave filifera* and *A. schidigera*, and *A. geminiflora* and *A. multifilifera*. The first two species are more similar to one another than the second two are. The two pairs differ primarily in leaf width, with *A. filifera* and *A. schidigera* having wider leaves than *A. geminiflora* and *A. multifilifera*.

Agave filifera versus Agave schidigera

Agave filifera

- Rosettes are 15–20 inches tall by 20–24 inches across (40–50 by 50–60 cm).
- Plants produce few offsets.
- Leaves are lance-shaped, measuring 6–12 inches long by 0.75–1.5 inches wide (15–30 by 1.9–4 cm).
- The terminal spine is 0.75 inch (1.9 cm) long, grayish, flat on top and rounded below.

Agave schidigera

- Rosettes are 18–30 inches tall by 36–40 inches across (45–75 by 90–100 cm).
- Leaves are lance-shaped, measuring 12–16 inches long by 0.5–1.5 inches wide (30–40 by 1.2–4 cm).
- The terminal spine is under 0.5 inch (1.2 cm) long, brown to gray, flat on top and rounded below.

COMPARISON

Distinguishing *Agave filifera* from *A. schidigera* requires looking out for subtle differences between the plants. First, in habitat, *A. filifera* is an offsetting type while *A. schidigera* is not, though under cultivation the occasional plant might throw out an offset or two. Next, mature plants of *A. filifera* tend to be a bit smaller than those of *A. schidigera*, both in individual leaf length and overall rosette size. Finally, the terminal spine is a bit longer on *A. filifera* than on *A. schidigera*. Younger plants show distinct growth differences. The leaves of *A. filifera* tend to be longer and narrower with a slight curve, and are more upright, while those of *A. schidigera* are usually shorter and wider relative to the length, lacking a slight curve, and lie flatter while radiating out from the center more symmetrically.

Young plants of *Agave filifera* (left) and *A. schidigera* (right)

Small plants of *Agave geminiflora* (left) and *A. multifilifera* (right) are easy to tell apart.

Agave geminiflora versus Agave multifilifera

Agave geminiflora

- Rosettes are solitary, measuring about 24–36 inches tall by 24–36 inches across (60–90 by 60–90 cm).
- Leaves are numerous, long, thin, and flexible, measuring 18–24 inches long by 0.25–0.33 inch wide (45–60 by 0.6–0.8 cm).
- Leaves may or may not have curly white fibers along the margins.

Agave multifilifera

- Rosettes are solitary, measuring about 24–36 inches tall by 36–48 inches across (60–90 by 90–120 cm).
- Leaves are long, thin, and rigid, measuring 20–30 inches long by 0.5–1.5 inch wide (50–75 by 1.2–4 cm).
- Leaves have many curly white fibers along the margins.

COMPARISON

The narrower leaves of both *Agave geminiflora* and *A. multifilifera* set them apart from *A. filifera* and *A. schidigera*, so we will turn our attention to distinguishing between *A. geminiflora* and *A. multifilifera*. These two narrow-leaved, offsetting types can be differentiated by the amount of give to their leaves; those of *A. geminiflora* are much more flexible and won't poke and prod the unsuspecting handler, while those of *A. multifilifera* are quite stiff and rigid, causing much longlasting pain if you are not careful.

Agave colorata, *Agave marmorata*, and *Agave zebra*

These similar-looking species all have powdery blue leaves (or, in one form of *Agave marmorata*, dark green ones) that feel like varying grades of sandpaper when stroked gently. These leaves have prominent teeth on large mammillate margins, and frequently have prominent crossbanding, yet each one has a distinctive look when fully grown. All three tend to lean over as they get larger, further tying them together.

Agave colorata

Agave colorata takes two distinct forms.

The common form
- Rosettes are 18–24 inches tall by 18–24 inches across (45–60 by 45–60 cm).
- Plants produce offsets.
- Leaves are powdery blue and crossbanded, spoon-shaped, and about 12 inches long by 4–6 inches wide (30 by 10–15 cm).
- Leaves have pronounced mammillate edges with large, formidable, dark brown teeth and a stout terminal spine.

The uncommon form
- Rosettes are larger, measuring about 36 inches tall by 36–48 inches wide (90 by 90–120 cm).
- Plants do not produce offsets.
- Leaves are long, sword-shaped, and 18–24 inches long by 4–6 inches wide (45–60 by 10–15 cm).
- Leaf margins are not as deeply scalloped, and the teeth are not quite as prominent.

Agave marmorata

There are two distinct forms of *Agave marmorata*.

The desert form
- Rosettes reach 45–50 inches tall by 60–78 inches across (115–130 by 150–200 cm).
- Plants are solitary or produce few offsets in cultivation.
- Leaves are 40–50 inches long by 7–12 inches wide (100–130 by 17–30 cm), deeply guttered, and colored blue-gray with prominent crossbanding.
- Leaf margins are distinctly mammillate.

The mesic form
- Rosettes reach 45–50 inches tall by 60–78 inches across (115–130 by 150–200 cm).
- Plants are solitary.
- Leaves are 40–50 inches long by 7–12 inches wide (100–130 by 17–30 cm) and colored light to medium green.

Agave zebra

- Rosettes are 24–36 inches tall by 36–48 (rarely 60) inches across (60–90 by 90–120 [rarely 150] cm).
- Plants are solitary in habitat, but in cultivation they will frequently produce offsets.

- Leaves are powdery blue-gray, lanceolate, deeply guttered, distinctively crossbanded, and 20–30 inches long by 4–6 inches wide (50–75 by 10–15 cm).

COMPARISONS

Even though all three species have similar leaf color with noticeable crossbanding, they are not too difficult to tell apart as mature plants.

First, we can pull *Agave colorata* out of the mix by noting its smaller, more closed rosettes and its shorter, obovate to nearly spoon-shaped leaves that are very wide relative to the length and nearly flat above. The leaves of both *A. marmorata* and *A. zebra* are more lance-shaped, longer and relatively narrower, and deeply guttered above.

Now the challenge is to separate *Agave marmorata* from *A. zebra*, which we can do with relative ease. First, as mature plants, the leaves of *A. marmorata* are much longer, narrower and more distinctly guttered than those of *A. zebra*. Second, the *A. zebra* terminal spine is longer and more lethal than that on *A. marmorata*.

Finally, as in humans, the teeth can be used for identification. Those on *A. zebra* are larger, more irregularly curved and more wicked-looking than those on *A. marmorata*.

When looking at young plants of these three, they are grouped a little differently. Leaves on young plants of *Agave marmorata* tend to be more linear-lanceolate in shape. Leaves on *A. colorata*, on the other hand, are broadly obovate (spoon-shaped), while those on *Agave zebra* can be broadly linear-lanceolate to broadly obovate. These two can usually be distinguished by the leaf margins and by touch. Leaves of *A. colorata* tend to have pronounced mammillate margins with large, breast-shaped teats, and are smooth to the touch. *Agave zebra* leaves have less pronounced mammillate margins and are slightly to noticeably rough to the touch.

Compare young plants of *Agave colorata* (left), *A. marmorata* (middle), and *A. zebra* (right).

Agave havardiana, Agave ovatifolia, Agave parrasana, and Agave parryi

Although closely related and somewhat similar-looking, adult plants of these species are generally readily separated; it is the young plants that are difficult to distinguish from each other. But with careful examination and experience, it can be done. The four species can be subdivided into two pairs, with *Agave havardiana* and *A. parryi* as one pair and *A. ovatifolia* and *A. parrasana* as the other, set apart primarily by close inspection of the terminal spine, the leaf margin, and the teeth along the margin.

Agave havardiana

- Rosettes reach 20–30 inches tall and about 48–60 inches across (50–75 by 120–150 cm). Plants are solitary, or rarely offsetting.
- Leaves are 12–24 inches long and 6 inches wide (30–60 by 15 cm), blue-gray, and ovate-acuminate, meaning that they are widest near the middle with a long taper to the tip.

Agave parryi

- Individual rosettes achieve a size of 15–20 inches tall and 24–36 inches across (40–50 by 60–90 cm).
- All forms are offsetting types.
- Leaves are 10–16 inches long by 3–5 inches wide (25–40 by 7.5–13 cm) and linear ovate, meaning that they are about equal width from near the base to above the middle, and then taper to the tip.

Agave ovatifolia

- Rosettes reach 32–36 inches tall by 48–60 inches across (80–90 by 120–150 cm).
- Plants are solitary, rarely producing an offset or two.
- Leaves are distinctive, 20–22 inches long by 9–11 inches across (50–55 by 22–28 cm), broadly ovate, silvery blue, and cupped on the upper surface.

Agave parrasana

- Rosette is tight and rounded, about 12–18 inches tall and 18–28 inches across (30–45 by 45–70 cm).
- Plants are solitary in habitat, but in cultivation some will produce offsets.
- Leaves are thick, rigid, blue-gray to gray-green, and 8–12 inches long by 4–5 inches wide (20–30 by 10–13 cm).

COMPARISONS

Let us divide the four species into two pairs before looking at the differences between the species in each pair.

The stout terminal spine on both *Agave havardiana* and *A. parryi* is dark brown to black, and decurrent to at least the first pair of teeth. The thin terminal spine on *A. ovatifolia* and *A. parrasana* is light to dark brown and not decurrent. The leaf margin on *A. havardiana* and *A. parryi* is typically straight with the small, slender teeth straight or reflexed towards the leaf base. Contrastingly, on *A. ovatifolia* and *A. parrasana* the leaf margin is typically more mammillate and the small teeth are more consistently recurved.

Agave havardiana versus Agave parryi

Separating *Agave havardiana* from *A. parryi* is not an easy task, especially when the plants are young. As with many closely related species, the differences are subtle and nuanced.

When looking at relatively young plants, with rosettes about 8 inches wide, note that the rosette for *Agave havardiana* has fewer, larger leaves that are thick and widest below the middle, with the shape described as ovate-lanceolate. The rosette for *Agave parryi* tends to have more leaves that are narrower, slightly thinner from topside to underside and widest at the middle, also with the shape described as ovate-lanceolate.

Older plants are a little easier to separate. *Agave havardiana* produces few, if any, offsets while those of *A. parryi* are generally pro-lific producers of baby plants. The rosettes of *A. havardiana* are larger and more open than those of *A. parryi*. Finally, the leaves of *A. havardiana* are wider and thicker with the widest point below the middle, and the leaves of *A. parryi* are generally narrower, with the widest point at the middle.

Agave ovatifolia versus Agave parrasana

While these two are quite easy to separate as mature plants, young plants can be somewhat difficult to tell apart owing to the variation within both species.

In young plants, the leaves of *Agave ovatifolia* are usually longer and narrower, with a length to width ratio of 3:1 or more, while those of *A. parrasana* tend to be shorter and wider with a length to width ratio of 2:1 or less. The marginal teeth on *A. ovatifolia* are usually shorter and darker, while those on *A. parrasana* tend to be longer, relatively thinner, either white or lighter tan, and make deep impressions on the surrounding leaves.

Larger plants are much easier to separate based on the size and shape of the rosette. At 32–36 inches tall by 48–60 inches across (80–90 by 120–150 cm), the rosette of *Agave ovatifolia* is much larger than that of *A. parrasana* which measures 12–18 inches tall by 18–28 inches across (30–45 by 45–70 cm) The overall shape of the rosette is relatively low and wide for *A. ovatifolia*, while rosettes of *A. parrasana* tend to be nearly equal in height and width.

Agave chrysantha and *Agave palmeri*

These two species are closely related, and have been known to hybridize in the wild. They are similar in appearance and very difficult to separate vegetatively. The bright golden yellow flower color of *Agave chrysantha* readily distinguishes it from the pale greenish cream flower color of *A. palmeri*. However, if flowers are not available, we must look to vegetative characteristics—which are not always consistent or readily apparent, causing us to throw our hands in the air and wait for flowers.

Agave chrysantha

- Rosettes are 18–36 inches tall by 30–72 inches across (45–90 by 75–180 cm).
- Leaves are variable, pale blue to green or yellowish green, linear-lanceolate to lanceolate, and deeply guttered.
- Teeth measure 0.16–0.39 inches (4–10 mm), with smaller teeth between the larger ones in the upper two thirds of the leaf.

Agave palmeri

- Rosettes are 18–36 inches tall by 30–48 inches across (45–90 by 75–120 cm).
- Leaves are variable, linear-lanceolate, and colored pale blue to green or yellowish green.
- The teeth measure 0.12–0.24 inches (3–6 mm) and are slender and evenly spaced, sometimes with smaller teeth between larger ones on the upper two thirds of the leaf.

COMPARISON

The flowers are a dead giveaway, with *A. chrysantha* having bright golden yellow flowers compared to the pale greenish yellow flowers of *A. palmeri*. Looking at maximum size of the individual rosettes is another surefire way to separate the two. *Agave chrysantha* can reach 6 feet (180 cm) or rarely 7 feet (215 cm) across while *A. palmeri* will top out at about 4 feet (90 cm) across. A close look at the leaf color reveals that both are variable, with color ranging from pale blue to green or yellowish green in both. But the leaf margins are slightly different: *Agave chrysantha* has mostly wavy to undulate edges while *Agave palmeri* has mostly straight margins.

Agave gentryi, Agave montana, Agave salmiana, and Agave shawii

These four are grouped together because of their vegetative similarities. Additionally, they all share the unusual feature of having large, congested bracts at the tops of their inflorescences. Although there are other species with this interesting characteristic, such as *Agave parrasana* and sometimes even *A. deserti*, they are not easily confused with these four.

Agave gentryi

There appear to be three distinct forms.

First form

- The rosette is the most massive and dense, growing to 48–60 inches tall by 60–72 inches across (120–150 by 150–180 cm).
- Plants produce offsets.
- Leaves are light green, 36–48 inches long by 8–10 inches wide (90–120 by 20–25 cm), very broad and thick, widest from the base to above the middle, with a long taper to the terminal spine.

Second form

- This one is more variable and a bit smaller than the first form, reaching a size of about 42–48 inches tall by 48 inches across (100–120 by 120 cm).
- Plants are either solitary or offset sparingly.
- Leaves are a medium to dark green, 30–36 inches by 6–8 inches (75–90 by 15–20 cm), slightly narrowed at the base, widest near the middle and then long tapering to the terminal spine.

Third form

- This one is by far the most variable; rosettes can reach 36–60 inches tall by 36–72 inches across (90–150 by 90–180 cm); offsetting.
- The leaves are dark green, 24–36 inches long by 6–8 inches wide (60–90 by 15–20 cm), and either broad from the base to mid-blade before tapering to the tip, or long triangular, broadest at the base, and with a long taper to the tip.

Agave montana

- Rosettes are hemispherical, 30–48 inches tall by 48–66 inches across (75–120 by 120–170 cm).
- Plants are solitary.
- Leaves are medium to dark green and measure 12–16 inches long by 6–7 inches wide (30–40 by 15–17 cm), flat on both surfaces, and broad from the base to above the middle before tapering quickly to the tip.

Agave salmiana var. ferox

- Rosette is urn-shaped, measuring 36 60 inches tall by 48–96 inches across (90–150 by 120–240 cm).
- Plants produce offsets.
- Leaves are bright green to dark green, 24–36 inches long by 7–12 inches wide (60–90 by 17–30 cm), narrow near the base, and widest above the middle.
- Leaves grow up and curve out and away from the center.

Agave shawii

- Rosettes are 12–24 inches tall and 12–36 inches across (30–60 by 30–90 cm).
- Plants can develop trunks that lie on the ground, and produce offsets, eventually forming huge colonies up to 6–9 feet (1.8–2.7 meters) across.
- Leaves are light to dark green, 8–20 inches long by 3–8 inches wide (20–50 by 7.5–20 cm), broad, and sword-shaped.

COMPARISONS

The best way to distinguish among these four species is to look closely at the rosette shape and the leaves, particularly the terminal spine and marginal teeth, and the relationship between them.

First, we should separate *Agave salmiana* var. *ferox* from the other three. This is relatively easily done by looking at the overall shape of each species' rosette. The rosette of *A. salmiana* var. *ferox* is upright to spreading with leaves that curve out and away from the center and then swoop back upright. Contrastingly, leaves of the other three are more or less straight with little or no curving.

While *Agave salmiana* var. *ferox* and *A. gentryi* both have long acuminate leaf tips leading to the terminal spine, the leaves of *A. salmiana* var. *ferox* are extremely broad near the middle and relatively flat from edge to edge. On the other hand, the leaves of *A. gentryi* are typically wider near the base and long triangular in shape, and have a definite U shape in cross-section—though given the amount of variability in *A. gentryi* there are exceptions in which the leaves are slightly narrower near the base, broader near the middle, and then long tapering to the spine. If you happen to have one of these forms, look closely at the leaf margins and apices. *Agave salmiana* var. *ferox* will have crenate margins and large teeth with a slightly less acuminate apex, and *A. gentryi* will have slightly less crenate margins with smaller teeth and a much more pronounced acuminate apex. If you still cannot tell which species you have, and suspect that it is either *A. salmiana* var. *ferox* or *A. gentryi* 'Jaws', check for the out-and-up curve to the leaves which indicates *A. salmiana* var. *ferox*, or the U-shaped cross-section that would indicate 'Jaws'.

Next, *Agave gentryi* is set apart from *A. montana* and *A. shawii* by the leaves. The leaves of *Agave gentryi* are concave to nearly folded on the upper surface, while those of the other two are flat to slightly concave. Also, the leaves on plants of *Agave gentryi* are generally broadest near the base and long triangular in shape, while the leaves on the other two are generally broad from the base to above the middle, and taper more quickly to the spine, forming a more acute angle.

Finally, to separate *Agave montana* from *A. shawii*, one must look at the overall shape of the rosette and think in broad generalities with respect to the leaves. The leaves on *A. montana* tend to be more spread out, making the rosette shape a little flatter and wider than it is tall. Conversely, the leaves on *A. shawii* tend to be more upright, giving the rosette a narrower form with height either equal to or greater than the width. Many, but not all, plants of *A. montana* will have a nice pattern of silvery frosting on the otherwise dark green leaves, while this characteristic is never seen on *A. shawii*. Also, the terminal spines on new leaves of *A. montana* are frequently reddish brown before quickly aging to grayish white, while those on *Agave shawii* tend to be black or dark brown and remain that color even on older leaves. If all else fails, put the names on a target, and then throw darts to determine which one you have.

In the mountains of northeastern Mexico there are plants that have been regarded as *Agave gentryi*, yet upon close inspection appear to have some characteristics of *A. montana*. The leaves are flatter and shorter acuminate than in typical *A. gentryi*, the teeth are larger than on typical *A. gentryi*, closer to the terminal spine, more closely set together, and leave larger bud imprints. These plants may simply be variants of a still-evolving *A. gentryi*, opening up the possibility of selecting some very cool forms if grown from seed.

Compare young plants of *Agave gentryi* (left) with those of *A. montana* (center) and *A. shawii* (right).

Plants by Size Categories

When there is a particular spot to be filled in the garden, you may want to choose a plant based on its size. I have divided the following agaves into categories based on their diameter. Because of the variability in sizes, several species will fall into more than one category. The same plant could easily achieve a different size due to cultural differences, such as climate, soil, use of fertilizer, amount of water applied, location, or whether the plants is grown in pots or in the ground. As agaves are living plants that refuse to follow the boundaries we set, the following tables are meant to be used as general guidelines and not used as gospel. The diameters are in inches and centimeters in order to maintain consistency between the tables, and I implore you, the reader, not to stab me with an *Agave gentryi* leaf for making you do any conversion to feet or meters.

Extra Small Plants

Agave albopilosa	white hair agave	8–16 inches (20–40 cm)
Agave isthmensis	isthmus agave	6–15 inches (15–36 cm)
Agave macroacantha	large spine agave	10–18 inches (25–45 cm)
Agave parviflora	small flower agave	6–12 inches (15–30 cm)
Agave polianthiflora	Polianthes red flower agave	8–15 inches (20–36 cm)
Agave toumeyana var. *bella*	Toumey agave	6–8 inches (15–20 cm)
Agave utahensis	Utah agave	10–16 inches (25–40 cm)

Agave gentryi

Small Plants

Agave albopilosa	white hair agave	8–16 inches (20–40 cm)
Agave 'Blue Glow'	blue glow agave	24–36 inches (60–90 cm)
Agave bracteosa	green spider agave	18–24 inches (45–60 cm)
Agave colorata, common form	mescal ceniza	18–24 inches (45–60 cm)
Agave deserti	desert agave	18–30 inches (45–75 cm)
Agave filifera	thread-edge agave	16–24 inches (40–60 cm)
Agave geminiflora	twin-flower agave	24–36 inches (60–90 cm)
Agave horrida	wicked agave	15–30 inches (36–75 cm)
Agave horrida ssp. *perotensis*	Perote, wicked agave	24–36 inches (60–90 cm)
Agave isthmensis	isthmus agave	6–15 inches (15–36 cm)
Agave 'Kichijokan'	happy crown agave	12–24 inches (30–60 cm)
Agave 'Kissho Kan'	happy crown agave	12–24 inches (30–60 cm)
Agave macroacantha	large spine agave	10–18 inches (25–45 cm)
Agave mitis	apple green agave	24–36 inches (60–90 cm)
Agave nickelsiae	Nickels' agave	30–36 inches (75–90 cm)
Agave ocahui	ocahui	20–36 inches (50–90 cm)
Agave palmeri	Palmer agave	30–48 inches (75–120 cm)
Agave parrasana	cabbage head agave	18–28 inches (45–70 cm)
Agave parryi var. *couesii*	Coues agave	15–30 inches (36–75 cm)
Agave parryi var. *huachucensis*	Huachuca agave	15–36 inches (36–90 cm)
Agave parryi ssp. *neomexicana*	New Mexico agave	15–24 inches (36–60 cm)
Agave parryi var. *truncata*	dwarf artichoke agave	15–24 inches (36–60 cm)

Agave pelona	bald agave	24–30 inches (60–75 cm)
Agave petrophila	rock-loving agave	20–30 inches (50–75 cm)
Agave potatorum	butterfly agave	20–36 inches (50–90 cm)
Agave 'Royal Spine'	royal spine agave	24–30 inches (60–75 cm)
Agave schidigera		24–36 inches (60–90 cm)
Agave shawii	Shaw agave	18–36 inches (45–90 cm)
Agave striata	needle leaf agave	18–30 inches (45–75 cm)
Agave stricta	needle leaf agave	18–30 inches (45–75 cm)
Agave titanota	alabaster white agave	24–40 inches (60–100 cm)
Agave toumeyana	Toumey agave	8–24 inches (20–60 cm)
Agave victoriae-reginae	Queen Victoria agave	10–24 inches (25–60 cm)

Medium-Sized Plants

Agave bovicornuta	cow's horns agave	36–48 inches (90–120 cm)
Agave chrysantha	golden flower agave	30–72 inches (75–180 cm)
Agave colorata, uncommon form	mescal ceniza	30–72 inches (75–180 cm)
Agave multifilifera	shaggy head agave, chahuiqui	36–48 inches (90–120 cm)
Agave nickelsiae	Nickels' agave	30–36 inches (75–90 cm)
Agave palmeri	Palmer agave	30–48 inches (75–120 cm)
Agave 'Sharkskin'	sharkskin agave	30–42 inches (90–105 cm)
Agave titanota	alabaster white agave	24–40 inches (60–100 cm)
Agave xylonacantha	woody spine agave	36–48 inches (90–120 cm)
Agave zebra	zebra agave	36–60 inches (90–150 cm)

Large Plants

Agave applanata	maguey de ixtle	42–72 inches (105–180 cm)
Agave asperrima	rough leaf agave	36–72 inches (90–180 cm)
Agave gentryi	Gentry agave, maguey, maguey verde	36–72 inches (90–180 cm)
Agave havardiana	Havard agave	48–60 inches (120–150 cm)
Agave montana	mountain agave	48–66 inches (120–165 cm)
Agave ovatifolia	whale's tongue agave	48–72 inches (120–180 cm)
Agave potrerana	potrero agave	48–72 inches (120–180 cm)
Agave salmiana var. *ferox*	maguey de pulque	48–96 inches (120–240 cm)
Agave vilmoriniana	octopus agave	48–72 inches (120–180 cm)
Agave wocomahi	wocomahi	48–60 inches (120–150 cm)

Extra Large Plants

Agave applanata	maguey de ixtle	42–72 inches (105–180 cm)
Agave asperrima	rough leaf agave	36–72 inches (90–180 cm)
Agave chrysantha	golden flower agave	30–72 inches (75–180 cm)
Agave gentryi	Gentry agave, maguey, maguey verde	36–72 inches (90–180 cm)
Agave marmorata	marble leaf agave	60–78 inches (150–195 cm)
Agave montana	mountain agave	48–66 inches (120–165 cm)
Agave ovatifolia	whale's tongue agave	48–72 inches (120–180 cm)
Agave potrerana	potrero agave	48–72 inches (120–180 cm)
Agave salmiana var. *ferox*	maguey de pulque	48–96 inches (120–240 cm)
Agave vilmoriniana	octopus agave	48–72 inches (120–180cm)

Glossary

ACUMINATE: describes a long taper, usually in reference to the agave's leaf tip

ACUTE: describes an abrupt taper of less than ninety degrees, usually in reference to the leaf tip

AFF.: abbreviation for affinity, used to indicate that a plant is possibly the same as the species indicated, but the identity has not been confirmed

BUD PRINT: a term coined by Howard Scott Gentry, describing the outline of the margins and teeth of one leaf impressed upon the surface of another leaf while leaves are in the bud

BULBIL: a small plant produced on the inflorescence

CLONE: a plant that is genetically identical to the parent plant. Examples include offsets and bulbils.

COLONY: a large cluster of clonal plants formed by the production of offsets identical to the parent plant

CORYMB: a flat-top cluster of flowers, with the pedicels of the lower flowers longer than those of the upper flowers

CRENATE: describes a leaf margin that is strongly and abruptly undulate

CROSSBANDING: horizontal color variation found on some agave leaves

FILIFEROUS: having thread-like structures, as found along some agaves' leaf margins

GLABROUS: lacking hairs

GLAUCOUS: having a waxy coating on the epidermis

HYDRIC: pertaining to abundant amounts of water

LANCEOLATE: lance-shaped, usually four to six times longer than wide, widest below the middle and nearer the base

LINEAR: long and narrow, with sides that are parallel

MAMMILLATE: describes a leaf margin that is extremely undulate and breast-shaped

MESIC: pertaining to moderate amounts of water. Compare to xeric or hydric.

MONOCARPIC: describes a plant or rosette that flowers once in its lifetime, and then dies

MULTIANNUAL: describes a plant that grows for many years before it finally flowers and dies

OBLANCEOLATE: lanceolate in reverse, with the widest part above the middle and nearer the leaf tip

OBOVATE: ovate in reverse, with the widest part nearer the tip

OBTUSE: broadly rounded, at an angle greater than ninety degrees, usually in reference to the leaf tip

OFFSET: a plant connected to the parent plant, usually by a rhizome or stolon

OVATE: egg-shaped, usually one and one half times as long as wide, with the widest part near the base

PANICULATE: having a compound inflorescence, a cluster of spikes, racemes or corymbs

PEDICEL: the stalk attaching the flowers to the main stalk or the branches of an inflorescence

PUP: an offset

RACEME: an unbranched inflorescence with the flowers attached to the main stalk by pedicels

RACEMOSE: in *Agave*, describes an inflorescence that is intermediate between spicate and paniculate, having a central stalk with many very short side branches

RHIZOME: an underground stem

SCABROUS: rough to the touch

SPATULATE: spoon-shaped

SPICATE: in *Agave*, describes an inflorescence with the flowers attached by pedicels directly to the main stalk

STOLON: an aboveground stem

TEATS: rounded, breast-like teeth bearing protrusions, found along the leaf margin of some agaves

UNDULATE: wavy

VALLECULATE: having grooves, channels or little valleys as found longitudinally on some agave leaves

XERIC: pertaining to minimal amounts of water

XERIPHYTIC: referring to plants adapted to dry, desert conditions

Bibliography

Baker, John. 1877. *The Gardeners' Chronicle.*

Berger, Alwin. 1915. *Die Agaven.* Jena, Germany.

Breitung, August J. 1959–1964. *Cactus and Succulent Journal.*

Breitung, August J. 1960. *Cactus and Succulent Journal.* 32: 35–38.

Linnaei, Caroli. 1753. *Species Plantarum.*

García-Mendoza, Abisaí. 2002. Distribution of *Agave* (Agavaceae) in Mexico. *Cactus and Succulent Journal.* 74: 177–187.

García-Mendoza, Abisaí and Felipe Palma Cruz. 1993. Una Nueva Especie de *Agave* (Agavaceae, Subgénero *Agave*) de Oaxaca y Chiapas, Mexico. *Sida.* 15: 565–568.

García-Mendoza, Abisaí and Esteban Martínez Salas. 1998. *Agave petrophila* García-Mend. & E. Martínez, nom. Nov. (Agavaceae). *Sida.* 18: 627.

Gentry, Howard Scott. 1982. *Agaves of Continental North America.* Tucson, Arizona: University of Arizona Press.

Heller, Thomas. 2003. *Agaven.* Natur und Tier-Verlag GmbH.

Ingram, Stephen. 2008. *Cacti, Agaves, and Yuccas of California and Nevada.* Los Olivos, California: Cachuma Press.

Irish, Mary. 2002. Growing Agaves in Cold Climates. *Cactus and Succulent Journal.* 74: 165–173.

Irish, Mary and Gary Irish. 2000. *Agaves, Yuccas, and Related Plants.* Portland, Oregon: Timber Press.

Jacobi, G. von. 1864–1867. *Versuch zu einer Systematischen der Agaven*, Vol. 20–21. Hamburger Garten & Blumen-Zeitung.

Reveal, James L. and Wendy C. Hodgson. 2001. Flora of North America, Vol. 26: Agavaceae. www.eFloras.org.

Salm-Dyck, J. H. 1834. *Annotationes Botanicae.* Hortus Dyckensis.

Sato, Tony. 1999. *Nishiki Succulent Handbook.* Fukushima-shi, Japan: Japan Cactus Planning Co. Press.

Staff of the L. H. Bailey Hortorium. 1976. *Hortus III.* New York: Macmillan Publishing.

Standley, Paul C. 1920. *Trees and Shrubs of Mexico.*

Starr, Greg and José A. Villarreal, Q. 2002. *Agave ovatifolia* (Agavaceae) Una Nueva Especie de Maguey del Noreste de México. *Sida.* 20: 495–499.

Thiede, Joachim. 2001. *Illustrated Handbook of Succulent Plants: Monocotyledons.* London: Springer-Verlag.

Trelease, William. 1920. In Standley, *Trees and Shrubs of Mexico.* 23: 107–142.

Ullrich, Bernd. 1990. *Agave macroculmis* Todaro en *Agave gentryi* Ullrich spec. nov. *Succulenta.* 69: 210–214.

Ullrich, Bernd. 1990. *Agave obscura* Schiede and *Agave horrida* Lemaire ex Jacobi ssp. perotensis Ullrich ssp. nov. *Cactaceas y Suculentas Mexicanas.* 35: 80.

Ullrich, Bernd. 1992. On the Discovery of *Agave schidigera* Lemaire and Status of Certain Xysmagave Berger. *British Cactus and Succulent Journal.* 10: 66.

Ullrich, Bernd. 1992. On the History of *Agave asperrima* and *A. scabra* (Agavaceae) as well as some taxa of the Parryanae. *Sida.* 15: 241–261

Ullrich, Bernd. 1993. Observations sur *Agave mitis* Martius, *A. celsii* Hooker et. *A. albicans* Jacobi. *Succulentes.* 16: 32

Villarreal, José A. 1996. Una Nueva Especie de *Agave* Subgénero *Agave* (Agavaceae) de Mexico. *Sida.*17: 191–195.

Watson, W. 1912. *Agave Leopoldii*: A Protest! *The Gardeners' Chronicle.*

Zuccarini, J. G. 1833. Ober Einige Pflanzen aus den Gattungen *Agave* und Fourcroya. *Nova Acta Physico-Medica Academiae Caesareae Leopoldino-Carolinae Naturae Curiosorum.* 162: 661–680.

Acknowledgments

Thank you to family, friends, and associates who have contributed to the development of this book. Thanks to Brian Starr for editing help and photography lessons. Pat McNamara, Bonnie Golden, and Brooke Gebow helped to make this more coherent, readable, and enjoyable; Tony Avent at Plant Delights Nursery in Raleigh, North Carolina, has been a valuable resource and sounding board; and the staff at Mountain States Wholesale Nursery provided continuous support. Thank you to Bill Broyles and Wendy Hodgson for their intense scrutiny of the manuscript and treasured advice. Kevin Barber planted the bug in my ear. Ron Gass deserves special thanks for his many years of general encouragement, moral support, and pleasant travels to study plants. Various traveling companions over the years have made for many delightful and memorable trips into the wilds of the U.S. Southwest and Mexico; Mark Aubrey, Chad Davis, George Hull, Kirti Mathura, and Rob Nixon all contributed to fun times. Brian Kemble spent many hours as a traveling partner while also reviewing parts of the manuscript. Thanks to Julie Hecimovich for the accurate climate zone map. Thanks to Ursula Schuch and Marie-Antoinette Keeran for translating plant descriptions from German to English and French to English. And finally, thanks to Scott Calhoun for his willingness to spend many grueling hours enduring long, bumpy dirt roads to visit yet another out-of-the-way species and still maintain his sense of humor while sharing critical advice on photography and writing techniques.

Index of Plant Names